Readers Rave about Previ
CorelDraw For Dummies:

"I never learned so much in a desktop publishing ?
educational."
— Kelli Scott, Albany, New York

"It doesn't treat you like a 'dummy.' Straightforward and simple, it's written like a person is talking to you, not like a manual."
— Alia Breyer, Venice, Florida

"This book proves that no matter how good you are, you can always learn a lot more."
— Steve LaForte, Winchester, Ontario

"Great writing! Easy to understand. Takes the fear out of learning the program. (I wish textbooks were written this well!)"
— Gary Parnell, Dallas, Texas

"Very humorous and entertaining. Took the fear out of learning what seemed like a rather daunting program."
— Ray Gorzynski, Sudbury, Ontario

"Written in a down-to-earth style. Made coping with CorelDraw very easy."
— Jacqueline Conway, London, England

"It covers *everything,* including the best shortcuts."
— Susie Held, Spring City, Pennsylvania

"The humor really helps non-technical Corel users master the ins and outs of the program. I laughed a lot! Thanks for publishing such a helpful tool!"
— Celia Ng, New York, New York

"I liked the lucid way the basic topics were covered. Now I feel I can make progress on my own. Corel should enclose a copy of this book with their software!"
— C. E. Smith, Trenton, Ontario

"This book gives me information fast and easy. I like it!"
— Michael Evan Carnes, Cincinnati, Ohio

"Clean and to-the-point. It is the only book that clearly identifies the differences between all parts of CorelDraw."
— Mel Knoyle, Salem, Oregon

"I was rolling on the ground at some of the comments — hilarious! It made the learning easier and enjoyable."
— William Dunlop III, West Chester, Pennsylvania

"Written in a very basic style that is easy to understand, and there are plenty of illustrations to guide us. This is the first *...For Dummies* book purchase I have made, and I plan to purchase more."
— Mardi MacLachlan, MacTier, Ontario

CORELDRAW!™ 6
FOR
DUMMIES®

CORELDRAW!™ 6 FOR DUMMIES®

by Deke McClelland

IDG Books Worldwide, Inc.
An International Data Group Company

Foster City, CA ♦ Chicago, IL ♦ Indianapolis, IN ♦ Braintree, MA ♦ Dallas, TX

CorelDRAW!™ 6 For Dummies®

Published by
IDG Books Worldwide, Inc.
An International Data Group Company
919 E. Hillsdale Blvd.
Suite 400
Foster City, CA 94404

Library of Congress Catalog Card No.: 95-78769

ISBN: 1-56884-901-x

Printed in the United States of America

10 9 8 7 6 5 4 3 2 1

1B/RZ/RQ/ZV

Distributed in the United States by IDG Books Worldwide, Inc.

Distributed by Macmillan Canada for Canada; by Computer and Technical Books for the Caribbean Basin; by Contemporanea de Ediciones for Venezuela; by Distribuidora Cuspide for Argentina; by CITEC for Brazil; by Ediciones ZETA S.C.R. Ltda. for Peru; by Editorial Limusa SA for Mexico; by Transworld Publishers Limited in the United Kingdom and Europe; by Al-Maiman Publishers & Distributors for Saudi Arabia; by Simron Pty. Ltd. for South Africa; by IDG Communications (HK) Ltd. for Hong Kong; by Toppan Company Ltd. for Japan; by Addison Wesley Publishing Company for Korea; by Longman Singapore Publishers Ltd. for Singapore, Malaysia, Thailand, and Indonesia; by Unalis Corporation for Taiwan; by WS Computer Publishing Company, Inc. for the Philippines; by WoodsLane Pty. Ltd. for Australia; by WoodsLane Enterprises Ltd. for New Zealand.

For general information on IDG Books Worldwide's books in the U.S., please call our Consumer Customer Service department at 800-762-2974. For reseller information, including discounts and premium sales, please call our Reseller Customer Service department at 800-434-3422.

For information on where to purchase IDG Books Worldwide's books outside the U.S., contact IDG Books Worldwide at 415-655-3021 or fax 415-655-3295.

For information on translations, contact Marc Jeffrey Mikulich, Director, Foreign & Subsidiary Rights, at IDG Books Worldwide, 415-655-3018 or fax 415-655-3295.

For sales inquiries and special prices for bulk quantities, write to the address above or call IDG Books Worldwide at 415-655-3200.

For information on using IDG Books Worldwide's books in the classroom, or ordering examination copies, contact Jim Kelly at 800-434-2086.

For authorization to photocopy items for corporate, personal, or educational use, please contact Copyright Clearance Center, 222 Rosewood Drive, Danvers, MA 01923, or fax 508-750-4470.

 is a trademark under exclusive license to IDG Books Worldwide, Inc., from International Data Group, Inc.

About the Author

Deke McClelland is the author of more than 30 books about desktop publishing and graphics programs for the Mac and Windows, including IDG's best-selling *Macworld Photoshop 3 Bible, Photoshop 3 For Macs For Dummies, CorelDRAW! For Dummies, Mac Multimedia & CD-ROMs For Dummies, Macworld FreeHand 4 Bible,* and *PageMaker 5 For Windows For Dummies.*

He is also a contributing editor to *Macworld* magazine and frequently pops up in *Publish* and *PC World.* He received the Ben Franklin Award for the Best Computer Book in 1989 and won prestigious Computer Press Awards in 1990, 1992, and 1994. When he isn't writing, he hosts the television series "Digital Gurus" for the Jones Computer Network. In his few minutes of spare time, he lives with his wife and aging cat in Boulder, Colorado.

ABOUT IDG BOOKS WORLDWIDE

Welcome to the world of IDG Books Worldwide.

IDG Books Worldwide, Inc., is a subsidiary of International Data Group, the world's largest publisher of computer-related information and the leading global provider of information services on information technology. IDG was founded more than 25 years ago and now employs more than 7,500 people worldwide. IDG publishes more than 235 computer publications in 67 countries (see listing below). More than 70 million people read one or more IDG publications each month.

Launched in 1990, IDG Books Worldwide is today the #1 publisher of best-selling computer books in the United States. We are proud to have received 8 awards from the Computer Press Association in recognition of editorial excellence, and our best-selling ...For Dummies® series has more than 19 million copies in print with translations in 28 languages. IDG Books Worldwide, through a recent joint venture with IDG's Hi-Tech Beijing, became the first U.S. publisher to publish a computer book in the People's Republic of China. In record time, IDG Books Worldwide has become the first choice for millions of readers around the world who want to learn how to better manage their businesses.

Our mission is simple: Every one of our books is designed to bring extra value and skill-building instructions to the reader. Our books are written by experts who understand and care about our readers. The knowledge base of our editorial staff comes from years of experience in publishing, education, and journalism — experience which we use to produce books for the '90s. In short, we care about books, so we attract the best people. We devote special attention to details such as audience, interior design, use of icons, and illustrations. And because we use an efficient process of authoring, editing, and desktop publishing our books electronically, we can spend more time ensuring superior content and spend less time on the technicalities of making books.

You can count on our commitment to deliver high-quality books at competitive prices on topics consumers want to read about. At IDG Books Worldwide, we value quality, and we have been delivering quality for more than 25 years. You'll find no better book on a subject than an IDG book.

John J. Kilcullen

John Kilcullen
President and CEO
IDG Books Worldwide, Inc.

WINNER
Eighth Annual
Computer Press
Awards ≥ 1992

WINNER
Ninth Annual
Computer Press
Awards ≥ 1993

IDG BOOKS WORLDWIDE

IDG Books Worldwide, Inc., is a subsidiary of International Data Group, the world's largest publisher of computer-related information and the leading global provider of information services on information technology. International Data Group publishes over 235 computer publications in 67 countries. More than seventy million people read one or more International Data Group publications each month. The officers are Patrick J. McGovern, Founder and Board Chairman; Kelly Conlin, President; Jim Casella, Chief Operating Officer. International Data Group's publications include: **ARGENTINA'S** Computerworld Argentina, Infoworld Argentina; **AUSTRALIA'S** Computerworld Australia, Computer Living, Australian PC World, Australian Macworld, Network World, Mobile Business Australia, Publish!, Reseller, IDG Sources; **AUSTRIA'S** Computerwelt Oesterreich, PC Test; **BELGIUM'S** Data News (CW); **BOLIVIA'S** Computerworld; **BRAZIL'S** Computerworld, Connections, Game Power, Mundo Unix, PC World, Publish, Super Game; **BULGARIA'S** Computerworld Bulgaria, PC & Mac World Bulgaria, Network World Bulgaria; **CANADA'S** CIO Canada, Computerworld Canada, InfoCanada, Network World Canada, Reseller; **CHILE'S** Computerworld Chile, Informatica; **COLOMBIA'S** Computerworld Colombia, PC World; **COSTA RICA'S** PC World; **CZECH REPUBLIC'S** Computerworld, Elektronika, PC World; **DENMARK'S** Communications World, Computerworld Denmark, Computerworld Focus, Macintosh Produktkatalog, Macworld Danmark, PC World Danmark, PC Produktguide, Tech World, Windows World; **ECUADOR'S** PC World Ecuador; **EGYPT'S** Computerworld (CW) Middle East, PC World Middle East; **FINLAND'S** MikroPC, Tietoviikko, Tietoverkko; **FRANCE'S** Distributique, GOLDEN MAC, InfoPC, Le Guide du Monde Informatique, Le Monde Informatique, Telecoms & Reseaux; **GERMANY'S** Computerwoche, Computerwoche Focus, Computerwoche Extra, Electronic Entertainment, Gamepro, Information Management, Macwelt, Netzwelt, PC Welt, Publish, Publish; **GREECE'S** Publish & Macworld; **HONG KONG'S** Computerworld Hong Kong, PC World Hong Kong; **HUNGARY'S** Computerworld SZT, PC World; **INDIA'S** Computers & Communications; **INDONESIA'S** Info Komputer; **IRELAND'S** ComputerScope; **ISRAEL'S** Beyond Windows, Computerworld Israel, Multimedia, PC World Israel; **ITALY'S** Computerworld Italia, Lotus Magazine, Macworld Italia, Networking Italia, PC Shopping Italy, PC World Italia; **JAPAN'S** Computerworld Today, Information Systems World, Macworld Japan, Nikkei Personal Computing, SunWorld Japan, Windows World; **KENYA'S** East African Computer News; **KOREA'S** Computerworld Korea, Macworld Korea, PC World Korea; **LATIN AMERICA'S** GamePro; **MALAYSIA'S** Computerworld Malaysia, PC World Malaysia; **MEXICO'S** Compu Edicion, Compu Manufactura, Computacion/Punto de Venta, Computerworld Mexico, MacWorld, Mundo Unix, PC World, Windows; **THE NETHERLANDS'** Computer! Totaal, Computable (CW), LAN Magazine, Lotus Magazine, MacWorld; **NEW ZEALAND'S** Computer Buyer, Computerworld New Zealand, Network World, New Zealand PC World; **NIGERIA'S** PC World Africa; **NORWAY'S** Computerworld Norge, Lotusworld Norge, Macworld Norge, Maxi Data, Networld, PC World Ekspress, PC World Nettverk, PC World Norge, PC World's Produktguide, Publish& Multimedia World, Student Data, Unix World, Windowsworld; **PAKISTAN'S** PC World Pakistan; **PANAMA'S** PC World Panama; **PERU'S** Computerworld Peru, PC World; **PEOPLE'S REPUBLIC OF CHINA'S** China Computerworld, China Infoworld, China PC Info Magazine, Computer Fan, PC World China, Electronics International, Electronics Today/Multimedia World, Electronic Product World, China Network World, Software World Magazine, Telecom Product World; **PHILIPPINES'** Computerworld Philippines, PC Digest (PCW); **POLAND'S** Computerworld Poland, Computerworld Special Report, Networld, PC World/Komputer, Sunworld; **PORTUGAL'S** Cerebro/PC World, Correio Informatico/Computerworld, MacIn; **ROMANIA'S** Computerworld, PC World, Telecom Romania; **RUSSIA'S** Computerworld-Moscow, Mir - PK (PCW), Sety (Networks); **SINGAPORE'S** Computerworld Southeast Asia, PC World Singapore; **SLOVENIA'S** Monitor Magazine; **SOUTH AFRICA'S** Computer Mail (CIO), Computing S.A., Network World S.A., Software World; **SPAIN'S** Advanced Systems, Amiga World, Computerworld Espana, Communicaciones World, Macworld Espana, NeXTWORLD, Super Juegos Magazine (GamePro), PC World Espana, Publish; **SWEDEN'S** Attack, ComputerSweden, Corporate Computing, Macworld, Mikrodatorn, Natverk & Kommunikation, PC World, CAP & Design, Datalngenjoren, Maxi Data, Windows World; **SWITZERLAND'S** Computerworld Schweiz, Macworld Schweiz, PC Tip; **TAIWAN'S** Computerworld Taiwan, PC World Taiwan; **THAILAND'S** Thai Computerworld; **TURKEY'S** Computerworld Monitor, Macworld Turkiye, PC World Turkiye; **UKRAINE'S** Computerworld, Computers+Software Magazine; **UNITED KINGDOM'S** Computing/Computerworld, Connexion/Network World, Lotus Magazine, Macworld, Open Computing/Sunworld; **UNITED STATES'** Advanced Systems, AmigaWorld, Cable in the Classroom, CD Review, CIO, Computerworld, Computerworld Client/Server Journal, Digital Video, DOS World, Electronic Entertainment Magazine (E2), Federal Computer Week, Game Hits, GamePro, IDG Books Worldwide, Infoworld, Laser Event, Macworld, Maximize, Multimedia World, Network World, PC Letter, PC World, Publish, SWATPro, Video Event; **URUGUAY'S** PC World Uruguay; **VENEZUELA'S** Computerworld Venezuela, PC World; **VIETNAM'S** PC World Vietnam.
08/30/95

Credits

**Senior Vice President
and Publisher**
Milissa L. Koloski

Associate Publisher
Diane Graves Steele

Brand Manager
Judith A. Taylor

Editorial Managers
Kristin A. Cocks
Mary Corder

Product Development Manager
Mary Bednarek

Editorial Executive Assistant
Richard Graves

Editorial Assistants
Chris Collins
Stacey Holden Prince
Laurie Maudlin
Kevin Spencer

Acquisitions Assistant
Suki Gear

Production Director
Beth Jenkins

**Supervisor of
Project Coordination**
Cindy L. Phipps

Supervisor of Page Layout
Kathie S. Schnorr

Pre-Press Coordination
Steve Peake
Tony Augsburger
Patricia R. Reynolds
Theresa Sánchez-Baker
Elizabeth Cárdenas-Nelson

Media/Archive Coordination
Paul Belcastro
Leslie Popplewell

Graphic Coordination
Shelley Lea
Gina Scott
Carla Radzikinas

Project Editor
Julie King

Technical Reviewer
Lee Musick

Project Coordinator
J. Tyler Connor

Production Page Layout
Shawn Aylsworth
Linda M. Boyer
Dominique DeFelice
Angela F. Hunckler
Jane Martin
Laura Puranen
Alicia Shimer

Proofreaders
Sandra Profant
Gwenette Gaddis
Dwight Ramsey
Robert Springer

Indexer
Sherry Massey

Cover Design
Kavish + Kavish

Acknowledgments

The author wishes to extend his grateful thank-you-very-kindly's to all the groovy folks who helped him with the book that you now hold in your hands. Julie Galla from Corel never once failed to return a phone call and kept me stocked with a steady stream of products. Lee Musick turned out to be one of the best technical editors I've ever had the pleasure of working with. And Julie King did her usual exemplary job of ensuring that the text is unambiguous, humorous, and grammaticologically correct.

No page of thank-yees would be complete without one directed at my charming and beautiful wife of ten years, Elizabeth. She's the cat's meow (which has confused our cat on more than one occasion).

(The Publisher would like to give special thanks to Patrick J. McGovern, without whom this book would not have been possible.)

Contents at a Glance

Cartoons at a Glance

By Rich Tennant

"Hey Dad - guess how many Milk Duds fit inside your disk drive."

page 7

"YOU'VE PLUGGED YOUR MOUSE INTO THE ELECTRIC SHAVER OUTLET AGAIN."

page 259

Determined to help Wanda find her lost file, Del connects his 'Royco 100 Fish Finder' to her hard disk.

page 372

"WELL'P — THERE GOES THE AMBIANCE."

page 272

THE GREAT THING ABOUT THIS DRAWING PROGRAM IS, ITS MADE CREATING SALES FLYERS AS EASY AS PUTTING ONE FOOT IN FRONT OF THE OTHER.

page 345

"OOPS, I FORGOT TO LOG OFF AGAIN."

page 43

"It says,' Seth- Please see us about your idea to wrap newsletter text around company logo. Production!"

page 235

"THE FUNNY THING IS, I NEVER KNEW THEY HAD DESKTOP PUBLISHING SOFTWARE FOR PAPER SHREDDERS."

page 63

"WOW! I DIDN'T EVEN THINK THEY MADE A 2000 DOT PER INCH FONT!"

page 189

"OK, TECHNICALLY THIS SHOULD WORK, JUDY. TYPE THE WORD 'GOODYEAR' ALL CAPS, BOLDFACE, AT 700-POINT TYPE SIZE."

page 124

Table of Contents

. . . .

Introduction

The *Guinness Book of World Records* doesn't seem to offer a category for the most immense software package. If it did, the prize would clearly have to go to CorelDraw 6. This ample, expansive, sprawling, capacious, comprehensive program is *so* large that it consumes four CD-ROMs. That's three gigabytes of stuff — more than would fit on the combined hard drives of your computer, your friend's computer, your boss's computer, and your grandma's programmable calculator.

Simply put, CorelDraw 6 is an all-in-one artist's studio. It enables you to create precise illustrations, draw free-form artwork, paint electronic masterpieces, edit digital photographs, and even design three-dimensional environments that look every bit as realistic — or surrealistic — as real life. The CorelDraw programs are so powerful that you need a 486 or better computer to run them. The package also includes thousands upon thousands of pieces of clip art, fonts, digital photographs, 3-D models, and other valuable stuff.

All this combined with the program's reasonable price may explain CorelDraw's phenomenal popularity. By some accounts, it's *the* most popular piece of graphics software for the personal computer.

Why a Book . . . For Dummies?

But all this power comes at a price. The CorelDraw 6 package comprises 13 programs. The central program is CorelDraw, which enables you to design professional-quality pages and artwork, but you also get Photo-Paint, Dream 3D, Presents, Depth, Move, Trace, Capture, Multimedia Manager, and a bunch of others. If Corel could come up with a way to market its KitchenSink and Swiss PocketKnife programs, they would be in the package as well.

Needless to say, there's no way to sit down cold with 13 programs and figure them out overnight — in fact, there's really no reason why you should even bother to learn all 13. How can you tell which of these programs are worth your time and which you should ignore? I can tell you from years of personal experience that a few Corel programs are very interesting, some are somewhat interesting, and the rest are pretty darn forgettable — so forgettable that I have to consult Corel's press information to remember them.

So instead of packing your brain full of a bunch of utter nonsense about a bunch of programs you'll *never* touch, I cover just those aspects of those programs that I think you'll find exciting, entertaining, and ultimately useful. Being a generous guy by nature, I leave the boring stuff for another book.

By the way, I should mention that this book is specifically about CorelDraw 6. I suppose that you *could* use it to learn about one of the other versions of the program, but quite a few commands would be different, some tools wouldn't be available, and your screen would look different than the ones pictured throughout this book. I can't say that I recommend this approach.

If you're using an older version of the program, your better bet is to look for an earlier edition of this book. Ask your bookseller for the edition that covers your version of the program. It'll make you smile again.

How to Use This Book

I tried to write this book so that you can approach it from several perspectives, depending on how you learn.

- ✔ If you're a reader — it's been my experience that only *hard-core* readers put up with book introductions — I hope that you'll find my writing lively enough to keep you from falling asleep or collapsing into an information-age coma.

- ✔ If you just want to find out how a command works and then toss the book back into a dusty corner, look up the topic in the index and then turn to the appropriate page. You'll find that this publisher creates an ample, expansive, immense, sprawling, capacious, and comprehensive index, on par with CorelDraw itself.

- ✔ If you already know your way around CorelDraw, flip through the book, check out a few of the tips here and there, and pay special attention to the information marked with the CorelDraw 6 icon.

- ✔ If you hate to read anything without pictures, just read Rich Tennant's comics. I fall into this learning group. (Good news, huh?) Folks like you and me won't learn anything about CorelDraw, but by golly, we'll get in a few yucks.

- ✔ If you want to get a quick idea of what this book is like, read the four chapters in Part V. Each chapter contains a series of short sections that not only give you an indication of the high-falutin' caliber of information in this book but also mesmerize you with my enchanting style and wit. Well, perhaps *mesmerize* is the wrong word. How about *clomp you over the head?*

- ✔ If you don't much like the idea of reading a computer book but you're so confused that you don't even know what questions to ask, start at Chapter 1 and see where it takes you. I promise that I won't leave you wallowing in the dust.

This book has been read and reread by folks who don't know the first thing about CorelDraw, and to this day, they are only marginally confused. Considering that they all led happy and productive lives before they read *CorelDRAW! 6 For Dummies* and that only three of them had to seek therapy afterwards, I think that this is one heck of a book.

How This Book Is Organized

I've divided *CorelDRAW! 6 For Dummies* into five digestible parts, each of which contains three to six chapters, which are themselves divided into gobs of discrete sections, which contain these funny little letter-units called *words*. I thought about including a synopsis of every sentence in the book in this introduction, but then I thought, no, it'd be better if you had a chance to read the book before the next Ice Age set in. So here are brief descriptions of the parts instead.

Part I: The Stuff Everyone Pretends They Already Know

We're all dumb about some things and smart about others. But however smart we may be about our key interests in life, we're afraid that our dumb topics will be the death of us. At any moment, someone may expose us for what we truly are — congenital half-wits. You know what I'm saying here? (Sob.) Pass me that tissue, would you? (Sniff.) Thank you. (Honk.)

So this part of the book is about answering all those questions that you had and didn't know you had, and even if you did know, you wouldn't have asked anyone because all your friends would have laughed at you and branded you an Industrial Age cretin. These chapters are like a CorelDraw information pill. Swallow them and be smart. Or at least, better informed.

Part II: Let the Graphics Begin

Now that you've bared your soul and learned the basics, it's time to start expressing yourself and creating some bona fide computer art. Not an artist? Not to worry. Neither are thousands of other folks who use this program. In fact, CorelDraw is specifically designed to accommodate artists and nonartists alike, enabling you to express the uniquely individual creative impulses that surge through, well, all those places that things tend to surge through. That is to say, you'll be able to get the job done. You can even throw in a few special effects for good measure.

Part III: Getting the Message Out There (Wherever There Is)

Many of us feel the special need to share things with other people. Reports, newsletters, and internal memos allow us to show off our personalities and mix in a bit of our literary expertise. Bold headlines like "Joe Bob Receives Employee of the Month Award" or "Sales Up in March" tell a little something about who we are and how we live.

CorelDraw knows that it's not enough to draw pretty pictures; you have to be able to back up those pictures with hard-hitting text. In these chapters, you'll discover that CorelDraw is half drawing program and half document-creation software. You can enter and edit text, design logos and special text effects, create multipage documents, and print the whole thing out on 20-pound bond paper.

Part IV: Corel's Other Amazing Programs

As I mentioned earlier, I try to steer you away from Corel's boring and mostly useless programs and concentrate on the good ones. This part of the book covers two good programs that you're sure to want to check out, Photo-Paint and Dream 3D. In fact, it devotes three full chapters to Photo-Paint, a program that is growing in popularity and is second only to CorelDraw in usefulness and artistic prowess. You'll even learn how to share graphics between Photo-Paint and CorelDraw.

Part V: The Part of Tens

This part of the book is a savory blend of real information and the sort of chatty top-ten lists that prevent us all from understanding too awfully much about anything. In these chapters, you'll find lists of special effects, time-saving shortcuts, obscure features, file formats, and advice for everyday living. Prepare to be entertained as you learn. Prepare to laugh and be studious. Prepare to chortle until factoids come out your nose.

Icons Used in This Book

To alert you to special passages of text that you may or may *not* want to read, the National Bureau of Wacky Graphics has designed the following universal margin icons and thoughtfully interspersed them throughout the book.

Here's an example of something you may want to avoid. This icon highlights a close encounter of the nerd kind, the variety of information that could land you in the intensive care ward if you were to utter it at the Annual Gathering of Hell's Angels. In other words, read if you must, but don't repeat.

Here's something you didn't know, or if you did know it, you're smarter than you thought. Don't be surprised if a single tip makes you fractions of a percentage point more efficient than you were before. It's been known to happen to people just like you.

This may be some bit of information that I've already mentioned. But you may have forgotten it, and I want to drill it into your head. Metaphorically, of course. Or it may be something that I just thought you might like to know — a friendly gesture on my part.

This icon spells danger. Or, at least, something to be watchful for. Try to steer clear of the stuff I describe here.

If you're at all familiar with CorelDraw 3, 4, or 5, you may be keenly interested in how CorelDraw 6 differs from its predecessors. This icon lets you in on the newest features so that you can make the transition to Version 6 in record time. I also point out a few old features that have been changed so dramatically that you may not recognize them without a little help.

This icon calls attention to information that, while mildly interesting, is not in the least bit important to your understanding of CorelDraw. I just throw it in to keep the scandal-mongers happy.

Where to Go from Here

Different people read in different ways. You may want to check out the index or table of contents and look up some bit of information that has been perplexing you for the past few days. Or you might just close the book and use it as a reference the next time you face an impasse or some horrible, confusing problem. Then again, you could just keep on reading, perish the thought. Personally, I couldn't put the book down, but you may have more willpower.

How to Bug Me

If you want to ask me a question, tell me about a mistake, or just share your opinions about this book, feel free to write me at one of these handy e-mail addresses:

America Online: DekeMc

CompuServe: 70640,670

If you're on the Internet, please write me at DekeMc@AOL.com. Those geeks at CompuServe charge a receiving fee for Internet mail.

Don't be discouraged if I don't respond for a couple of weeks. It just means that I'm in over my head with projects and deadlines (as usual). I eventually respond to every e-mail I get. If you write me by regular mail, please include a phone number or e-mail address so that I can respond.

Good luck with the book, and may CorelDraw treat you with the dignity that you — a superior, carbon-based life form — deserve.

Part I

The Stuff Everyone Pretends They Already Know

The 5th Wave   By Rich Tennant

"Hey Dad - guess how many Milk Duds fit inside your disk drive."

In this part . . .

1 magine this: You're enrolled in an introductory computing course. The professor asks you to write a simple computer program. Let's say that you're to create a program that types out a series of *A*s in a column or something equally pointless. Who cares? It's not important. Anyway, the professor takes time to carefully explain the language and logic behind the exercise. Because you secretly harbor an unusually immense brain — granted, you only use it on special occasions — you understand thoroughly. No sweat.

But when you sit down in front of a terminal at the computer lab, you realize that you lack a key bit of information. How are you supposed to get to the point where you start entering your programming instructions? The computer is on, but it just sits there blinking at you. Anything you enter results in an error message. You're so utterly clueless and overwhelmingly frustrated that you don't even know how to ask one of the pompous lab assistants what the heck is going on.

I've been there. I empathize. It stinks. The fact of the matter is, any amount of knowledge is worthless if you don't know the basics. The difficulty, of course, is that lots of folks act as if they already know the basics because they don't want to look like, well, a dummy. But let's face it, when it comes to computers, remarkably few people know what's going on. And those who do tend to be insufferable.

So here are the basics. The following chapters explain all the easy stuff that you've been pretending to know, little realizing that 90 percent of the people around you don't know it either. Soon, you'll be welcomed into the the ranks of the Insufferable Computer Dweebs, a group we're all dying to join.

Chapter 1

What's with All These Programs?

· ·

In This Chapter

- ▶ The uses for CorelDraw
- ▶ Where CorelPhoto-Paint fits in
- ▶ The differences between Draw and Photo-Paint
- ▶ The lowdown on CorelOCR-Trace
- ▶ Should you worry about CorelCapture?
- ▶ The business end of Presents
- ▶ How CorelDream 3D will boggle your mind
- ▶ The utter wackiness of Depth and Motion 3D
- ▶ Why Multimedia Manager wants to be your electronic librarian

· ·

*O*nce upon a time, back when dinosaurs roamed the earth, CorelDraw used to be a single program. Weird, huh? Nowadays, the CorelDraw 6 box includes more than ten separate programs, each of which you can use independently or in tandem with its little electronic friends. This chapter introduces many of the programs and explains their relative benefits and degrees of usefulness, which range from truly stupendous to barely worth yawning over. I also tell you which chapters in this book, if any, contain more information about each program.

Lots of computer companies try to increase the value of their core products by including additional programs. In commercial circles, this technique is called *bundling*. For students of bundling, Corel is about the most aggressive case study around.

You Bought What?

You know you're in trouble when just purchasing a program is complicated. Over the last few years, CorelDraw's marketing has become more and more convoluted. Unlike most vendors — which release a new version of a product and discontinue the old one — Corel still sells most versions of the CorelDraw package, from Version 3 on up.

✔ The most recent upgrade, CorelDraw 6, is compatible exclusively with Windows 95 and Windows NT 3.5.1. If you're still using Windows 3.1, you'll have to upgrade. CorelDraw 6 has a suggested retail price of $700 (though you can expect to pay about $200 less than that) and includes all the programs discussed in this chapter.

✔ CorelDraw 5 runs fine on Windows 3.1, but it doesn't run so well under Windows 95. If you're running Windows 95 on your PC, you'll want to install CorelDraw 6 instead of Version 5. Currently priced the same as Version 6 — 700 smackers — CorelDraw 5 includes the desktop publishing program Ventura, which is missing from all other versions, including Version 6.

✔ Even so, I don't know why anyone would buy Version 5 these days. Ventura is an okay program and all, but it isn't a sufficient motivation for paying full price for CorelDraw 5. And at $200 retail, CorelDraw 4 is half the price and nearly as capable. It seems to me that you'll either want the newest of the new — CorelDraw 6 — or an older, cheaper version that functions just fine.

✔ CorelDraw 3 is the best value. Costing a mere $100 retail — I've seen it as low as $55 in discount stores — the darn thing includes seven separate programs — more than enough to please the casual graphics enthusiast.

Isn't that confusing? And better still, it may all change. Corel may dump one of the programs, most likely Version 3 or 4, and possibly lower the price of Version 5. It's like trying to predict the price of pork belly futures.

I'm not sure whether this weird sales strategy is profitable for Corel, but I sure hope that it catches on with other software publishers. After all, it's confusion like this that keeps computer authors like me employed.

CorelDraw

This is the program that started it all. Not only is CorelDraw — or just Draw for short — the program after which the package is named, it's the most powerful and the most useful of the bunch. Not surprisingly, therefore, it's the one I talk about in the most detail. Chapters 2 through 13 blather on at length about this wonderful piece of software.

What can you draw with Draw? Why, you can draw *anything*. Free-form graphics of butterflies or unicorns engaged in some ridiculous activity, architectural plans for a bathroom off the linen closet (I wish *I* had one of those), maps of downtown Disney World, technical drawings of car engines before and after reassembly, anatomical illustrations that show food going down the trachea (and the ensuing coughing fit that follows) . . . the list is endless, or at least close enough to endless that I'd run the risk of boring you into a coma if I were to continue.

Wait, there's more. You can open and edit clip art — you know, those drawings that other people create specifically so that you can mess them up. You can create wild text effects, such as a logo or two for Stuckey's. You can even design documents such as advertisements for Stuckey's, fliers for Stuckey's, and posters for Long John Silver's. (What does Stuckey's need with posters, anyway? We're all familiar with their pecan logs.)

Thar's math in them thar objects d'art

Math is the driving force behind CorelDraw. I know, it's sick, but it's true. When you draw a wiggly line, for example, Draw takes down the coordinates of the first and last points and calculates a mathematical description of the curve between the two points. Draw thinks of each line, shape, or character of text as a mathematical object, which is why Draw and programs like it are sometimes called *object-oriented* software. Later, when you print your drawing, the program explains all this math to the printer, which in turn draws the objects as smoothly as it can so that they all look like you drew them by hand and not with a computer.

If your printed drawings look jagged, it's because you're using a cheap printer. You can improve the appearance of your drawings by buying a better printer or by paying to have your drawing printed at a service bureau. Either way, it involves the outlay of some additional cash. For the whole story on printing, read Chapter 13.

CorelPhoto-Paint

The primary purpose of CorelPhoto-Paint, discussed in Chapters 15 through 17, is to enable you to make changes to photographic images. You can change the color scheme of a photo so that everyone in your family looks like they had the sense not to wear bright orange and avocado green in the seventies. You can apply special effects so that Grandma Edna's face appears molded in lead. You can retouch subtle or bothersome details such as Junior's unusually immense chin wart. You can even combine the contents of two different photos so that Uncle Mike and Aunt Rosie are standing shoulder to shoulder, even though the two of them would just as soon hang out in the same room together as take a flying leap into the Grand Canyon. And if that sounds like an accurate description of your family, you need all the help you can get.

CorelPhoto-Paint was originally sold by ZSoft — the same folks who make PC Paintbrush — under the name PhotoFinish. Corel has made some pretty significant changes over the years, so most folks would hardly recognize the program. Wow, titillating stuff, eh?

Finding photos to edit

The following list explains a few ways to get photos on a floppy disk or Photo CD so that you can edit them in Photo-Paint:

✔ You can take a photograph to a service bureau and have it *scanned* onto a floppy disk, which means to read the photo and convert it to a digital image, sort of like recording music to a CD. Some folks call scanning *digitizing.* This is generally a pretty expensive proposition, around $2 to $10 per photo, depending on whether you scan the photo in black and white or in color.

✔ To locate a service bureau, look in the Yellow Pages under "Desktop Publishing." Some cities have lots of them. San Francisco, Los Angeles, Seattle, Chicago, New York, and all those other coastal towns have as many service bureaus as they have adult book stores. But out in the heartland, they're a little harder to come by. You may have to search around a little bit. If you have friends in the computer graphics biz, ask them for recommendations.

- ✔ If you intend to do a lot of scanning, you may want to purchase your own scanner. Prices range from a few hundred bucks for a cheesy hand-held scanner to $1,000 and up for a top-of-the-line color model.

- ✔ Kodak's Photo CD technology provides a better alternative to scanning your images to disk, both in terms of quality and economy. For around $100, you can transfer up to 100 photos from slides, negatives, or undeveloped rolls of film to a compact disc that's identical in appearance to CDs that play music. Of course, to take advantage of Photo CD, you need a CD-ROM drive, which can cost $300 or more.

- ✔ For service bureaus that can put your images on Photo CD, look in the Yellow Pages under "Photo Finishing-Retail." Word has it that some Wal-Mart stores are even offering this service in their film processing departments.

- ✔ You can also buy CDs filled with photographs shot by professional photographers. Called *stock photos,* these images run the gamut from famous landmarks to animals, from textures to people engaged in people-like pursuits. Corel sells its own line of stock photo CDs, which you can buy for a little as $15 a pop.

- ✔ If you subscribe to an on-line service such as CompuServe or America Online, you can download photos using your modem. Watch out, though. Because of their large file size, photos take several minutes — sometimes hours — to download. You can waste some major bucks in access charges if you're not careful.

Painting from scratch

You don't have to edit photos in Photo-Paint. You can also paint images from scratch. The difference between drawing in CorelDraw and painting in Photo-Paint is that the painting process is a lot more intuitive. In fact, you don't need my help to paint an image. It's totally easy. You sketch a little here, erase a little there, fill in some details, and keep working on it until you get it right. Kids love painting on a computer. You'll love it too. It's the easiest thing you can do with *any* computer program, I swear.

Picture yourself done up in pixels

Ah, even in the Simple-Simon world of computer painting, Technical Stuff rears its nerdy head. Remember that I said that CorelDraw defines lines, shapes, and text using complex mathematical equations? (If not, and assuming you care, check out the sidebar "There's math in them thar' objects d'art," earlier in this chapter.) Well, Photo-Paint defines the entire image — whether it's a photograph or something you painted from scratch — using thousands or even millions of tiny colored squares called *pixels*.

A Photo-Paint image is similar to a mosaic. When you get close to a mosaic, you can see the individual colored tiles. When you get far away, the tiles blur into a recognizable picture. Pixels work just like those tiles. When you magnify an image in Photo-Paint, you can see the individual pixels. When you restore the image to its regular size, the pixels blur together.

Draw and Photo-Paint Duke It Out

Although both drawings and images are forms of computer artwork, the two are very distinct. Drawings created in CorelDraw feature sharp edges, as demonstrated in Figure 1-1. The second half of the figure shows an enlarged detail so that you can see what a difference math makes. Even when printed at a really large size, a drawing retains its detail.

Figure 1-1:
No matter how large or small you print a drawing, it's all smooth lines and high contrast.

Images created with Photo-Paint feature softer edges. One shade flows continuously into the next. *C'est magnifique, trés* artsie fartsie, *n'est-ce pas?* But like Achilles — you know, that Greek guy with the bad heel — images have a fatal flaw. They look better when printed at small sizes. When they're printed large, you can see the jagged transitions between colors, as illustrated in Figure 1-2. (If you read the last Technical Stuff sidebar, you'll recognize the colored squares as pixels.)

Figure 1-2:
When printed small, paintings look fine, but when printed large, they look like a stinky pile of goo.

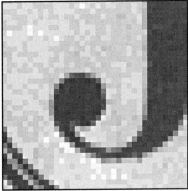

You can't use CorelDraw to edit scanned photos. Because photos are images, you can only edit them in Photo-Paint. Likewise, you can't edit stuff that you create in a drawing program in Photo-Paint.

CorelOCR-Trace

CorelOCR-Trace is a conversion program. It converts Photo-Paint images to CorelDraw drawings by tracing the outlines of lines and shapes in the image. Suppose that you've put pen to paper and sketched out that plan of the bathroom off the linen closet discussed earlier. Now you want to convert the plan to a CorelDraw drawing. How can you get your hand-drawn sketch into Draw? Scan it, open and modify it in Photo-Paint, and then convert it using CorelOCR-Trace, that's how.

Unfortunately, converting an image to a drawing is an iffy proposition. It relies on something called artificial intelligence, which is about as reliable as military intelligence. The program tries to emulate your brain, but it invariably does a pretty poor job. That's why you have to be prepared to edit the drawing in CorelDraw.

Oh, yes, that's the word *ojoucd* — no wait, it's *qohoot*

CorelOCR-Trace can also read. If you scan in a page of text, the program can convert the page to a computer text document that you can open and edit in a word processor such as WordPerfect or Microsoft Word. This capability is called *optical character recognition,* or simply by its initials, *OCR.*

Unfortunately, OCR involves even more artificial intelligence than converting images to drawings.

Depending on the quality of the page you want Trace to read, the program can easily confuse one letter for another. For example, the word *optical* might be read as *optkal, ogucd, ojoucd,* or *qohoot.* Don't get me wrong — CorelOCR-Trace is as good as most other OCR programs on the market. But it's highly unlikely that it will read *any* page 100 percent correctly. In some cases, it's easier to enter the text from scratch.

In a time when magazine articles, TV commercials, and CNN news blips remind you on a daily basis how much new stuff is out there that you're totally unaware of, isn't it nice to know that you can get away with *not* knowing something? The fact is, most folks don't need to learn CorelOCR-Trace. Oh sure, *you* might. But you won't. And neither will you, over there. No, not you, ma'am. In the blue. Yes, that's right, *you.* See, although it's very capable, CorelOCR-Trace is a special-interest program, of very limited value to most people. I never use it myself. And if *I* never use it, well, need I say more?

CorelCapture

This program is hardly a program at all. It barely cuts the mustard, as 'twere. It holdeth ne'er so much as a candle to those whose company it keeps.

What I'm trying to say is that CorelCapture barely warrants my mentioning it. In fact, why don't you go ahead and skip to the next section. You have better things to do than read about CorelCapture. Iron your socks, for example. Learn how to play the pan pipe. Make noises with your armpit.

Okay, now that I've gone and gotten you all excited about this program, I'll tell you a little about what it does. CorelCapture takes pictures of your screen that are called *screen shots.* This book is chock full of such pictures. They allow me to describe CorelDraw's interface while at the same time showing it to you.

Pretty cool, huh? The only problem is, you'll probably never need to use this program. What do you need with screen shots? Do you want to wallpaper your room with the insides of CorelDraw? Heck no. So unless you're documenting a program like I am in this book, CorelCapture is of no use to you.

Just in case you find yourself loving this program in direct violation of my specific instructions, here's a little something you should know: You can use Photo-Paint to edit the pictures you shoot with CorelCapture. In fact, that's exactly what I did to refine many of the figures in this book.

CorelPresents

Previous versions of CorelDraw included three programs that you could use to create business presentations (assuming, of course, that you had the slightest interest in creating business presentations):

- ✔ CorelChart enabled you to create business graphics. You know — bar charts, pie charts, anything to show how well the company is doing, how much market share everyone can expect, how much money is going down the tubes, and the like.

- ✔ CorelMove was an animation package that enabled you to make an image move about the screen and generally attract attention.

- ✔ CorelShow enabled you to put it all together in a presentation. You could print Show files to slides or play them on-screen, complete with whiz-bang effects.

This multiprogram approach was inconvenient at best, and Corel has wisely combined Chart, Move, and Show into a single program called Presents. Now you can create stunning slide shows that would impress Ross Perot from the safety and comfort of a single program.

The thing is, few folks seem to use CorelDraw for presentations. In the hundreds of response cards that wonderful, delightful, beautiful readers sent in about previous editions of this book, about a quarter of them asked for more concentration on Photo-Paint. No one — not a single soul — asked for more presentation information. So guess what? I tossed the presentation chapters into a fiery pit and wrote three new Photo-Paint chapters. Hey, that's just the kind of democracy-loving, responsive, and all-around considerate kind of guy I am.

CorelDream 3D

When most folks think of computer graphics, they conjure up vivid three-dimensional images, the sort of stuff you simply can't create without computers. You know, like that cool ballroom scene in Disney's *Beauty and the Beast* or the new Pixar movie, *Toy Story,* which was created using nothing but computers. And it seems as if the intro to every TV show includes some kind of 3-D graphics, whether it's a spinning logo or a bunch of wacky letters whizzing across the screen. Whatever the case, every image is rendered in incredible, hyper-realistic detail, as if you died and went to Bizarro World.

CorelDream 3D is a new program that lets you create your own hyper-realistic, Bizarro-World, 3-D graphics. The problem is that it's pretty darn complicated — like any 3-D drawing program. First you have to build a model of an object, which is roughly equivalent to constructing a geodesic dome out of Tinker Toys. Then you have to wrap a surface around the shape, which is kind of like stretching a balloon or some other elastic plastic around your Tinker Toys. Next, you have to amass all your models together and set up lights and camera angles. And when you're finished, you don't print the drawing. That would take too long. Instead, you render it out to an image file, which may take a few minutes or a few hours, depending on the complexity of the graphic. After that little process is completed, you can open the image in Photo-Paint and print it.

Sound hard? Well, it is hard. The truth is, 3-D drawing is one of the most complicated pursuits humans and computers can engage in. But what the heck, Dream 3D is worth a look-see anyway, which is what Chapter 18 is all about. There I tell you how to get to first base with this powerful but difficult program. The rest of the bases are up to you.

CorelDepth and CorelMotion 3D

Just in case CorelDream doesn't fit all your 3-D needs, CorelDraw 6 includes two additional programs, CorelDepth and CorelMotion 3D. The former (Depth) lets you create three-dimensional text effects. The latter (Motion 3D) is an animation program that's great for making type and logos fly across the screen through the simulated confines of three-dimensional space.

Both Depth and Motion 3D can be fun. But it takes a lot of time and effort to produce decent effects. You need not only talent but extraordinary patience and determination as well. And though these are great qualities — I've often yearned for a little bit of talent, patience, and determination myself — they are well outside the scope of this ignoble little book.

Dream, Depth, and Motion were all snatched up from programs that run on the PC's main competitor, the Macintosh. CorelDream is based on a popular 3-D drawing program called Ray Dream Designer. CorelDepth was originally AddDepth, also from the company Ray Dream. And CorelMotion began as LogoMotion, a program sold by Specular International. This is the kind of stuff we technology writers know about because we're inundated by daily bucketloads of press releases. No doubt, you couldn't care less where these programs came from, but I just hate to let this precious information go to waste.

Multimedia Manager

With all the stuff you'll be creating with these programs, Corel thought you might need a librarian to keep track of it all. That's where Multimedia Manager comes in. This program is capable of generating thumbnail — that is, tiny — previews of every drawing, image, chart, animation, and presentation stored on a disk. This way, you don't have to open each file one at a time to see what's inside it.

You can also use Multimedia Manager to organize just about any kind of files on the planet. Suppose that you've set up your disk so that one directory contains drawings of African animals and another contains a few North American varieties. But you also want to keep track of the horse-like animals — the zebras, the mustangs, the Triggers — regardless of their home turf. Multimedia Manager is your tool. To create a catalog of horse-ish critters, you just drag files from a file list into a little album window on-screen, and you're in business. You get previews and everything. You can even listen to sound files and watch movies. Cool.

Theoretically groovy as Multimedia Manager might be, it differs from Corel's other programs in that it doesn't let you *create* anything. It's just a muck-about-and-organize-things tool. That's why I don't discuss it in this book. You can get by without it. Later, when you've mastered everything else, you may want to check it out. But in the meantime, you and I have more important territory to cover. Hi ho!

This program used to be called CorelMosaic, but given the popularity of a completely unrelated program also called Mosaic — which lets you browse through the vast Internet — it seemed a wise idea to pick a new name. Besides, Multimedia Manager is a lot more meaningful, don't you think?

And the Rest . . .

Remember the intro to the early episodes of "Gilligan's Island," in which the Gleeful Castaway Singers sang "and the rest" instead of "the Professor and Mary Anne"? Well, that's how I feel about the other programs bundled with CorelDraw 6, including Dialog Editor, CorelScript, and the others — they're not really worth special mention. Oh sure, Font Master lets you monkey around with typefaces, and Color Wizard supposedly ensures that the colors you see on-screen match the ones that come out of your printer (in case you've found that to be a problem). But these programs are about as effective as the Professor was at fixing the Minnow — and that's why I don't cover them in this book.

But Wait, There's More

That's right, if you act now, you'll also receive thousands of clip-art drawings, hundreds of typefaces, lots and lots of photos, and more animation, sound, and movie files than you can shake a Douglas Fir at. No other program comes close to providing this variety of ready-to-use stuff. It's truly amazing and well worth the price of admission on its own. I'll be featuring much of this artwork throughout this book in the hopes that it will make it easier for you to follow along. I'm just that kind of guy.

Because these files take up so much digital storage space — enough to fill literally thousands of disks — they're included on CD-ROM. This means that you need a CD-ROM drive to access this stuff. If your computer doesn't have a CD drive, you may have a friend that has one. Or maybe some other computer in your office is equipped with CD-ROM. Either way, I suggest that you borrow the services of a machine with CD-ROM to copy some of your favorite clip art, fonts, photos, and so on to disk so that you can use them with your computer. If you don't know how to copy files, ask a friend for help or go out and buy a copy of *Windows 95 For Dummies.*

Feeling Overwhelmed?

I don't blame you. Corel has gone a little nuts in the value department. But the fact is, Draw and Photo-Paint are far and away the most useful programs of the bunch. Frankly, few users would even buy a program like OCR-Trace or Multimedia Manager if it weren't bundled with Draw.

To wit, most of this book is devoted to Draw, with the secondary emphasis going to Photo-Paint. But I'll bet you ten comes a runnin' to five (actually, I don't gamble, so I'm a little rusty on the vocabulary) that after you learn how to use these two wonderful programs, you'll find that you can pick up on the others with remarkable ease. No doubt, then, you'll be wanting to take a gander at my next book, *CorelDRAW! For Bionic Brained Ultra-Dweebs.* I'll probably devote the whole thing to CorelMotion 3D.

Chapter 2
See CorelDraw Run

CorelDraw is one son-of-a-gun program. But you don't have a prayer of mastering it until you and the program get a little better acquainted. You have to learn its nuances, understand some of its clockwork and gizmos, study its fruity yet palatable bouquet, and make yourself familiar with its inner psyche. In short, you need to read this chapter. Herein lies the answer to that time-honored question, "What makes Draw draw?"

Draw on the March

Entering the world of CorelDraw is a mysterious but surprisingly straight-forward process. It goes a little something like this:

1. **Turn on your computer.**

   Imagine how embarrassed you'd be if you skipped this step.

2. **Wait for your computer to start up.**

   Dum dee dum. Be patient, it'll be finished soon. This might be a good time to go get some coffee, buy a doughnut, or use the little whatever-sex-you-are's room. Dum dee dum.

3. Enjoy a close encounter with Windows 95.

Yes, CorelDraw 6 requires the newest in new operating systems, Windows 95. If you're looking at some older version of Windows (or DOS, heaven help you), you won't be able to use CorelDraw 6. That's just the way it goes, I'm afraid. Check out the appendix, "Installing CorelDraw 6," for the whole story.

4. Start up CorelDraw.

The easiest way to do this in Windows 95 is to use the Start menu. Use the left mouse button to click on the Start button in the lower-left corner of the screen. A menu of items appears. Move the cursor over the first item in the menu, <u>P</u>rograms, to display a list of folders and programs that you can run. Next, move the cursor over the Corel Applications item to display yet another menu filled with programs that are included in the CorelDraw 6 package. Finally, move the cursor over the CorelDraw 6 item and click on it. Figure 2-1 demonstrates this process in graphic detail.

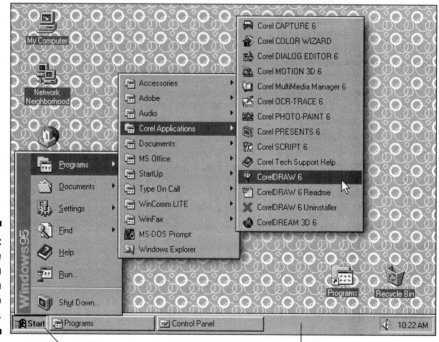

Figure 2-1:
Use the
Start menu
to gain
entrance to
Corel Draw 6.

The all-important Start menu   The taskbar

Don't panic if you have problems with menus and mouse clicks. I cover this stuff in more detail later in this chapter.

Oh, happy day, CorelDraw is now starting. In mere moments, you'll be able to use the program. In the meantime, let me share with you a few tidbits of information designed to increase your enjoyment of this terrific program.

✔ There's more than one way to start CorelDraw. If you like pressing keys more than clicking mouse buttons, try this: Click on the background pattern to deactivate everything. Press Alt+S to display the Start menu and then press P to display the Programs submenu. Assuming that Corel Applications is the only item that begins with a C, press C to display its menu. (Otherwise, press C as many times as it takes to highlight the Corel Applications item and then press the right-arrow key.) Use the up- or down-arrow key to highlight the CorelDraw 6 item and press Enter. To recap, that's Alt+S, P, C, up-arrow key several times, Enter. Piece of cake.

✔ In all likelihood, you can see a window labeled Corel Applications, much like the one in Figure 2-2, on the Windows 95 desktop. If you click on the CorelDraw 6 icon inside this window — spotlighted in the figure — and then press Enter, the program dutifully starts up.

✔ You can also double-click on the CorelDraw 6 icon — that is, press the left mouse button twice in rapid succession — to start the program.

✔ If you figure that you'll be using CorelDraw a lot — as I guess you do if you bothered to purchase this book — you can create a handy-dandy shortcut for it. Click with the right mouse button on the CorelDraw 6 icon spotlighted in Figure 2-2. A little pop-up menu appears. Click on the Create Shortcut item in the menu (or press the S key) to create a new icon labeled CorelDraw 6 [2]. You can drag the icon out onto the desktop to make it accessible whether the Corel Applications window is open or not. To rename the icon, press the F2 key to highlight the current name and then enter a new one from the keyboard.

✔ You can even assign a keyboard shortcut to CorelDraw 6. Right-click on the shortcut icon or the original to bring up the same old pop-up menu and then click on the Properties item or press R. A dialog box named CorelDraw 6 Properties comes up. Click on the Shortcut tab in the top-left corner of the dialog box and then press Alt+K to activate the Shortcut Key option. Now press C (or some other choice you think you can remember). Windows 95 automatically assigns the shortcut Ctrl+Alt+C. (It's always Ctrl+Alt+something.) From now on, when you press Ctrl+Alt+C, Windows 95 starts up CorelDraw 6. It's so convenient, you'll swear you were living in the 21st century.

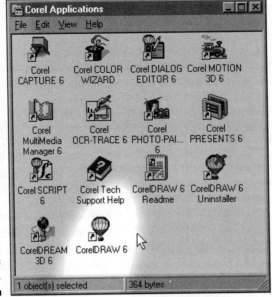

✔ If you don't see a Corel Applications folder loitering about on your Windows 95 desktop, check out the taskbar at the bottom of the screen. There may be a Corel Applications button. Click on it to display the window.

✔ If you can't locate anything with the word Corel in it, whether on the desktop, in the taskbar, or in the Start menu, right-click on the My Computer icon in the upper-left corner of the screen to display a pop-up menu. Then either click on Find or press F. After the Find dialog box appears, type **Corel** and press Enter. Locate the Corel Applications item in the list at the bottom of the dialog box and then double-click on it to open the Corel Applications window.

✔ If you can't find the Corel Applications folder, you need to ask yourself a difficult question. Are you sure that someone installed CorelDraw on this computer? If you aren't sure, ask the person in charge of installing things at your home or office. If the answer turns out to be, "No, why would I install that piece of junk?", consult the appendix in the back of this book for installation instructions. As they say, if you want it done right, you gotta do it yourself.

Interface in Your Face

When you first start CorelDraw, the program produces a welcome screen that contains a bunch of buttons. You have the option to start a new drawing, open a drawing saved to disk, or even peruse the on-screen tutorial. Feel free to check out the tutorial, if you so desire, by clicking on the bottom button. (The first CorelDraw 6 CD-ROM must be in your CD-ROM drive for the tutorial to work.) Otherwise, click on the check box labeled Show This Welcome Screen at Startup to turn off the option. Then click on the Start a New Corel Draw Graphic button in upper-left corner of the welcome screen to make the screen go away forever.

What you see next and what I show you in Figure 2-3 is CorelDraw 6's *interface* (pronounced *in-yur-face*). The interface is your means for working in and communicating with CorelDraw 6. All the bits and pieces that you see labeled in Figure 2-3 are bravely covered at great length and personal risk in the following sections.

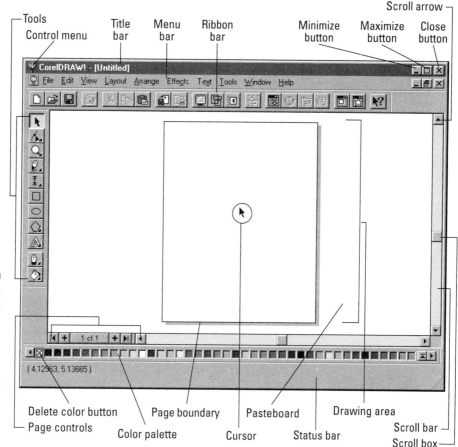

Figure 2-3:
All the stuff that goes into the CorelDraw 6 interface.

If you're familiar with previous versions of CorelDraw, this new interface may come as something of a shocker. Corel's always monkeying around with the buttons and menus, and Version 6 is no exception. But though the new interface may look different, it's remarkably similar to its predecessors. Just take a few deep breaths and walk this way.

Title bar

Topping it all off, the *title bar* tells you the title of the program — in this case, CorelDraw — followed by the name of the document you're working on — in this case, Untitled, because you haven't assigned a name to the document. CorelDraw always creates a new, untitled window when you start the program so that you can begin working right away. On the left side of the title bar is the *Control menu.* On the right side of the title bar is the *Minimize button,* which has a little bar at the bottom of it. To the right of that is either the *Maximize button* (a box with a bar at its top) or the *Restore button* (two little boxes). And to the right of that is a *Close button* with an X in it. These items are common to all Windows 95 programs, but I'll tell you how they work just to while away the time.

✔ When you first start CorelDraw 6, the interface appears inside a window that hovers in front of the Windows 95 desktop and any other programs you may be using. How distracting! To cover up all that background stuff, click on the Maximize button. Now the interface fills the screen in floor-to-ceiling cinematic splendor.

✔ To restore the CorelDraw interface to its cramped quarters in a floating window, click on the Restore button. The background stuff becomes accessible again.

✔ You can move the floating CorelDraw window around by dragging on the title bar — that is, pressing and holding the left mouse button on the title bar while moving the mouse.

✔ To change the size of the floating window, position your cursor over one of the window's four corners or one of its four sides. Your cursor changes to a line with arrowheads at either end. Drag the corner or side as desired.

✔ If you want to get CorelDraw out of your face for a moment and you're really feeling daring, click on the Minimize button to hide the CorelDraw window entirely. A CorelDraw button appears in the taskbar at the bottom of the screen to show you that CorelDraw is still running but has gone into hiding. Click on the button to bring the interface back into view.

✔ To quit CorelDraw 6, click on the Close button. More on this topic in the "Put Your Drawing to Bed" section of Chapter 3.

> ✓ All these options are available as commands from the Control menu, but you'd have to be a nut to use them when the title bar and buttons are so much more convenient.

Menu bar

A single *menu bar* appears just below the title bar. The menu bar is another one of those traits CorelDraw shares with all other Windows 95 programs. Each word in the menu bar — File, Edit, View, Quagmire — represents a *menu*. A menu contains a list of *commands* that you can use to manipulate the various lines and shapes you've drawn, change the way text looks, and initiate other mind-bogglingly sophisticated procedures.

On either side of the menu bar are the familiar Control menu and buttons that you find on the title bar. They work the same way as the title bar Control menu and buttons, too, with one exception. Instead of controlling the entire interface, they affect a single open drawing only. If you click on the Minimize button, for example, the drawing shrinks to a little title bar in the lower-left corner of the interface. To see the drawing again, click on the Maximize button in the little title bar or double-click anywhere on the little title bar.

Menus are a pretty big topic, so I talk more about them later in this chapter (in the continental "Les Menus sans Soup du Jour" section, to be exact).

Ribbon bar

The *ribbon bar* is a bunch of buttons that you can click on to access certain commands or functions, such as New, Open, Print, and so on. If you want to find out what one of these buttons does, just let your cursor hover over it. A little yellow box springs to life, saying something helpful, such as "Copy."

Quite frankly, I hate the ribbon bar. It's a stupid Microsoft idea that serves no real purpose and just clutters up the interface. Why do I harbor such hostile feelings? I'll tell you why:

> ✓ First, you can't do anything with the ribbon bar that you can't do with the menu bar. Instead of clicking on the Open button, for example, you can choose File⇨Open. Better yet, you can press the keyboard shortcut, Ctrl+O.

> ✓ Second, the little button icons are so dinky that you can hardly tell one from another, and when you can, you can't tell what they do. Quick, tell me which button is the Align/Distribute button? Or Snap To Guidelines? Call me an anarchist, but I reckon that such unintelligible buttons make the program harder to use, not easier.

✔ Third, the ribbon bar reduces the size of the drawing area, which is really a problem when you're working on a 13- or 15-inch monitor.

✔ And finally, Corel implemented the ribbon bar out of peer pressure. All the other Windows programs were doing it, so Corel hopped on board. Just imagine what would happen if all the other Windows programs jumped off a cliff.

To get rid of the ribbon bar — honestly, you'll be glad you did — right-click on the ribbon between a couple of icons. (Don't right-click on the far right side of the ribbon bar where it's empty, or you'll get the wrong menu.) A pop-up menu appears, starting off with a Toolbars option. Click on the second option, Standard, to hide the ribbon bar.

Alternatively, you can choose the Toolbars command from the Views menu. Inside the Toolbars dialog box, click on the Standard option to turn it off and then press Enter. Either way, the ribbon bar vanishes and frees up valuable screen space.

Tools

CorelDraw 6 provides 11 tools, 2 more than Version 5. In fact, these tools are the first additions to the core tools since Teddy Roosevelt quit the Rough Riders.

To select a tool, click on its icon. Then use the tool by clicking or dragging inside the drawing area. To find out more about tools and even give one or two a test run, skip ahead to the "How to Deal with Complete Tools" section. Or better yet, just keep reading. You'll get there soon enough.

Drawing area

Smack dab in the middle of the drawing area is the *page boundary,* which represents the physical size of the printed page. If you position a shape inside the page boundary, it prints. If you position a shape outside the page boundary, it doesn't print. The area outside the page boundary is called the *pasteboard.* It's the surface on which the page sits. You might think of the pasteboard as a kind of drawing repository, because you can use it to store shapes temporarily while you try to figure out what to do with them. It's also a great place to set copies of logos, headlines, ornamental graphics, and other stuff that you use repeatedly throughout a drawing.

Scroll stuff

The *scroll bars* let you navigate around and display hidden portions of your drawing inside the drawing area. CorelDraw offers two scroll bars: one vertical bar along the right side of the drawing area and one horizontal bar along the bottom. If you click on a *scroll arrow,* you nudge your view of the drawing slightly in that direction. For example, if you click on the right-pointing scroll arrow, an item that was hidden on the right side of the drawing slides into view. Click in the gray area of a scroll bar to scroll the window more dramatically. Drag a *scroll box* to manually specify the distance scrolled.

Navigation is another big topic, one to which I devote significant energies in Chapter 3.

Page controls

To the left of the horizontal scroll bar is a clump of *page controls,* which let you advance from one page to another inside a multipage drawing. I explain the nuances of these controls in Chapter 12. In the meantime, just ignore them.

Color stuff

You can change the colors of the outlines and interiors of shapes in the drawing area using the color controls at the very bottom of the CorelDraw interface. Click with the left mouse button on a color in the *color palette* to change the color assigned to the interior of a selected shape. Click with the right mouse button to change the color of a shape's outline. Use the Delete Color button to make an interior or outline transparent.

This topic is another biggie. I cover it in my usual rough-and-tumble style throughout the rolling sagebrush and hilly terrain of Chapter 7.

Status bar

The status line keeps you apprised of what's going on. For example, anytime your cursor is in the *drawing area* — the place where you create your drawing, naturally — the status line tells you the exact coordinate location of your cursor. Cool, huh? It also tells you a load of information about selected shapes or anything else you might want to create.

For more information about this splendid feature, check out "The status bar tells all" section of Chapter 6.

The Mouse is Your Willing Slave (and Other Children's Stories)

So far, I've casually mentioned several ways to use your mouse. Well, it's high time I explained what I'm talking about.

Very likely, you've already noticed that when you move the mouse, the cursor moves on-screen. Way to use those deductive reasoning skills. But that's not all the mouse does. In fact, it's your primary means of communicating with CorelDraw. Oh sure, the keyboard is great for entering text and performing the occasional shortcut, but the mouse is the primo drawing and editing tool. In other words, you need to become familiar with the thing.

The typical mouse features two buttons on top, which register clicks, and a trackball underneath, which registers movement. If your mouse offers three buttons, you'll quickly discover that the center button doesn't work in CorelDraw.

Here's a quick look at some common mouse terminology (not how mice talk, mind you, but how we talk about them, sometimes behind their furry little backs):

- ✔ To *move* your mouse is to move it without pressing any button.

- ✔ To *click* is to press the left button and immediately release it without moving the mouse. For example, you click on a tool icon to select a tool.

- ✔ To *right-click* is to press and release the right mouse button. In the old days, you rarely right-clicked — just to apply color to an outline and that sort of thing. But under Windows 95 and CorelDraw 6, the right mouse button takes on new meaning. In fact, I recommend that you take a moment and right-click on everything you can see. Every time you do, a pop-up menu appears, offering a list of specialized options. When in doubt, right-clicking may very well solve your problem.

- ✔ To *double-click* is to press and release the left button twice in rapid succession without moving the mouse. As discussed earlier in this chapter, you can open a program by double-clicking on its icon. Some programs even accept *triple-* and *quadruple-clicks*. CorelDraw does not go to such extremes.

- ✔ To *press and hold* is to press the button and hold it down for a moment. I refer to this operation very rarely — an example is when some item takes a moment or two to display.

✔ To *drag* is to press the left button and hold it down as you move the mouse. You then release the button to complete the operation. In CorelDraw, for example, you drag with the Pencil tool to draw a free-form line.

✔ To *crush* the mouse is to set it on the floor and stack heavy rocks on it. You are almost never called on to perform this technique. In fact, I recommend crushing only to very desperate performance artists, and then only if running the mouse over with a station wagon fails to get a rise.

You can also use the keyboard and mouse in tandem. For example, in CorelDraw, you can draw a perfect square by pressing the Ctrl key while dragging with the Rectangle tool. And you can press Shift and click on shapes with the Arrow tool to select multiple shapes at a time. Such actions are so common that you often see key and mouse combinations joined into compound verbs, such as *Ctrl+dragging* or *Shift+clicking*. Don't you love the way computer marketing and journalism abuses the language? i THinX IT/z Grait.

How to Deal with Complete Tools

You can liken CorelDraw's tools to the pencils, compasses, and French curves that technical artists used back in the bad old days. The difference is that in CorelDraw, a tool never wears out, stains, runs dry, gets lost, or gets stepped on. The tools are always ready to use on a moment's notice.

A quick experiment

To familiarize yourself with the basic purpose of tools as a group, try this brief exercise:

1. **Click on the Pencil tool icon.**

   It's the fourth one down — it looks like a pencil drawing a wiggly line. Select the tool, and it's ready to use.

2. **Express yourself.**

   I don't want to give away too much stuff about the Pencil tool — I'd spoil the many surprises awaiting you in Chapter 5 — but you drag with the tool to create free-form lines. It works just like a pencil. So draw something. Figure 2-4 shows a line I drew, if that's any help.

Pencil tool

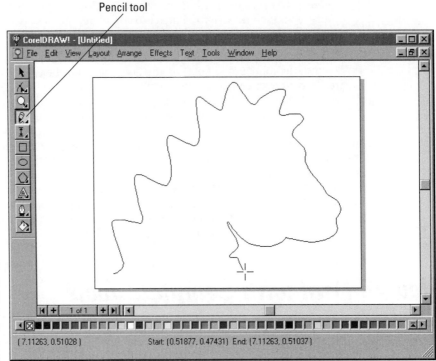

Figure 2-4:
A spiked
thing drawn
with the
Pencil tool.

3. Roam freely. Recognize no boundaries.

Even though I stayed inside the page boundaries in Figure 2-4, you don't
have to. You can draw anywhere you want inside the drawing area, either
in the page boundary or on the pasteboard. Just remember, if it's outside
the page, it won't print.

4. Keep on drawing.

Don't stop. After you finish drawing one line, start another one. Draw
something really complicated or something really messy. Drawing with a
mouse can be a real chore if you're not experienced with it. So I suggest
that you spend some quality time moving your mouse around. I want you
two to get acquainted.

5. Okay, that's enough already.

I mean, don't get obsessed with it or anything.

6. Grab the Arrow tool.

Click on the Arrow tool — at the top of the toolbox — to select it. (Corel calls this tool the _Pick tool._ But if the tool looks like an arrow, I say, call it an arrow. Besides, I don't like to talk about "picking" in mixed company.) The Arrow tool lets you manipulate the stuff you've drawn.

7. Select one of the lines.

Click on some line that you added to the drawing area. Make sure to align the tip of the arrow with the line before you click. The tip of the arrow is the _hot point._ I selected my wacky animal's wacky eye, as shown in wacky Figure 2-5.

8. This is the end of the line, folks.

See those enormous squares that surround the line you just clicked on? They show that the line is selected. Try pressing Delete. Oops, the line's gone. You just killed it. Way to go.

See, that was pretty easy, huh? With some time, effort, patience, and a few other rare commodities, you'll have the whole drawing-with-a-mouse thing down cold.

Arrow tool

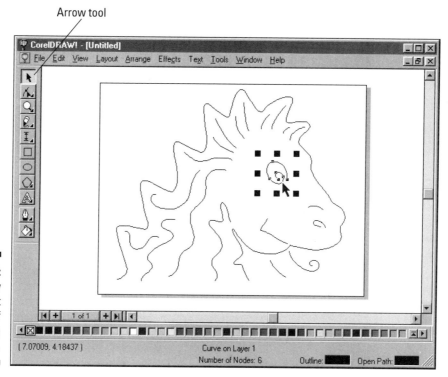

Figure 2-5:
The Arrow tool caught in the act of selecting a line.

Tool tricks

You should know a couple more things about tools before continuing on to the next subject, whatever that may be. First, some tools offer these weird things called *flyout menus.* When you click on either of the last two icons in the tool box — known respectively as the Outline and Fill tools — CorelDraw displays a flyout menu like the one shown in Figure 2-6. Click on an icon inside the menu to select the specific option you want to apply. For example, the Fill tool fills the interior of a selected shape according to the option you select from the flyout menu.

Many other tools — namely those that have little triangles in their lower-right corners — also offer flyout menus. But rather than simply clicking to display the flyouts for these tools, you have to press and hold on the tool icon. Then click on an icon in the flyout menu to make it the active tool in the toolbox.

For example, CorelDraw 6's new Polygon tool is one of the tools that offers a flyout menu. Press and hold on the tool to display a flyout menu filled with three icons — a polygon, spiral, and graph paper — as shown in Figure 2-7. If you select the spiral or graph paper icon, it becomes the new occupant of the Polygon tool slot, as the figure shows.

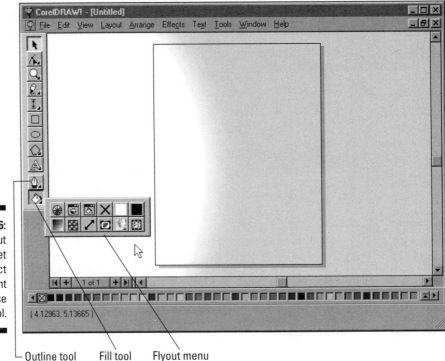

Figure 2-6:
Flyout
menus let
you select
different
ways to use
a tool.

└ Outline tool　　Fill tool　　Flyout menu

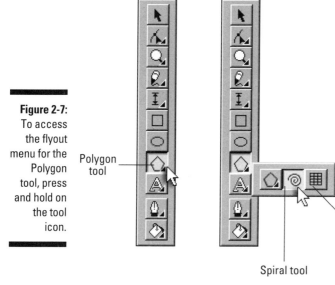

Figure 2-7:
To access the flyout menu for the Polygon tool, press and hold on the tool icon.

Polygon tool

Spiral tool   Graph paper tool

More tool tricks

Normally, the tool icons adhere to the left side of the CorelDraw interface as if they were stuck there with Polygrip. But you can move the toolbox easily: Simply drag it by its left or right edge as demonstrated in Figure 2-8. (Don't drag the empty area below the toolbox, or you won't get anywhere.) After you release the mouse button, you get a new, independent toolbox complete with a title bar. You can drag the title bar to move the toolbox around on-screen.

TECHNICAL STUFF

Something you don't need to know about flyouts

The flyout options for the Outline and Fill tools aren't really tools at all. They're just bogus graphical menus. Rather than allowing you to monkey around in the drawing area — a tool's sacred right and responsibility — they perform immediate effects, just like menu commands.

By contrast, the flyout options for the Shape, Zoom, Pencil, Dimension, Polygon, and Text tools are true tools that you can use to create and edit shapes, lines, and text in the drawing area. These are tools as they were meant to be.

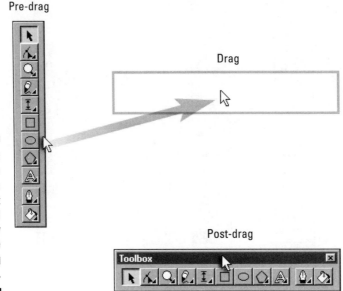

Pre-drag

Drag

Post-drag

Figure 2-8:
Drag the
toolbox to
let it float
around
independently
inside the
drawing
area.

Just for laughs, here are some things you can do with the toolbox:

🖈 Another way to make the toolbox float independently is to double-click in the gray area around the tools.

🖈 You can resize the toolbox by dragging any side or corner.

🖈 To restore the tools to their original moorings, double-click on the Toolbox title bar.

🖈 In CorelDraw 6, the tool icons are pretty tiny. To make them larger, right-click inside the gray area around the tools and select the Toolbars option. (Alternatively, you can choose View⇨Toolbars.) The Toolbars dialog box appears, offering three Size options that affect the size of icons in the toolbox and ribbon bar. Small is the default setting. Figure 2-9 shows how the tool icons grow when you select Medium, which is a great option for working on large monitors. If you still have problems seeing the tool icons, select the Large setting.

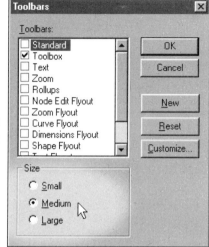

Figure 2-9:
Select the
Medium
option to
make the
tool icons
bigger.

Les Menus sans Soup du Jour

Instead of listing hors d'oeuvres and other tasty morsels, CorelDraw's menus enable you to do stuff, such as open a drawing, abuse the drawing so that it's no longer recognizable, and save it to disk under the name Mud.

To choose a command from a menu, click on the menu name and then click on the command name. For example, if I were to ask you to choose File⇨Open, you would click on the File menu name to display the File menu and then click on the Open command.

Les equivalents du keyboard

In the case of File⇨Open (and many other commands), there's no reason to go to all the effort of using menus. You can simply press Ctrl+O — that is, press and hold the Ctrl key, press the O key, and then release both keys — to achieve the same results. This technique is called using a *keyboard equivalent.*

Most keyboard equivalents are listed along the right side of a menu. Some keyboard equivalents select tools and perform other functions instead of accessing menu commands. Either way, I'll keep you apprised of the keyboard equivalents throughout this book. If you take the time to memorize a few here and there, you'll save yourself a heck of a lot of time and effort.

Alt, ma chère amie, oui?

Not satisfied? Well, there is yet another way to access commands from the keyboard that is common to all Windows programs. Windows provides special Alt+key equivalents. The following steps (with French translations) demonstrate one scenario for exploiting Alt:

1. **Press the Alt key to activate the menu bar.**

   No need to hold the key down. Just press and release Alt, and the menus become active.

2. **If you want to browse through the menus, press the down-arrow key to display the current menu.**

   Then use the left- and right-arrow keys to change menus; use the up- and down-arrow keys to highlight command names.

3. **If the command has a submenu, press the right-arrow key to display that menu.**

   A submenu is simply an additional list of commands designed to further refine your choice of operations. Press the left-arrow key to hide the menu.

4. **Press Enter to choose the highlighted command.**

5. **To abandon the whole menu bit, press Alt again.**

   Or press the Esc (Escape) key. Each time you press Esc, CorelDraw hides a level of menus.

Alternatively, after pressing Alt, you can press the key for the underlined letter in the menu name, followed by the key for the underlined letter in the command name. For example, to choose File⇨Open, press Alt, followed by F and then O.

The Incessant Chatter of Dialog Boxes

Some menu commands react immediately. Others require you to fill out a few forms before they can be processed. In fact, any command that's followed by an ellipsis (three dots, like so: . . .) displays either a *dialog box* or a *roll-up*. A dialog box asks you to answer some questions before CorelDraw implements the command; a roll-up stays on-screen so that you can perform an operation repeatedly without having to choose the command over and over again.

Figure 2-10 shows a sample dialog box. Though this specific dialog box is a figment of my imagination — I pieced it together from a couple of different sources — it illustrates the different kinds of options that dialog boxes can contain. (I had to create this dialog box because none of Corel's real dialog boxes show all the possible options you may encounter.)

Check boxes   Option boxes   Tabs   Title bar

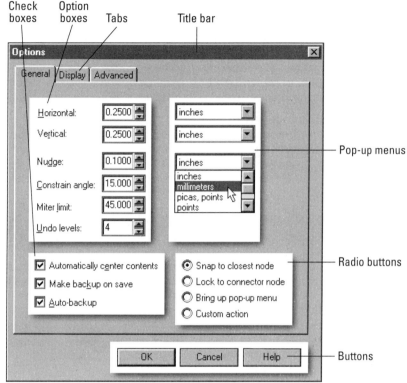

Pop-up menus

Radio buttons

Figure 2-10:
The anatomy of an imaginary dialog box.

Buttons

The dialog box options work as follows:

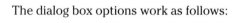

✔ Many of CorelDraw 6's dialog boxes contain multiple panels of options. To get to a different panel, click on one of the *tabs* at the top of the dialog box.

✔ An option in which you can enter numbers or text is called an *option box.* (Propeller heads also like to call these options *fields,* strictly because it sounds more technical.) Double-click on an option box to highlight its contents and then replace the contents by entering new stuff from the keyboard. Or, if you prefer, use the arrow icons to the right of an option box or press the arrow keys on the keyboard to incrementally raise or lower a numerical value. All without hydraulics, mind you.

✔ To conserve space, some multiple-choice options appear as *pop-up menus* (also known in some circles as *drop-down lists*). Click on the down-pointing arrow icon to display a menu of options. Then click on the desired option in the menu to select it, just as if you were choosing a command from a standard menu.

✔ You can select only one circular *radio button* from any gang of radio buttons. To select a radio button, click on the button or on the option name that follows it. The selected radio button gets a black dot; all deselected radio buttons are hollow.

✔ You can select as many *check boxes* as you want. Really, go nuts. To select a check box, click on the box or on the option name that follows it. Clicking on a selected check box turns off the option.

✔ Not to be confused with the radio button, the normal, everyday variety of *button* allows you to close the current dialog box or display others. For example, click on the Cancel button to close the dialog box and cancel the current command. Click on OK to close the dialog box and execute the command according to the current settings. If a button name includes an ellipsis, clicking on it brings up another dialog box.

As you can with menus, you can select options and perform other feats of magic inside dialog boxes from the keyboard. To advance from one option to the next, press the Tab key. To back up, press Shift+Tab. To select any option, press Alt along with the key for the underlined letter (or just press the letter by itself as long as no option box is highlighted). Press Enter to select the button that's surrounded by a heavy outline, such as OK. Press Esc or Alt+F4 to select the Cancel button.

Roll-Ups, Now in Eight Fruity Flavors

Roll-ups, like the one shown in Figure 2-11, are basically dialog boxes that can remain on-screen while you work with other functions in CorelDraw. They float above the surface of the drawing area, just like the toolbox. CorelDraw 6 offers a whopping 30 roll-ups that you can display on-screen all at once, just a few at a time, or whatever. Each roll-up provides so many individual options that there's no point in running through them all here. Suffice it to say that roll-ups let you do some pretty amazing stuff.

The roll-up in Figure 2-11, for example, lets you add depth to an otherwise two-dimensional shape. You can stretch the shape off the page, much like you'd . . . well, frankly, there's no real-life equivalent. It's way cool, which is why I describe it in Chapter 9.

Anchor   Roll-up
button   button

Figure 2-11:
Roll-ups
float above
the drawing
area like
flat,
rectangular,
non-rain-
bearing
clouds.

Roll 'em up and tack 'em down

Roll-ups are called roll-ups because you can roll them up. Strange but true. Click on the up-pointing arrow in the upper-right corner of the roll-up window to hide everything but the title bar. This way, you can have several roll-ups on-screen at once without cluttering up the interface. Click on a roll-up's arrow again — it's a down-pointing arrow now — to restore the full window.

By default, a roll-up is anchored so that it remains on-screen regardless of other activities you perform. However, if you want the roll-up to disappear after it's used once, click on the thumbtack icon just to the left of the arrow icon in the title bar. The thumbtack appears to raise up, showing that the roll-up is no longer anchored. The next time you click anywhere outside the roll-up, it disappears. If you're having problems with screen clutter, this is another way to eliminate it.

But if you want my opinion, you should leave the thumbtack down. Having the roll-up disappear every time you click outside it can be terribly disconcerting and is rarely useful. I mean, if you want to close the darn thing, why not just click on the Close button?

Breakaway roll-ups

One more thing about roll-ups in CorelDraw 6: Because there are so many of them, Corel combined some roll-ups into related groups. For example, the Position, Rotation, and Size roll-ups are all included in a single Transform group, as shown in Figure 2-12.

- ✔ You can switch to a different roll-up in the group by clicking on its name in the scrolling list at the top of the roll-up window.

- ✔ To separate an item in the group into an independent roll-up, drag the item's name outside the roll-up window, as in Figure 2-12. Give me your roll-ups, yearning to be free.

- ✔ You can also combine roll-ups into your own groups, whether the roll-ups are related or not. Ctrl+drag the title bar of one roll-up and drop it onto some neutral area inside another roll-up. When the cursor is properly aligned, the white arrow points downward to show that the two roll-ups are ready to group. That's when you release the mouse button.

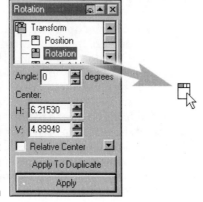

Figure 2-12: Drag a roll-up name outside the window to separate it from its group.

The 5th Wave — By Rich Tennant

"OOPS, I FORGOT TO LOG OFF AGAIN."

Chapter 3

Ladies and Gentlemen, Insert Your Pocket Protectors!

. . . .

In This Chapter

▶ Creating a new document

▶ Importing clip art

▶ Magnifying your drawing for a closer look

▶ Using other zooming options

▶ Exploring the past and present virtues of scrolling

▶ Modifying the screen display

▶ Looking at a rat in startling ways

▶ Saving a drawing to disk

▶ Updating files and making backups

. . . .

*W*ith CorelDraw, you're the omnipotent master of your creation. You can add whatever flair or flourish you deem appropriate, using whatever tool strikes your fancy. You have total artistic freedom (as much as your client or boss allows, that is). But you can't experience the heady joys that come with this absolute power until you master three basic tasks: creation, navigation, and storage. *Creation* is giving birth to the drawing; *navigation* is tooling around the on-screen landscape, moving from one part of your drawing to the next; and *storage* is the small but essential ceremony that ensures that all your hard work doesn't go in the tank when you quit the program. This chapter gets you up to speed on all three subjects, plus a few others for good measure.

Spank the Baby

You probably don't remember this, but when the doctor whisked you out of your mom, he smacked your rump to make you take in that first lungful of air and bellow like a stricken — well . . . baby. Now here you are, several thousand days later, wondering why I'm bringing up such a painful subject. The truth is, you have to perform a similar maneuver before you can begin drawing in CorelDraw. You don't have to literally spank any babies — that would be too extreme, even for this book — but you do have to give CorelDraw the equivalent of the welcoming paddle.

How do you do that? Well, here's your chance to see whether you've managed to learn anything about computers so far. Which of the following actions do you suspect results in a new document in CorelDraw?

A. Gently but firmly slap the disk drive. There's no time like the present to teach your computer who's boss.

B. Taunt the computer mercilessly until it cries.

C. Choose File⇨New or File⇨Open.

Four out of five computer scientists agree that B is the best way to humble your computer into producing a new document. But recently, a significant minority of dissenting scientists have come out in support of answer C. In the interest of fair and unbiased journalism, I test this strange theory in the following pages.

How do I start a new document?

Assuming that you turned off the welcome screen as I instructed you to in the "Interface in Your Face" section of Chapter 2, CorelDraw automatically produces an empty drawing area after you start the program. (If CorelDraw does something else after you start it, choose Tools⇨Options or press Ctrl+J. Then select Start a New Document from the On Startup pop-up menu in the lower-left corner of the Options dialog box and press Enter. From now on, an empty drawing area greets you every time you start CorelDraw 6.)

The empty drawing area represents a brand new document. It has no preconceived notions of what a drawing is or what it should be. You can mold it into anything you want. You are master of the page.

Problem is, an empty drawing area can be terrifying. It's like looking inside the deepest recesses of your soul and seeing nothing — except that it's not nearly so profound. Suffice it to say, a new document is the surest formula for performance anxiety.

If for some reason — like, you're a masochist or something — you want to start a document from scratch after you've been working in the program for a while, all you need to do is select File⇨New or press Ctrl+N.

The enlightening Chihuahua scenario

Luckily, the empty drawing area isn't the only route available. You can approach your drawing from a different angle, namely that of opening or importing an existing drawing that can serve as a starting point.

Let's say that you want to draw a Chihuahua. Now there's a puzzle for you. Where are you going to find a yippy little dog on the third floor of an air-conditioned building in an office park surrounded by shopping malls? And even if you had a Chihuahua on your desk, baring its teeth at you in domesticated terror, you wouldn't have a hope of drawing it, because the degree of difficulty for creating a realistic Chihuahua from scratch in CorelDraw is somewhere in the neighborhood of 13 on a 10-point scale. (For that very reason, there are no Chihuahuas in this book.)

So what's the solution? Well, in and amongst CorelDraw's vast library of clip art, there's a drawing of a small animal that it is generally accepted to be the direct ancestor to the Chihuahua. I am referring, of course, to the rat. All you have to do is shorten the tail, snip the claws, enlarge the ears, remove some whiskers, bulge out the eyes, reduce the size of the brain cavity, and add a little balloon above its head that says "Yip yip," and the evolutionary transformation is complete.

But before you can do any editing, you have to add the rat to your new drawing using the File⇨Import command, discussed next. You can find the rat on the fourth CD-ROM included in your CorelDraw 6 package.

How do I import a piece of clip art?

The following steps tell you how to import the rat or any other piece of clip art into a drawing.

1. **Choose File⇨Import or press Ctrl+I.**

   The Import dialog box appears, as shown in Figure 3-1.

2. **Select a disk drive from the Look In pop-up menu.**

   Click anywhere on the option box at the top of the dialog box to display a pop-up menu. Then click on the drive in which you think your file is stored. To find the rat clip art, you should select your CD-ROM drive, which is probably the D drive.

3. **Open the desired directories in the central scrolling list.**

   Double-click on a folder name to open it. The list then displays all folders inside that directory. Double-click on another folder to open it, and so on.

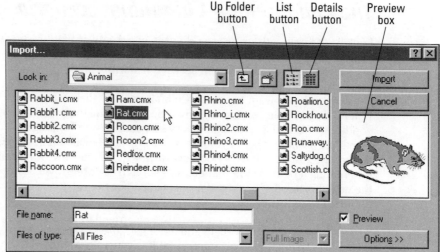

Up Folder button List button Details button Preview box

Figure 3-1:
Use this dialog box to locate and open clip art and other existing drawings.

For example, to get inside the Animal folder, which resides inside the Clipart folder, double-click on the word *Clipart* in the scrolling list and then on the word *Animal*.

4. Select the drawing that you want to open.

To open the rat, first click on any file name in the scrolling list. This activates the list. Next press R to scroll to the drawings that begin with that letter, including such hits as Rabbit, Raccoon, and Ram. Then click on the right scroll arrow a couple of times to advance to the Rat.CMX file. Click on it to select it. Assuming that the Preview check box is selected, a preview of the drawing appears on the right side of the dialog box so that you can see what it looks like.

5. Click on the Import button or press Enter.

That's all there is to it. CorelDraw plops the rat inside the drawing area so that you can manipulate it at will.

I wish that I could tell you how to change a rat into a Chihuahua in five easy steps, but I can't. Instead, I devote Chapters 4 through 9 to the topic of drawing and editing in CorelDraw. I don't specifically address Chihuahua illustrations, but you can tell that they're constantly in the back of my mind.

In the meantime, here are a few additional notes on importing clip art to carry you through your working day.

✔ To close a folder and look at the contents of the directory that contains that folder, click on the Up Folder button (labeled in Figure 3-1).

- If you want to find out more information about a file — such as its size on disk and the last time it was modified — click on the Details button (also labeled in Figure 3-1). You can then change the order in which the files are displayed by clicking on the buttons along the top of the list. For example, to list the files alphabetically, click on the Name button.

- To hide that technical stuff and just see the file names again, click on the list button.

- Use the preview box to help identify drawings. For example, if you or someone you work with named a drawing GT12_RRX (or something equally meaningless), you can click on the file name and view a really tiny version of the drawing that may or may not be identifiable. But, hey, it's better than nothing.

- You can add as many pieces of clip art to a drawing as you like. For example, if you wanted to give the rat a friend to play with, you could choose File⇨Import again, select the Hamster.CMX file, and press enter.

- CorelDraw always imports all the little bits and pieces of stuff that go into a clip art graphic as something called a *group*. In order to select an individual eye, ear, or whisker, you have to first *ungroup* the graphic. To do this, choose Arrange⇨Ungroup or press Ctrl+U. Go ahead, do it now. I explain more about groups in the "Gang Behavior" section of Chapter 6.

- If CorelDraw can't import a file, there's a slim chance that the file is damaged and no longer usable. But it's more likely that the file was created in some program other than CorelDraw. Ask around and see whether anyone knows anything about the file, including where it came from.

And how do I open a drawing?

The reason I discussed the Import command in the preceding section was because Corel now ships all its clip art files in a special format called CMX. Although you can open this wonderful format in lots of different Corel programs — including Presents, Dream 3D, and others — you can open CMX files by using the Import command only.

However, if you want to open a drawing that you saved in CorelDraw or open clip art from an older CorelDraw collection (Version 4 or earlier), you use File⇨Open. As fortune would have it, the Open command works almost identically to File⇨Import, with two important exceptions:

- The Open command recognizes CDR files, which are files created and saved with any version of CorelDraw.

- When you open a drawing, a new window appears on-screen. Unlike Import, Open does not add the artwork to the existing drawing but instead opens it inside its own, independent window.

Otherwise, Open and Import are spiritual twins, offering an identical collection of pop-up menus and buttons. Become familiar with one, and you should have no problem using the other.

Tools for Getting Around in the Drawing Area

Ah, getting around, a favorite pursuit of the Beach Boys. Of course, we all know that in reality, the Beach Boys were about as likely to get around as a parade of go-carting Shriners. I mean, it's not like you're going to confuse a squad of sandy-haired Neil Bush look-alikes with the Hell's Angels. John Denver, Richie Cunningham, and James Watts could play kazoos on "The MacNeil/Lehrer Report" and come off as more streetwise than the Beach Boys.

Now that I've offended everyone who's ever surfed or enjoyed falsetto harmonies, I will say two things in the Beach Boys' defense. First, "Help Me, Rhonda" and "Good Vibrations" are crankin' tunes. And second, even a bunch of squares like the Beach Boys can get around in CorelDraw. (Nice tie-in, huh?)

Miracles of magnification

When you first open a drawing, you see the full page, as in Figure 3-2. To fit the page entirely inside the drawing area, CorelDraw has to reduce the page so that it appears considerably smaller than it will print. It's as if you're standing far away from things, taking in the big picture.

Although the big picture is great and everything, it lacks detail. Imagine trying to edit the claws, the eyes, or some other minute feature from this vantage point. That's why CorelDraw lets you zoom in to magnify the drawing and zoom out to make it smaller.

1. **Select the Zoom tool.**

   To magnify the drawing, click on the Zoom tool, which is the one that looks like a magnifying glass.

   To access the Zoom tool at the touch of a key, press F2. The cursor changes to a magnifying glass without your ever selecting a tool.

2. **Click in the drawing area.**

   CorelDraw magnifies the drawing to twice its previous size, as demonstrated in Figure 3-3. The program centers the magnified view at the point

Zoom tool

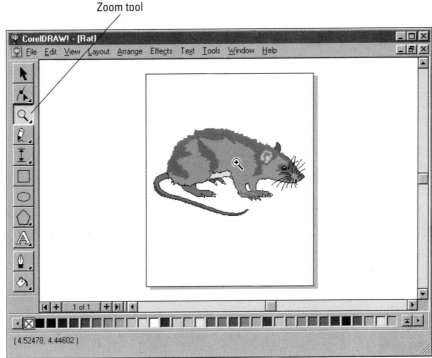

Figure 3-2:
Use the
Zoom tool to
magnify
your
drawing on-
screen.

where you click. In Figure 3-4, for example, I clicked on the eyeball to center the magnified view on the eyeball.

Alternatively, you can drag with the Zoom tool to surround the area that you want to magnify with a dotted outline. Using this technique, you can zoom in to more than twice the previous level of magnification.

3. Repeat Steps 1 and 2 till your wrist gets tired.

If you selected the Zoom tool by clicking on its icon in the toolbox, you can use it as many times as you like. If you selected it by pressing F2, CorelDraw reverts back to the selected tool after you finish zooming. This means that you have to press F2 each time that you want to zoom.

Figure 3-4 shows the result of pressing F2 and clicking a total of three times. The magnified rat is 800 percent as large as its counterpart in Figure 3-2 and 400 percent as large as the one in Figure 3-3.

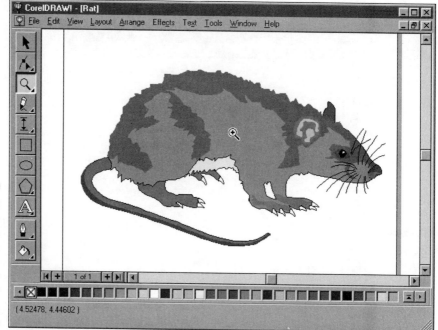

Figure 3-3:
Click with
the Zoom
tool to
magnify the
drawing by
a factor of
200 percent.

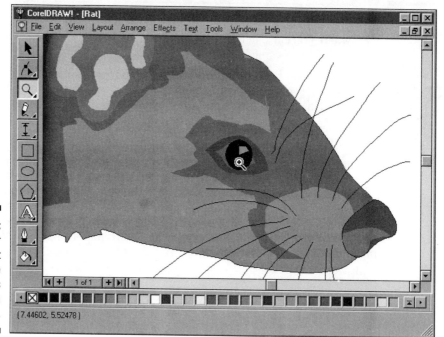

Figure 3-4:
The closer
you inspect
a rat, the
more it looks
like a
Chihuahua.

Zooming doesn't change the size at which your drawing prints. It just affects the size at which you see the drawing on-screen. It's like looking at an amoeba under a microscope. The creature doesn't actually grow and shrink as you vary the degree of magnification, and neither does your drawing.

Lightning-fast zooms

Magnification is only half the zoom formula. After all, that which zooms in must ultimately zoom out. CorelDraw also offers several automatic zoom controls that zoom in and out to predefined intervals. Here's the scoop:

- ✔ To zoom out, Shift+click or right-click with the Zoom tool. CorelDraw reduces the drawing to 50 percent of its former glory.

- ✔ You can also zoom out by pressing F3. The screen zooms at the touch of the key. No clicking, soaking, or whittling is required.

- ✔ To zoom in on a selected portion of your drawing, press Shift+F2. For example, assuming that you ungrouped the rat as I advised a few pages ago (by pressing Ctrl+U), you can select the rat's nose by clicking on it with the Arrow tool. Then press Shift+F2 to zoom in and get a close-up view of the critter's nostrils.

- ✔ To reduce the view so that every line, shape, and character of text is visible, press F4.

- ✔ To return the view so that you can see the entire page, press Shift+F4.

Your very own zoombox

If trying to remember all those keyboard shortcuts makes your brain hurt, you can use a special palette of Zoom tools, as shown in Figure 3-5. (If you don't see the zoom palette, right-click in the gray area around the tools to display a pop-up menu and then choose the Zoom option. A nice little Zoom palette springs to life. You can also double-click on the Zoom tool icon in the toolbox to display a zoom palette of sorts called the View Manager, but that palette contains lots of extraneous view controls that you quite honestly do not need.)

The buttons in the Zoom palette work just like the keyboard shortcuts I mentioned above. Click on the Zoom Out button to zoom out to 50 percent; click on the Show Page button to view the entire page at once; and so on. The only button that doesn't have a shortcut is the Actual Size button — the one labeled 1:1. This button displays the lines and shapes in your drawing at the same size that they actually print.

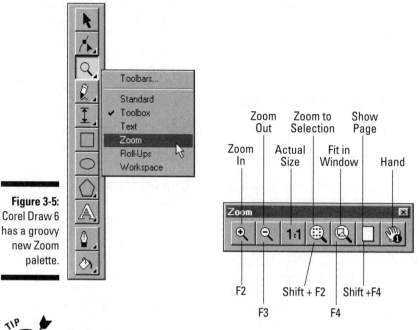

Figure 3-5:
Corel Draw 6
has a groovy
new Zoom
palette.

To fix the Zoom palette in place along the top of the window, double-click on some gray area inside the palette. Double-click again to make the palette float independently. Click on the Close button to put the palette away.

The secret magnification menu

If you don't like the keyboard shortcuts or the Zoom palette, select the Zoom tool and right-click anywhere in the drawing area. Up comes a pop-up menu, offering you a series of zoom options. You can even select from a submenu of specific zoom ratios, from 10 to 400 percent. Click on the option that you want to select — it's that easy.

A New Way to Scroll

As you doubtless have already noticed, you can see only bits and pieces of your drawing when it's magnified. The scroll bars and CorelDraw 6's new Hand tool allow you to control which bits and pieces are visible.

Suppose that you can only see the nose of the rat, as shown in Figure 3-6. You want to view the animal's face and neck, an inch or so to the left. To do so, you can do the following:

- ✔ Drag the scroll box on the horizontal scroll bar to the left. The drawing moves in the opposite direction.

- ✔ Select the Hand tool from the Zoom tool flyout, as shown in Figure 3-6. Then drag to the right with the Hand tool, as in Figure 3-7. After you release the mouse button, the drawing moves to the right.

- ✔ You can also select the Hand tool from the Zoom palette, shown back in Figure 3-5. The only difference is that the Zoom palette's Hand tool becomes deselected as soon as you finish scrolling, whereas you can use the Hand tool in the flyout menu several times in a row.

If you get lost when scrolling your drawing and can't figure out where it's gone, just press Shift+F4 to zoom all the way out so that the page fits inside the window. Then zoom and scroll as desired.

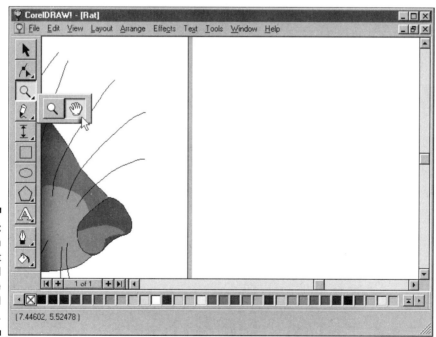

Figure 3-6:
You can now select a Hand tool from the Zoom tool flyout menu.

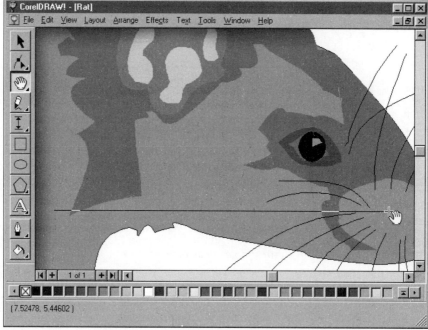

Figure 3-7:
Drag with
the Hand
tool to scroll
the drawing
in the
direction of
the drag.

The Screen is What You Make It

Another way to change how CorelDraw shows you a drawing on-screen is to switch *display modes.* Normally, you see the drawing in full, glorious color with all fills and outlines intact. This view is called the *editable preview mode.* This mode is excellent in that it shows the drawing as it will print. The only problem with this mode is that it can be slow, especially when you're viewing a complex drawing.

String art revival

To speed things up, choose View⇨Wireframe or press Shift+F9. In the *wireframe mode,* CorelDraw displays each shape in your drawing as if it were transparent and endowed with only a thin black outline, as shown in Figure 3-8. Compare this figure to Figure 3-3, which shows the rat at the same zoom ratio in the editable preview mode.

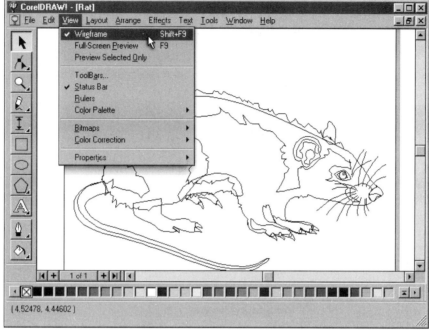

Figure 3-8:
A rat
caught in
the
wireframe
mode is a
sad sight
indeed.

The wireframe mode speeds things up considerably because CorelDraw can display a bunch of black outlines way faster than colors, gradations, arrowheads, and other attributes that you learn about in Chapter 7. But the wireframe mode also makes it more difficult to edit the drawing. It's like trying to imagine how a house will look when it's still in the framing stage. It's like reconstructing the *Venus de Milo* out of toothpicks and tissue paper. It's like removing your skin and going out in public with your bones showing. I could come up with lots more analogies, but suffice it to say that it's an underlying structure kind of thing, and it takes some getting used to.

You only need to use the wireframe mode if CorelDraw is running exasperatingly slowly, as Version 6 has a habit of doing on 386 and some 486 computers. And even then, you'll probably want to regularly switch back and forth between it and the editable preview mode to keep track of what's going on.

To return to the editable preview mode, press Shift+F9 or choose View➪Wireframe, just as you did to enter the wireframe mode. When a single command switches you back and forth like this one does, it's called a *toggle.*

Die, you gravy-sucking interface

Although it's absolutely essential to communicating with CorelDraw, the interface can occasionally prove distracting. To temporarily hide everything but the drawing itself, press F9 or choose View⇨Full-Screen Preview. Whether you were previously working in the wireframe or editable preview mode, CorelDraw shows the drawing in full color, as shown in Figure 3-9.

I like to call this mode the *hands-off preview mode* because you can't do anything in it besides look at the drawing. The second you click the right mouse button or press a key on the keyboard, CorelDraw exits the hands-off preview mode and restores the interface. Clicking the left mouse button forces CorelDraw to refresh the screen, but that's the extent of it. The hands-off preview mode is just a means of looking at your drawing without having to print it.

Occasionally, novices get all panicky when the interface disappears and assume that the only way to return to CorelDraw is to turn off the computer, pawn it, and buy a new one. I don't want this to happen to you. So at the risk of sounding repetitive, I'll repeat myself: Just press *any* key on the keyboard, and the interface returns.

Figure 3-9:
Unencumbered
by the
CorelDraw
interface,
the rat
appears
perceptibly
more at
ease with its
surroundings.

Preview bits and pieces

CorelDraw provides one additional method for previewing a drawing. The benefits of this method become more apparent as you become more familiar with the program. When you're working with a complex drawing, some shapes can get in the way of other shapes. You may be tempted to delete shapes just to get them out of your way. But don't, because there's a better way.

1. **Select the lines, shapes, and text that you want to preview.**

   I don't explain how to select stuff until Chapter 4. But to get you started, you can select a single object by clicking on it with the Arrow tool. You select multiple objects by clicking on one and then Shift+clicking on the others.

2. **Choose <u>V</u>iew⇨Preview Selected <u>O</u>nly.**

   After you choose this command, it remains in effect until you choose the command again.

3. **Press F9.**

   Only the selected objects appear on-screen. The rest temporarily vanish.

Figure 3-10 shows the result of selectively previewing a few shapes that make up the rat. The poor animal looks like a gang of field mice stripped it down to its underwear.

Figure 3-10:
Transforming a rat into a mole through selective previewing.

Save or Die Trying!

Saving your drawing is like locking your car. After you get in the habit of doing it, you're protected. Until then, life can be traumatic. A stereo stolen here, a crucial drawing lost there. During my formative desktop publishing years, I managed to lose so many drawings that I finally taped the message "Save or die trying" to the wall above my computer. If you're new to computers, I suggest that you do something similar. You look up, you save your drawing, and you live happily ever after.

After all, there's nothing like spending an hour or so on a complex drawing that you've neglected to save, only to be greeted by a system error, power outage, or some other electronic tragedy. It makes you want to beat the old fists on the top of the monitor, strangle the computer with its own power cord, or engage in other unseemly acts of computer terrorism.

To avoid the trauma, save your document to disk early and update it often.

Saving for the very first time

The very first time you save a new drawing, you have to name it and specify its location on disk. Here's how:

1. **Choose File⇨Save or press Ctrl+S.**

   The Save Drawing dialog box appears, as shown in Figure 3-11.

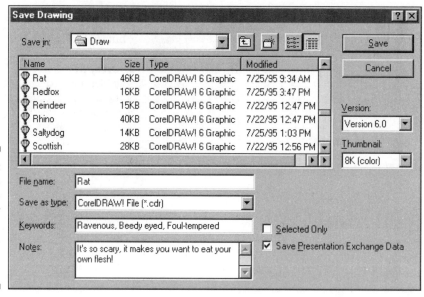

Figure 3-11: Use this dialog box to name your drawing and specify its location on disk.

2. Enter a name into the File Name option box.

Gone are the days when file names could only be eight characters long. Now you can go as high as you like. Heck, you can name the file *Scurvy, flea-bitten, no-good Chihuahua wannabe* if you like. As long as the name is shorter than 256 characters, you're okay.

It's also worth noting that you don't have to enter **.CDR** at the end of the file name. CorelDraw does that for you without you ever knowing. Isn't progress wonderful?

3. Select a disk drive from the Save In pop-up menu.

Use the pop-up menu to select the drive to which you want to save your drawing. Incidentally, you can't save a drawing to CD-ROM. If you opened a piece of CorelDraw's clip art, you need to save it to your hard drive or some other disk.

4. Select a directory inside the central scrolling list.

Double-click on folder names to enter and exit them just as you did when importing a drawing.

5. **Click on the Save button or press Enter.**

Your drawing is now saved! Come heck or high water, you're protected.

Updating the drawing

After you name your drawing and save it to disk for the first time, press Ctrl+S every time you think of it. Doing so automatically updates your drawing on disk without requiring you to work your way through dialog boxes, options, or any other interface artifacts. If you remember to update your drawing regularly, you won't lose hours of work when something goes wrong — notice that I said *when,* not *if.* You'll lose a few minutes, maybe, but that comes with the territory.

If you don't trust yourself to save your drawing every five to ten minutes, you can tell CorelDraw to do it for you. Choose Tools⇨Options (or press Ctrl+J) and then click on the Advanced tab near the top of the dialog box. Select the Auto-backup check box. To specify how often CorelDraw automatically saves your drawing, enter the number of minutes between saves into the option box just to the right of the check box. Then press Enter. Now your saving worries are gone.

Creating a backup copy

If you spend longer than a single day creating a drawing, you should create backup copies. That's not a hard and fast rule, mind you, but it is a sound principle of drawing management. The reasoning is, if a drawing takes longer than a day to create, you're that much worse off if you lose it. By creating one backup copy for each day that you work on the project — for example, *Rodent*

01, Rodent 02, Rodent 03, and so on — you're much less likely to lose your work. If some disk error occurs or you accidentally delete one or two of the files, one of the backups will probably survive the disaster, further protecting you from developing an ulcer or having to seek therapy.

At the end of the day, choose File⇨Save As. The Save Drawing dialog box opens, as when you first saved the drawing. Change the file name slightly and then click on the Save button. Way to be doubly protected!

Put Your Drawing to Bed

To leave CorelDraw, choose File⇨Exit or press Alt+F4. I know that Alt+F4 doesn't make anywhere near as much sense as Ctrl+O to open and Ctrl+S to save, but it's not Corel's fault. Microsoft demands the Alt+F4 thing from all its Windows programs. Where Microsoft came up with Alt+F4 is anyone's guess. I think that they made it confusing on purpose. This is the same company that brought you DOS, so what do you expect?

But Microsoft decided to make a little more sense with Windows 95. In addition to using Exit and Alt+F4, you can now click on the Close button in the upper-right corner of the CorelDraw interface. It wins my vote as the easiest way to quit the program.

Anyway, when you press Alt+F4 or click on the Close button, CorelDraw may warn you with a message that says, "Rat has changed. Save current changes?" or words to that effect. Unless you have some reason for doing otherwise, press Y or click on the Yes button. Then the program quits, leaving you back at the Windows 95 desktop.

To shut down Windows and turn off your computer, choose Start⇨Shut Down or press Alt+F4 again. A dialog box lists your options, allowing you to shut down the computer or simply restart Windows 95. Just press Enter to put your computer to sleep for the day. Then, when Windows tells you to turn off your computer, flick the power switch.

Part II
Let the Graphics Begin

The 5th Wave   By Rich Tennant

"THE FUNNY THING IS, I NEVER KNEW THEY HAD DESKTOP PUBLISHING SOFTWARE FOR PAPER SHREDDERS."

In this part . . .

Traditional art tools are messy. Real-life ink, for example, bleeds into the fibers of the paper, goops and glumps onto the page, and stains if you accidentally spill some on your clothes. Real-life pens clog; real-life paintbrushes need washing; and real-life paintings flop over accidentally and get dust and hairs stuck all over them. Real life, in other words, is for the birds (which is only fitting because birds are wholly unequipped to use CorelDraw, what with their puny little brains and their sad lack of opposable thumbs).

CorelDraw, being a figment of your computer's imagination, is very tidy and orderly. There's nothing real to deal with. The pencil draws a line that remains the same thickness throughout its entire length. Whoever heard of such a thing? You can edit lines and shapes after you draw them. Unbelievable. And if you make a mistake, you can choose the Undo command. The real world has no equivalent. CorelDraw provides a flexible, forgiving interface that mimics real life while at the same time improving on it.

In the next six chapters, I show you how to draw, how to edit what you've drawn, how to apply colors, how to duplicate portions of your artwork, and how to create special effects. By the time you finish with Chapter 9, those Number 2 pencils you've been storing all these years will be history.

Chapter 4

The Secret Society
of Simple Shapes

. . . .

In This Chapter

▶ Drawing rectangles, squares, ovals, and circles

▶ Introducing nodes

▶ Rounding off the corners of rectangles

▶ Converting ovals into pies and wedges

▶ Moving shapes with the Arrow tool

▶ Scaling and flipping shapes

▶ Deleting shapes and subsequently freaking out

▶ Using the Undo command

. . . .

*E*ver try to draw a perfect square the old-fashioned way? Regardless of how many metal rulers, drafting arms, and absolutely 100-percent-square stencils you have at your disposal, you're liable to miss the mark to some extent, however minuscule. And that's if you kill yourself over every corner and use the highest-grade engineering pens and acetate.

If you want to keep the Euclideans happy — and God knows, none of us wants to attract the wrath of an angry Euclidean — there's nothing like a drawing program for accuracy, simplicity, and downright efficiency. Suddenly, squares and circles are as easy to draw as, well, those smiley faces that little girls frequently use in their letters as punctuation at the end of jokes. You know, like "Sam caught a swordfish. It's so big and scary, I asked Sam if he was sure the fish didn't catch him!" followed by a smiley face. A semicircle mouth and two dots for eyes. Not even a circle to identify the boundaries of the head. Just a face in space, like some minimalist version of the Cheshire cat.

Well, anyway, the point is, smiley faces are ridiculously easy to draw, and so is the stuff in this chapter.

Shapes from Your Childhood

Wow, is this going to be easy! In about five minutes, you are going to laugh out loud at the idea that you once viewed computers as cold-blooded machines intent on the overthrow of humanity. It's not that computers *aren't* cold-blooded machines intent on the overthrow of humanity, mind you, but at least they won't seem quite so menacing.

Rectangles and squares

Click on the Rectangle tool (sixth from the top, the one that looks like a rectangle) to select it. Or if you prefer, press F6. Now drag in the drawing area. A rectangle grows from the movement of your cursor, as demonstrated in Figure 4-1. One corner of the rectangle appears at the point at which you begin dragging. The opposite corner appears at the point at which you release. What could be simpler?

Rectangle tool

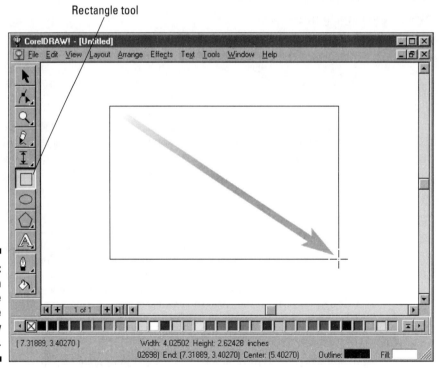

Figure 4-1:
Drag with the Rectangle tool to draw a rectangle.

Here's some more stuff you can do with this tool:

- ✔ Press and hold the Ctrl key while dragging with the Rectangle tool to draw a perfect square. The Ctrl key *constrains* the rectangle so that all four sides are the same length. Be sure to hold the Ctrl key down until you release your mouse button.

- ✔ Shift+drag with the Rectangle tool — that is, press and hold the Shift key while dragging — to draw the rectangle outward from its center. CorelDraw centers the rectangle about the point at which you begin dragging. A corner appears at the point at which you release.

- ✔ Ctrl+Shift+drag to draw a square outward from the center.

Ovals and circles

The Oval tool — the next tool down from the Rectangle tool — works the same way as the Rectangle tool. It even has a keyboard equivalent, which is F7. You drag inside the drawing area to define the size of an oval, as shown in Figure 4-2. You can draw a perfect circle by Ctrl+dragging with the Oval tool. Shift+drag with the tool to draw an oval from the center outward.

Oval tool

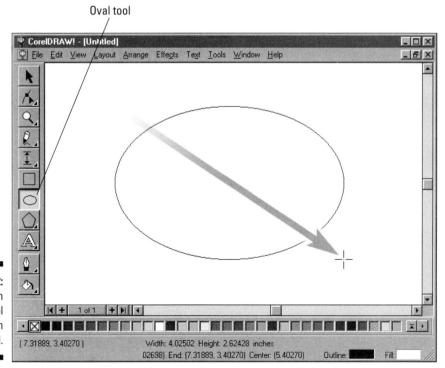

Figure 4-2:
Drag with
the Oval tool
to draw an
oval.

Within every oval there lurks an ellipse

Euclideans call the oval an *ellipse,* which is a shape whose outline travels at a fixed distance from two central points. You can draw an ellipse by hammering two nails into a board, tying a string between the two nails so that it has a lot of slack, and tracing the path of the string as shown in the following figure. The slack in the string determines the size of the ellipse.

Who cares? Well, technically, an oval is less structured than an ellipse. An oval can be anything from oblong to egg-shaped to lumpy-bumpy, whereas an ellipse is always perfectly formed and exactly symmetrical vertically and horizontally, just like shapes drawn with the Oval tool. And besides, I wanted to make sure that you appreciate the little things in CorelDraw. I mean, you wouldn't want to have to go back to board, string, and pencil, now would you?

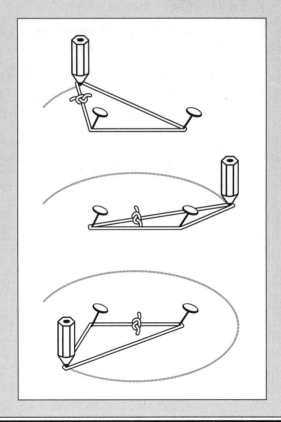

Shapes with lots of sides

After the Oval tool is the Polygon tool. New to CorelDraw 6, this tool lets you draw shapes with lots of sides, such as triangles, pentagons, octagons, and all those other 'gons. You can even draw stars. Boy howdy.

To draw a polygon — the generic name for any shape with three or more straight sides — select the Polygon tool by clicking on it. Then drag away, as shown in Figure 4-3. Ctrl+drag with the tool to draw a shape in which all sides are the same length (called an *equilateral polygon,* for those of you interested in tossing about the technical lingo). Shift+drag to draw the shape from the center out.

By default, CorelDraw creates a pentagon, which is a polygon with five sides. But you can draw as many sides as you want. To change the number of sides, do either of the following:

> ✔ To change the default setting, double-click on the Polygon tool icon in the toolbox. The setting affects the next shape you draw.

Polygon tool

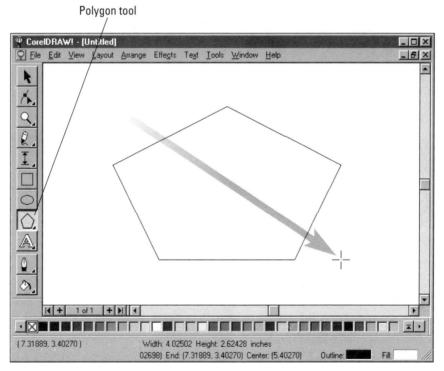

Figure 4-3:
Drag with
the Polygon
tool to draw
a multisided
shape.

✔ To change the number of sides assigned to a shape you've already drawn, select the Arrow tool and then right-click on the shape. Choose the Properties option from the bottom of the pop-up menu that appears.

Either approach brings up a dialog box similar to the one shown in Figure 4-4. The dialog box contains anywhere from three to five panels, but you only care about the one shown in the figure, which just so happens to be the one that first greets you. What luck.

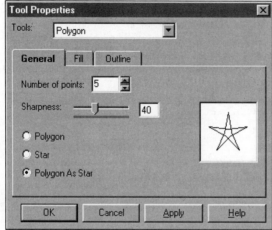

Figure 4-4:
You can decide whether to draw polygons or stars using this dialog box.

After the dialog box appears, proceed thusly:

1. Select the kind of shape you want from the radio buttons at the bottom of the dialog box.

You can draw a polygon, a star, or a third shape, which Corel calls Polygon As Star. Technically, this means that lines in the star don't cross, but more practically, the option gives you absolute control over the sharpness of the star's points. Suffice it to say, if you can't get the shape you want by selecting the Star option, try Polygon As Star instead.

The Polygon As Star option is available only if you double-click on the Polygon tool icon in the toolbox. If you want to convert an existing polygon to a Polygon As Star, you have to do it manually with the Shape tool, as explained in "Making a wacky shape wackier," later in this chapter.

2. Enter the number of sides for your shape into the Number of Points option box.

You can go as low as 3 for a triangle or as high as 500, which is, of course, an insanely large value.

Remember, when an option box is active, you can raise or lower the value in the box by pressing the up- or down-arrow key.

3. Adjust the Sharpness value, if you can.

If you select Polygon As Star or if you select Star and the Number of Points value is 7 or larger, the Sharpness option is active. A higher value increases the sharpness of the star's points.

4. Click on the Apply button to see how the settings affect your shape.

Or just press Enter to accept the changes and close the dialog box.

I should mention that you can similarly change the properties of rectangles and ovals. In other words, you can produce a Tool Properties dialog box either by double-clicking on the Rectangle or Oval tool or by right-clicking on a rectangle or oval in the drawing area and choosing the Properties option. But frankly, the changes you can make inside these dialog boxes are easier to apply using a special tool called the Shape tool, which I describe next.

Ways to Change Shapes

After you finish drawing a rectangle, oval, polygon, or star, take a look at it. You'll see one or more tiny, square *nodes* on the outline of the shape. At least that's what Corel calls them. Webster's says that a node is a "knotty, localized swelling." If I were you, I'd try not to think about that.

As illustrated in Figure 4-5, different shapes include different numbers of nodes (the nodes are highlighted in the figure).

 ✔ A rectangle sports a node on each of its four corners.

 ✔ An oval features just one node. If you draw the shape by dragging the cursor downward on-screen (as shown back in Figure 4-2), the node appears along the top of the shape, as in Figure 4-5. However, if you drag upward to draw the oval — which almost no one does — the node appears along the bottom. Either way is okay.

 ✔ A polygon or star has one node in each corner and one in the middle of each side. So a triangle has six nodes, while a pentagon or five-pointed star has ten.

Although they're certainly decorative and particularly festive during the holidays, nodes also provide a bona fide function. You can change a shape by dragging a node with the Shape tool — second in line, just below the Arrow tool — CorelDraw's mysterious tool of a thousand faces. Were he alive today, Lon Chaney would undoubtedly sue.

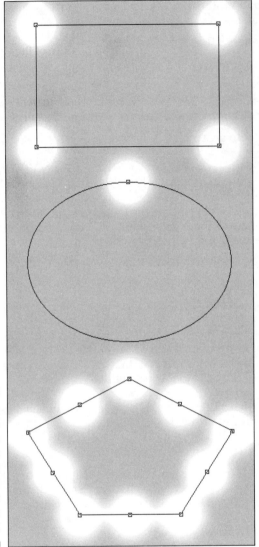

Figure 4-5:
Rectangles
and ovals
include
nodes that
you can
drag with
the Shape
tool.

Sanding off the corners

When applied to one of the nodes of a rectangle, the Shape tool rounds off the corners of the shape, as shown in Figure 4-6. Here's how it works:

1. Draw a rectangle.

You can't edit a rectangle until you draw it.

2. Click on the Shape tool to select it.

Or press F10.

3. Drag one of the rectangle's nodes toward the middle of the shape.

Regardless of which node you drag, CorelDraw rounds off all four corners in the shape to the same extent. Notice that you now have eight nodes, which mark the transitions between the straight and curved edges of the shape. Release the mouse button when you have sufficiently rounded off the corners.

To restore the rectangle's sharp corners, drag any of the eight nodes back to the corner position. Your corners should now be considered dangerous. Don't play too close to the rectangle or run around it with scissors in your hands.

Shape tool

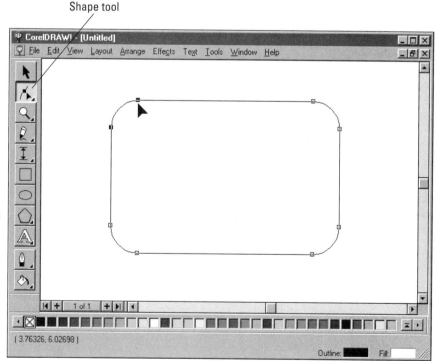

Figure 4-6:
Drag any node in a rectangle with the Shape tool to round off the corners.

Turning an oval into a tempting dessert

I speak, of course, of a pie. When you drag the node of an oval with the Shape tool, you change the oval to a piping hot pie with a node on each side of the wedge. Truth be told, you can actually create either a pie or an arc, depending on how you drag the node, as illustrated in Figure 4-7.

- ✔ Move the Shape tool cursor inside the oval during your drag to create a pie shape (top two objects in Figure 4-7). Like any shape, the pie has an interior that you can fill with a solid color, gradation, or what have you. (Chapter 7 talks about fills.)

- ✔ Move the cursor outside the oval during the drag to create an arc (bottom two objects in Figure 4-7). Notice that with an arc, the slice segments that form a *V* between the two pie nodes disappear. An arc is therefore a curved line with no scrumptious filling.

- ✔ Drag the node to the right to draw a pie with a wedge cut out of it or a long arc, as with the left two objects in Figure 4-7. (This assumes that you created the oval by dragging downward from left to right, which most folks do without thinking. If you create your ovals by dragging from right to left, you nonconformist you, drag the node to the left to cut out a wedge.)

- ✔ Drag the node to the left to throw away most of the pie and retain a slim wedge or a short arc, as with the right-hand objects in Figure 4-7. (If you created the shape by dragging right to left, drag the node to the right instead.)

- ✔ Press Ctrl while dragging to constrain the wedge angle to the nearest 15-degree increment. Because a circle is 360 degrees — I don't know where Euclid got that number, maybe he had 36 toes or something — Ctrl+dragging ensures 24 equal increments around the perimeter of the oval. (360 ÷ 15 = 24, in case you're interested.)

After you change the oval to a pie or arc, you can continue to apply the Shape tool to either node, creating all sorts of wedges and curves. To restore the pie or arc to a circle, drag one node exactly onto the other while keeping the cursor outside the shape. Don't worry about positioning the cursor directly over either node during the drag; the two nodes automatically snap together when they get close enough to one another.

Giving the pie a wedgie

Creating a pie is pretty straightforward. But because of the right/left thing discussed in the preceding section, it's kind of hard to create the pie-and-floating-wedge effect shown in Figure 4-8. I mean, you drag one way for the pie and the other way for the wedge, so how are you supposed to get the pie and wedge to match? Well, I'll tell you how, but it involves a couple of tricks that I haven't discussed yet. Assuming that you're willing to jump boldly into the unknown, here's how it works:

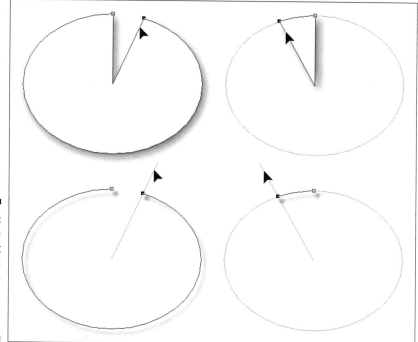

Figure 4-7:
The different ways to turn an oval into a pie or arc using the Shape tool.

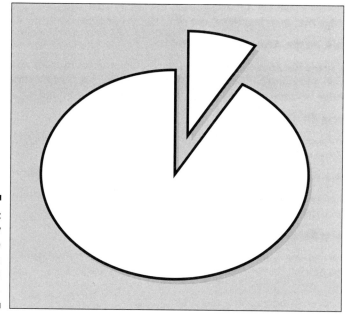

Figure 4-8:
The very popular pie shape with a floating wedge.

1. Select the Oval tool.

Remember, you can select the Oval tool by pressing F7.

2. Draw an oval with the Oval tool.

To keep things simple, make sure to drag from the upper-left portion of the drawing area to lower-right. This way, we'll be operating on the same wavelength.

3. Select the Shape tool.

Or press F10.

4. Ctrl+drag the oval's node to the right. Be sure to keep your cursor on the inside of the shape.

This creates a slice in the pie. Because the Ctrl key constrains your drag in increments, it makes it easier to match the wedge to the slice later on. Otherwise, it's all up to you. It doesn't matter how far you drag. You can create a thin slice or a big chunky one. Depends on what you want to represent. Or how hungry you are.

5. Press Ctrl+D.

Or choose Edit⇨Duplicate. The Duplicate command makes a copy of the shape. I discuss this command in Chapter 8, but for now, just accept it.

6. Reselect the Shape tool (F10) and Ctrl+drag the right-hand node of the new shape to the left.

Ctrl+drag past the upper node and toward the inside of the shape to create a wedge that matches the slice out of the original pie, as shown in Figure 4-9.

7. Click on the Arrow tool to select it.

Or press the spacebar. I explain how to use the Arrow tool with rectangles, ovals, pies, and all the rest in the next section. But for now, notice that the wedge becomes selected, with big corner handles around it.

8. Press Alt+F9.

Or choose Arrange⇨Transform⇨Scale & Mirror. Either way, the Scale & Mirror roll-up appears on-screen.

9. Click on the Flip Horizontal button, labeled in Figure 4-10.

Then press Enter or click on the Apply button. The wedge flips upside-down, as the figure shows.

10. Press the up-arrow key three or four times.

The arrow key nudges the shape incrementally. The wedge is now moved into place.

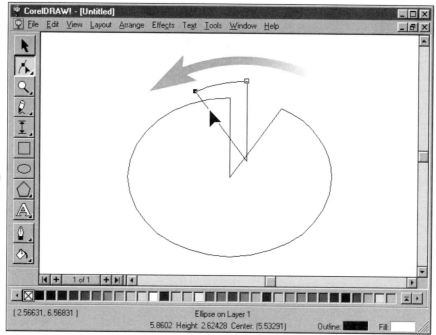

Figure 4-9:
Ctrl+drag
upward with
the Shape
tool to
create a
wedge that
matches the
slice.

Making a wacky shape wackier

Reshaping rectangles and ovals is a great way to while away the occasional rainy day, but you can have the most fun reshaping polygons and stars. Here's how it works:

✓ Regardless of which node you drag in a polygon, the related nodes move in kind. All side nodes move together (as you can see in shapes 2, 3, and 4 in Figure 4-11), and all point nodes move together (shapes 5 and 6). This feature ensures that the polygon or star is forever symmetrical.

✓ Just so that you can impress your friends, this kind of symmetry is known as *radial symmetry.*

✓ Try dragging a side node past a point node or vice versa to create Spirograph-like effects, including double stars. The effects look really great on shapes with ten or more sides.

✓ You can add or subtract sides by right-clicking on the polygon and choosing the Properties option, as explained in the "Shapes with lots of sides" section earlier in this chapter. The polygon retains its new, weird shape however you change the Number of Points values.

✓ Click on a side node and then Shift+click on a point node. Both nodes become selected. Now when you drag one of the two nodes, both side and point nodes move together. If this isn't worth an ooh or ah, I don't know what is.

Flip Horizontal button

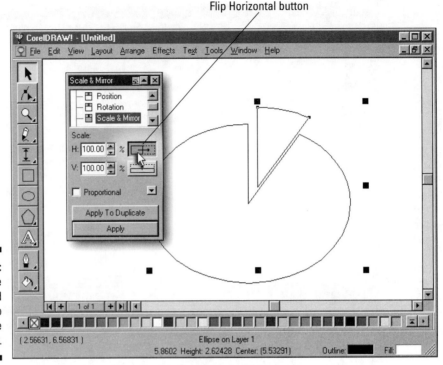

✔ Ctrl+drag a node to move side or point nodes in and out along a constrained axis. Ctrl+dragging is great if you want to keep things from getting
too out of hand.

 More than any other option I've discussed so far, reshaping polygons is something you should experiment with a lot. There's simply no limit to the number
of wild effects you can achieve.

Arrow Tool Techniques (or Tricks of the Pick)

 Every drawing and desktop publishing program on the planet offers a tool that
looks like an arrow. Some companies call their arrows *Selection tools*. Others
call them *Edit tools*. But wouldn't you know it, Corel — roughly the 500th
company to implement such a tool — went and renamed it the *Pick tool*. It
follows, therefore, that when you select something, you're actually "picking" it.
Just imagine if I had employed official Corel vernacular when instructing you to
select the rat's nose in Chapter 3.

Everyone I know calls the tool that looks like an arrow the *Arrow tool.* First tool among tools, the Arrow tool is an editing tool, much like the Shape tool. However, instead of enabling you to change details in an object like the Shape tool does, the Arrow tool changes the object as a whole.

Maybe an analogy will help. In sculpture, the Arrow tool would be a hammer and chisel, and the Shape tool would be one of those little things dentists use to scrape plaque off your teeth. Okay, how about this instead: In the demolition business, the Arrow tool would be a big charge of dynamite, and the Shape tool would be like a bug bomb. Oh, I have another one: In bricklaying, the Arrow tool would be a cement truck dumping liquefied concrete all over the place, while the Shape tool would, uh . . . well, again, it's one of those little dental things, because they might need to clean the bricks off when they get dirty . . . just forget it.

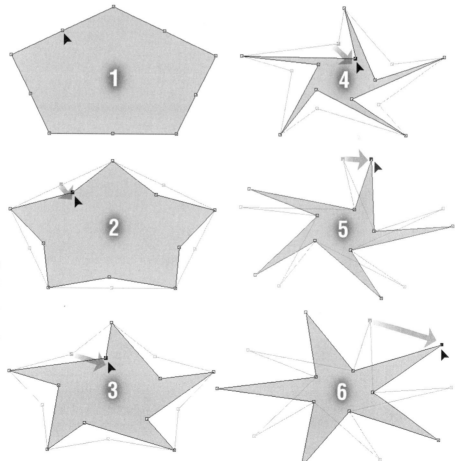

Figure 4-11:
Though you can apply an amazing range of adjustments to a polygon, the shape always remains symmetrical.

Select the Arrow tool and then click on a shape to select the shape. Be sure to click on the outline of the shape (because so far, all the shapes you've drawn are transparent, unless you've been experimenting without me).

To switch between the selected tool and the Arrow tool, just press the spacebar. Press the spacebar again to return to the previously selected tool. If text is active, press Ctrl+spacebar to switch between the selected tool and the Arrow tool.

If you just drew the shape or you were editing it with the Shape tool, you don't need to click on it with the Arrow tool. It remains selected automatically.

Once selected, the shape displays eight big black *handles* in a rectangular formation, as shown in Figure 4-12. The handles enable you to change the dimensions of the shape. The following list explains some basic ways to change a rectangle or ellipse with the Arrow tool.

✔ To scale the shape horizontally, drag the handle on the left or right side of the shape. Drag toward the center of the shape to make the shape skinnier; drag away from the shape to make it fatter.

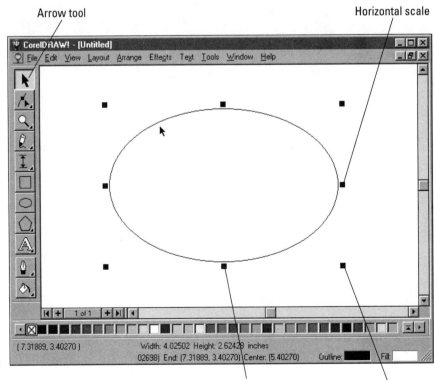

Figure 4-12: Click with the Arrow tool on a shape to select it and display the handles.

✔ To scale the shape vertically, drag the handle on the top or bottom side of the shape. Drag in to make the shape shorter; drag away to make it taller.

✔ You can also scale the shape proportionally, so that the horizontal and vertical proportions remain equal. To do so, drag one of the four corner handles. Drag in to reduce; drag away to enlarge.

✔ If you press Shift while dragging a handle, you scale the shape about its center. In other words, the center of the shape remains stationary throughout your drag. Normally, the opposite side is stationary.

✔ Ctrl+drag a handle to scale in 100 percent increments. You can scale a shape to twice, three times, or four times its previous size and even larger. You generally need a lot of extra room on-screen to pull this off. Try zooming out a few times (by pressing F3) before embarking on a Ctrl+drag.

✔ Ctrl+drag a side handle past the opposite side to flip the shape. For example, if you Ctrl+drag the left handle rightward past the right handle, you flip the shape horizontally. Drag the top handle down past the bottom handle to flip the shape vertically.

✔ To move a shape, drag its outline (not on the handles).

✔ If you click on the outline of a selected shape, the handles change to double-headed arrows. These arrows enable you to rotate and slant the shape as discussed in Chapter 9. To return to the big black handles, click on the shape again.

Kiss It Good-bye

To delete a shape, press Delete. It doesn't matter whether you selected the shape with the Shape tool or the Arrow tool or whether you just finished creating it with the Rectangle or Oval tool. Don't press the Backspace key, by the way. It won't do anything except cause your computer to beep at you.

Aaaugh, It's Gone!

Relax. Everything I've discussed in this chapter can be undone. You can undraw a rectangle or oval, restore a shape that you changed with the Shape tool, return a shape to its original size, and even bring back a shape you've deleted. To undo something, choose Edit⇨Undo or press Ctrl+Z or Alt+Backspace.

Not only can you undo the last operation, you can undo the one before that and the one before that. In CorelDraw, you can undo multiple operations in a row. For example, if you draw a rectangle, round off the corners with the Shape tool, and then scale it, you can press Ctrl+Z three times, first to return the rectangle to its original size, then to restore its sharp corners, and finally to delete it.

If you then change your mind, you can restore operations that you undid by choosing Edit⇨Redo.

It is possible to run out of undos. By default, you can undo no more than four operations *in a row.* So if you deleted something five operations back, you probably won't be able to retrieve it. (For more info, see the upcoming sidebar.)

Raising the Undo ceiling until the rubble falls on your head

You can find out for sure how many operations you can undo in a row by pressing Ctrl+J (Tools⇨Options) and looking at the value in the Undo Levels option box, highlighted below. If the value is more than 4, someone has changed it. You can change it, too, to any number from 1 to 99, but you should be careful. Depending on your computer, CorelDraw may not function as well if you raise the value. It may crash more often or it may prevent you from using other Windows 95 programs.

I recommend that you raise the Undo Levels value no higher than 10 unless someone who is familiar with the inner workings of your computer tells you to do otherwise. And even then, ask for credentials. It's always those computer know-it-alls who tell you to do something and then go on vacation when the entire system breaks down. Personally, I live by the credo, "If it ain't broken, don't fix it."

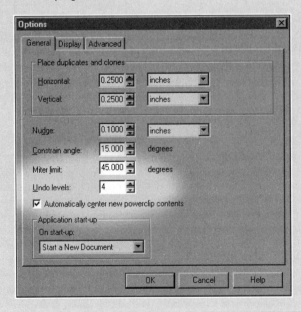

Chapter 5

Drawn It, Shaped It, Ready to Go Free-Form

In This Chapter

▶ Meet Shenbop, crazed adventure seeker

▶ Draw with the Pencil tool

▶ Learn all about paths, segments, and control points

▶ Go on a rampage with the Shape tool

▶ Wake the neighbors with your endless curve bending

▶ Face the Node Edit roll-up without fear

▶ Hack away extraneous nodes

▶ Convert simple shapes to free-form paths

*R*emember those Mountain Dew commercials from a few years back? A bunch of ripped guys poke their faces into the camera and express with virile bravado that they've "Jumped it," "Scaled it," yada yada yada, while visions of stunt men flinging themselves into and off of everything imaginable reel across the screen. Restless daredevils overcome nature. Fledgling Odysseuses on dangerous doses.

I'm not a parent, but if I were, I think I'd have been unnerved. These young men, juiced up on too much caffeine, overconfident beyond their levels of skill and endurance, were quite obviously destined to crack their skulls open during miscalculated bungie jumps, pound their kayaks into unyielding underwater boulders, smash their ultralights into low-flying crop dusters, and invite blood blisters when constructing spice racks without adult supervision. I mean, are we really comfortable handing over the leadership responsibilities of this great nation to a bunch of super-charged yahoos? Haven't we learned anything from the super-charged yahoos currently at the helm?

I'm not sure what all this is leading up to, but I think it's a cautionary note. Some of you, Mountain Dews in hand, are naturally pumped about the skills you have acquired so far. You're drawing pies with flying wedges and polygons with sharp corners while bandying about terms such as *ellipse* and *node* like a veteran CorelDraw hack. With the maddening rush of adrenaline surging through your temples combined with the dizzying sensation of newfound knowledge, you're practically psycho to throw off the chains of geometric shapes. You're itching to go free-form!

All right, I see nothing wrong with that. Just don't overdo it the first time out. I think Edgar Alan Poe said it best: "Quoth the raven, 'Chill, homie.' "

Do Some Doodling with the Pencil

Figure 5-1 shows an amphibian of dubious heritage whose name happens to be Shenbop. The major factor in Shenbop's favor is that he's ridiculously easy to draw. After selecting the Pencil tool — which you can do by clicking on the tool's icon or by pressing F5 — you can draw Shenbop in six steps, as demonstrated in Figure 5-2. Just drag with the tool as if you were doodling with a real pencil. Your lines may look a little shakier than mine — not that mine are all that smooth — but you can do it.

Pencil tool   Shenbop (a frog)

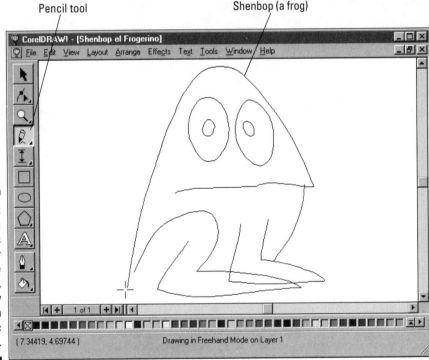

Figure 5-1:
If you can draw this cute critter with the Pencil tool, you may have hidden artistic abilities.

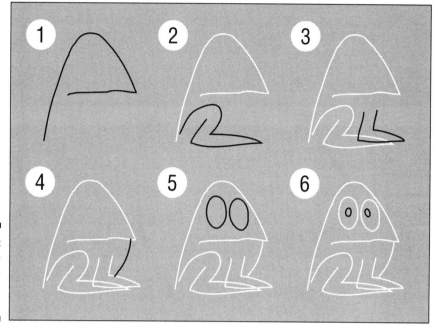

Figure 5-2:
The six-step
Shenbop
creation
program.

Understanding paths, lines, and shapes

Before I go any further, I need to introduce a few basic concepts. First of all, anything you draw — whether it's with the Rectangle tool, the Oval tool, the Pencil, or some future tool I haven't mentioned yet — is called a *path.* The reason behind the term has to do with the way some printers draw mathematical objects, but just think of it this way: If you blew up a rectangle or some other line or shape onto a sheet of paper the size of a city block, the shape's outline would become as wide as a sidewalk. You could follow it around the block, hence, it's a path. The only difference is that paths in CorelDraw are for extremely small people.

In each of Steps 1 through 4 of Figure 5-2, you draw an *open path,* in which the beginning and end of the path don't touch. An open path is therefore the same as a *line.* Steps 5 and 6 show *closed paths,* which are paths that loop around continuously with no obvious beginning or end. In laymen's terms, a closed path is a *shape.* It may seem silly for me to have to define common words like *line* and *shape,* but they lie at the core of CorelDraw. In fact, everything you draw falls into one of these two camps.

In Chapter 1, I introduced the term *object,* which can also mean either a line or shape. But unlike a path, an object can also be a block of text. For an object to qualify as a path, you have to be able to edit its outline. So paths are a subset of objects that include lines and shapes only. Figure 5-3 shows the family tree of CorelDraw objects.

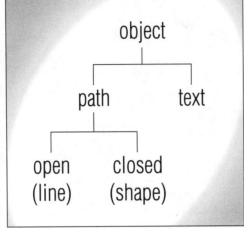

Figure 5-3:
Objects
include
paths and
text. Paths
include
lines and
shapes.

Dissecting a drawing

Now that I've completed the tiresome task of establishing the vocabulary, here are a few slightly more lively pointers on using the Pencil tool:

- ✔ Immediately after you draw a line or shape, CorelDraw performs some intense calculations and assigns nodes to the path automatically. The length of the path from one node to the next is called a *segment* (see Figure 5-4). And you thought we were finished with the vocabulary.

- ✔ If the path is fairly simple — say, requiring ten nodes or fewer — CorelDraw displays all the nodes. If the path is more complex, the program shows only the first and last nodes. It's just a display thing; all the nodes are present, they're just hiding. (If you were a node, wouldn't you be shy?)

- ✔ The total number of nodes for a path appears in the middle of the status bar at the bottom of the screen.

- ✔ CorelDraw has a habit of depositing nodes based on the speed at which you draw. When you draw fast, it lays down a node here, another there. When you draw slowly, the program riddles the path with nodes because it thinks that you're slowing down for emphasis. Unfortunately, densely concentrated nodes result in abrupt transitions and zigzags that make the path look jagged and irregular, as demonstrated in Figure 5-4. So try to maintain a quick and consistent drawing speed.

✔ If you're inexperienced at drawing with a mouse, nearly all your first hundred or so paths will be jagged and irregular. What can I tell you? It takes time to get it down. But don't let it bother you. As long as you draw approximately what you want, you can shape and mold it as discussed later in this chapter.

✔ To draw a straight line, click with the Pencil tool to establish the first node and then click at a new location to establish the second. CorelDraw automatically draws a straight line between the two nodes.

✔ To draw an irregular polygon — such as a triangle in which every side is a different length — click to create the first node, double-click at a new location to create the second node, and continue double-clicking to establish additional nodes in the path. The program draws a straight segment between each pair of nodes. To end the polygon, click once.

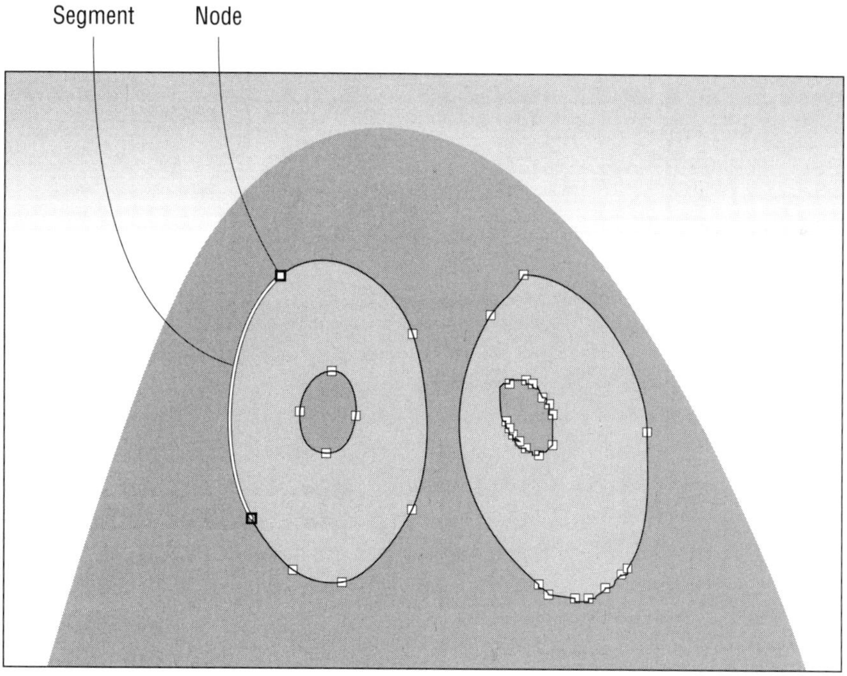

Segment   Node

Figure 5-4:
Paths with
moderate
numbers of
evenly
spread
nodes are
smooth
(left), while
paths with
densely
concentrated
nodes are
jagged
(right).

✔ To draw a closed path, you have to connect with the point at which you began dragging or clicking. If you miss, the path won't close properly. You can't fill an open path. (See Figure 5-5.)

✔ If a path does not close as you had hoped, you can press Delete and redraw it. But you can also close the path with the Pencil. Immediately after drawing an open path, drag from the first node to the last node to add a few more segments and close the path to form a shape. To close the path with a straight segment, click on the first node and then click on the last.

✔ You can extend any open path with the Pencil. After drawing the path, drag from either the first or last node. Or click on either node to add straight segments.

Closed path   Open path

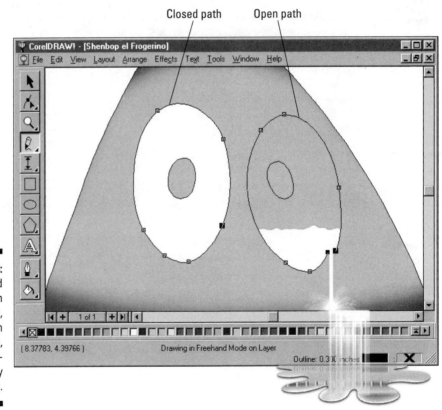

Figure 5-5:
A closed path can hold its fill, but an open path leaks, metaphorically speaking.

Nodes as You Never Knew Them

As I said earlier, it's no big deal if you don't draw your paths correctly right off the bat. Even the best and most knowledgeable CorelDraw artists spend a significant portion of their time editing and generally rehashing paths with that tool of tools, the Shape tool. You can move nodes, change the curvature of segments, add and delete nodes, close open paths, open closed ones, and otherwise change a haphazard scrawl into a gracefully sinuous line or shape.

A thousand nodes of light

To view and edit the nodes in a Pencil path, select the Shape tool — or press the shortcut key, F10 — and click on the path. The nodes in the path light up like candles on a Christm . . . er, tree of ambiguous religious origin. (We must always be PC when discussing PCs.)

Click on an individual node in the path to select the node. It changes from hollow to black. You may also see one or two *control points* extending from the node, as shown in Figure 5-6. A purely decorative dotted line — called a *lever* — connects each control point to its node.

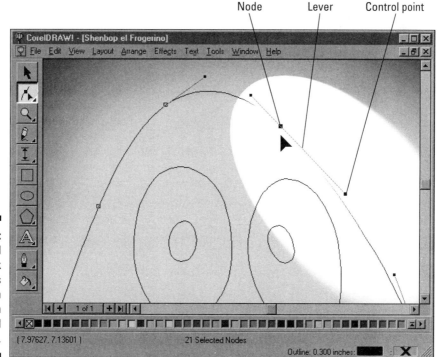

Figure 5-6:
Control points flank most nodes in a path drawn with the Pencil tool.

Control points determine the curvature of segments. And yet, unlike nodes, they don't actually reside on the path; they float above it like little satellites. In fact, a control point tugs on a segment in much the same way that the moon tugs at the ocean to create tides. It's like a detached ethereal force with special gravitational powers. But unlike the moon, a control point doesn't inspire men to howl or turn into werewolves when it's full.

The Shape tool in action

The following items explain how to use the Shape tool to select nodes and control points as well as change the appearance of a path. I've also tossed in a few general notes and bits of wisdom to help you along your way.

 ✔ Click on a node to select it and display any control points associated with the node. A node can have no control points, or it can have as many as two, one for each segment.

 ✔ Segments need control points to bend them. If a segment is not bordered on either side by a control point, the segment is absolutely straight.

 ✔ Drag a node to move it and its control points. The segments that border the node stretch to keep up, as demonstrated in Figure 5-7. You can drag the node as far as you want; segments are infinitely stretchy.

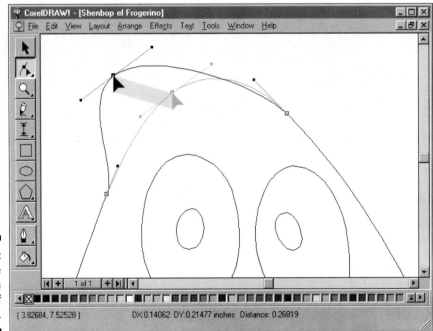

Figure 5-7:
Drag a node
to extend a
portion of
the path.

✔ Drag a control point to bend and tug at the corresponding segment, as shown in Figure 5-8. Notice that the node remains stationary, anchoring the segment.

✔ If the node is a *smooth node,* the opposite control point also moves, bending its segment as in Figure 5-8. This is because in a smooth node, the control points are locked into alignment to ensure a seamless arc. If the node is a *cusp node,* you can move one control point independently of its neighbor. The cusp node permits you to create corners in a path.

✔ Still vague on the whole control point thing? It may help to envision a typical Pencil path as a rubber band wrapped around a pattern of nails, as dramatized in Figure 5-9. The nails represent nodes in the path; the rubber band represents its segments. A sample control point appears as a round knob. The rubber band is starched to give it tension and prevent it from crimping. A path in CorelDraw likewise bends evenly in the direction of its handle.

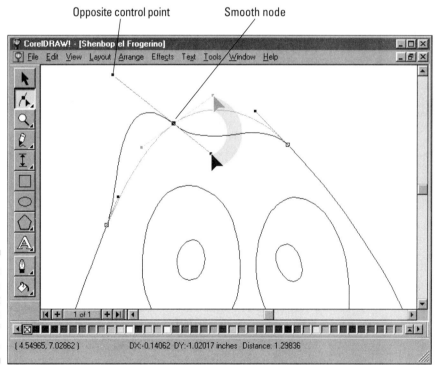

Figure 5-8:
Drag a control point to alter the curvature of a segment.

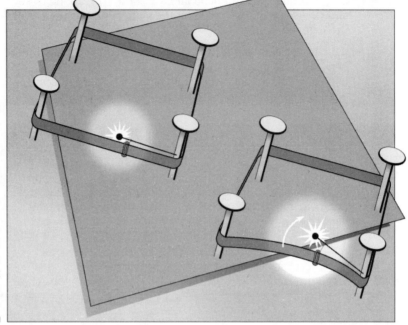

Figure 5-9:
By dragging
the control
point from
its original
position
(left), you
bend the
rubber band
segment in
that
direction
(right).

✔ If you don't want to deal with control points — believe me, everybody hates them — you can drag directly on a curved segment. The segment bends and stretches as shown in Figure 5-10.

✔ When you drag a segment bordered by a smooth node, the segment on the other side of that node bends and stretches with your drag. In Figure 5-10, both bordering nodes are smooth nodes, so three segments are affected.

✔ You can't drag a straight segment. Well, you *can,* but it doesn't do any good.

✔ To drag a node, control point, or segment in a strictly horizontal or vertical direction, press the Ctrl key while dragging.

✔ To select more than one node, click on the first node and Shift+click on each additional node. Then drag any one of them to move all the selected nodes at the same time.

✔ If the nodes that you want to select border each other, you can select them by dragging around them. As you drag, CorelDraw displays a dotted rectangle called a *marquee,* as shown in Figure 5-11. Any nodes surrounded by the marquee become selected.

✔ Don't forget to press Ctrl+Z or choose Edit⇨Undo if you make a mistake. Or, if you prefer, you can press Alt+Backspace. No change is irreparable if you catch it in time.

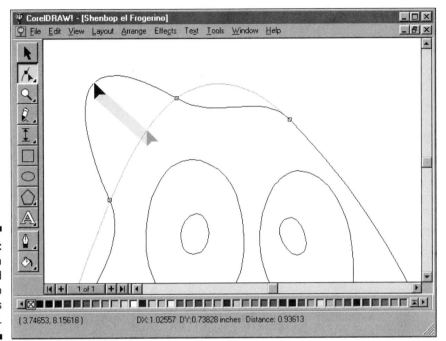

Figure 5-10:
Drag a curved segment to change its curvature.

Marquee

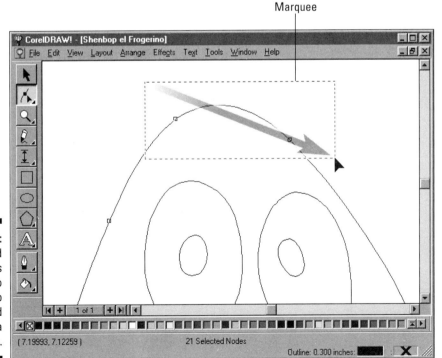

Figure 5-11:
Drag around the nodes you want to select to surround them in a marquee.

Meet the Node Edit Thingie

To perform any other node-editing function, such as adding and deleting nodes, joining and splitting paths, and all the rest of that stuff, you have to use the trusty Node Edit roll-up. To display the roll-up, featured in Figure 5-12, double-click on a node with the Shape tool or press Ctrl+F10.

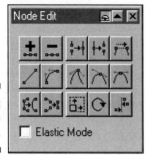

Figure 5-12:
The Node
Edit roll-up.

In earlier versions of CorelDraw, most buttons in the Node Edit roll-up were labeled with words. The meanings of the buttons weren't always crystal clear — To Line and Symmet took some figuring out — but at least you had a clue. In CorelDraw 6, all the buttons are marked with icons, few of which are the least bit recognizable.

Fortunately, Figure 5-13 includes helpful labels for each button. I also describe all the buttons in detail in the following three sections and show each icon in the margin when discussing it. And in case that's still not enough, I refer to each icon in the text by its order in the Node Edit roll-up. The fourth icon in the first row, for example, is the one labeled *Break one node in two* in Figure 5-13. Hopefully, the result is a crystal-clear discussion of this wacky roll-up.

Your first tentative node edits

The following list explains how to use the most essential options in the Node Edit roll-up to add nodes, delete nodes, and otherwise wreak havoc on the whole node-oriented world. Get psyched, because this is about the most exciting list you'll ever read. Short of the phone book, of course.

Oh, by the way, all of these items assume that you've already displayed the Node Edit roll-up. It's a good thing to keep on-screen. If it gets in your way, click on the up-pointing arrow icon on the right side of the title bar.

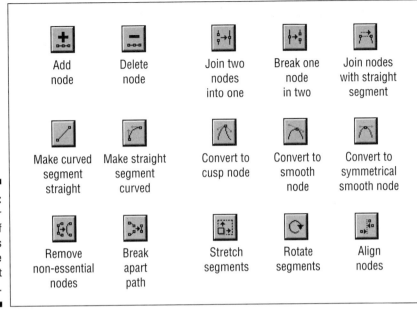

Figure 5-13:
Closer
scrutiny of
the buttons
from the
Node Edit
roll-up.

✔ To add a node to a path, click on the spot in the segment where you want to add the node. A round sort of blob appears. It's not a node yet; it's sort of a fetal node. Then click on the plus-sign icon in the roll-up to bring the node into the world of the living.

✔ You can also add nodes to a shape drawn with the Polygon tool. Try this: Draw a polygon and then select the Shape tool and drag one of the side nodes to make the shape look like a star. Now click on any segment to create a fetal node and click on the plus-sign icon in the Node Edit roll-up. Not only does a new node appear at the spot when you clicked, but additional nodes also spring up at symmetrical points around the shape. Drag any of these new nodes, and all the new nodes move in kind. It's very cool.

✔ To delete one or more nodes, select all the nodes you want to delete and then press Delete. Why bother with that button with the minus sign on it when the Delete key is so much more convenient?

✔ If you can add nodes to a polygon, it stands to reason that you can select a polygon node and delete it as well.

✔ You can also press the + or – key on the keypad to respectively add or delete a node. These keys work even when the Node Edit roll-up is hidden.

A little something you really don't need to know

When you draw with a real pencil, you smudge graphite directly onto the page. It's a cause/effect thing, a simple law of nature. When you draw with the Pencil tool, CorelDraw tries to imitate nature using math. But because math isn't the natural state of anything except computer programs and high school calculus teachers, the line has to undergo a conversion. You can tweak this conversion — thereby affecting how the Pencil tool draws — using the good old Tool Properties dialog box.

Double-click on the Pencil tool icon in the toolbox to display the Tool Properties dialog box. Three options have a bearing on Pencil paths, as spotlighted in the figure. The first, Freehand Tracking, controls how accurately the path follows your drag. The second, Corner Threshold, controls CorelDraw's tendency to insert jagged corners in a path. And the third, Straight Line Threshold, determines the likelihood of straight segments in a path.

In all three cases, the values in the option boxes can vary between 1 and 10. If you develop uncanny dexterity with the mouse, you may want to test out lower values, which — taken to their extremes — encourage the path to follow every nuance and jiggle in your drag. If your drags exhibit the kinds of tremors normally associated with small earthquakes, or if folks have a tendency to ask you why you write your letters in moving vehicles when you actually write them at a desk with optimal lighting during the stillest of evenings while listening to endless loops of Pachelbel's *Canon in D minor*, you may want to avail yourself of higher values, which result in smoother and less jagged paths, however less accurate.

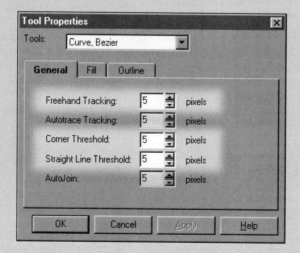

Excuse me for interrupting, but I feel it my duty to come out in hearty support for the flagrant clear-cutting of nodes. The fact is, CorelDraw invariably assigns too many nodes to Pencil paths. It verges on criminal overpopulation. It's not rare to see nodes stuck one right on top of the other, like procreating cockroaches, or wet Skittles, or some equally disgusting fluke of nature. As a rule of thumb, you need a cusp node for every corner in a path. You need a smooth node for every quarter-circle's worth of curve. Anything beyond that is garbage. Figure 5-14 shows a path before and after deleting extraneous nodes.

How to open, split, close, and join paths

To recap, I've so far explained how to add and delete nodes, which amounts to super common stuff. If only for the sake of strip-mining paths, you may be engaging in these operations frequently. The next functions I describe are slightly less common, but rank right up there nonetheless. You learn how to open closed paths, close open ones, slice and dice paths without the aid of a Vegematic, and join them back together as effortlessly as a supercollider bonds kernels of creamed corn back onto the cob.

Figure 5-14:
Bad Shenbop's nodes are many and crowded. Good Shenbop's nodes are few and far between.

Bad Shenbop   Good Shenbop

✔ To open a closed path, select a node that you want to split into two nodes and click on the Break button (the fourth icon in the first row) in the Node Edit roll-up. What was once one node is now two nodes. You can drag each node wherever you please.

✔ If the closed path was filled with a color before you opened it, the color disappears.

 ✔ To split an open path into two independent paths, select the node at which you want the split to occur and then click on the Break button. The path is now split, but it remains a single unit in CorelDraw's mind. To finalize the divorce, click on the second button in the third row of the roll-up. Or you can choose Arrange⇨Break Apart or press Ctrl+K. The two paths can now go their separate ways.

 ✔ To close an open path, select both the first and last nodes in the line and then click on the Join button (the third icon in the first row) in the roll-up. The two nodes are fused into one, and the line is transformed into a shape.

 ✔ The problem with the Join button is that it moves the nodes when joining them. If you want the nodes to remain in place and connect them with a straight line, click on the fifth button in the first row.

Joining two completely independent open paths into a single longer path is a little tricky. So instead of explaining it in a list item, I'll present it in steps.

1. Select the Arrow tool.

See, it's tricky already.

2. Click on the first open path that you want to join.

Don't try this on a closed path. If you want to extend a shape, make sure that you first open it by selecting a node with the Shape tool and clicking on the break icon in the roll-up (fourth button, first row).

3. Shift+click on the second open path that you want to join.

Now both paths are selected.

4. Press Ctrl+L.

Or choose Arrange⇨Combine. CorelDraw now recognizes the paths as a single unit.

5. Press F10 to select the Shape tool.

Getting trickier.

6. Click on the first or last node in one path and then Shift+click on the first or last node in the other path.

In other words, select the two nodes you want to fuse together.

7. Click on the Join button.

That's the third button in the first row. The two short lines are now one long line.

New ways to make a break

CorelDraw 6 introduces two new tools that let you break segments and paths apart. Both tools are available from the Shape tool flyout menu. Click and hold on the Shape tool icon in the toolbox to display a flyout containing a Knife tool and an Eraser tool, as demonstrated in Figure 5-15.

- After selecting the Knife tool, click on a path to cut it apart at that point. (If you miss the path, Corel beeps at you in a highly irritating manner.) You can click on a node or on a segment. Either way, a precise incision is made.

- By default, the knife tool closes any path it touches, whether the path was originally open or closed. If you click on a line drawn with the Pencil tool, for example, CorelDraw automatically adds new segments to the severed paths and creates two closed shapes. Makes about as much sense as cutting a piece of string and getting two pieces of dinnerware.

- To instruct CorelDraw to stop this nonsensical closing of knifed paths, double-click on the Knife tool icon in the toolbox. The Tool Properties dialog box comes to the rescue. Turn off the Automatically Close Object check box and press Enter.

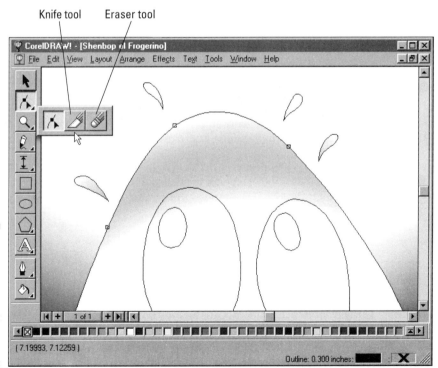

Figure 5-15: Shenbop sheds some sweat in anticipation of being put under the knife.

✔ The Eraser is another cutting tool, but rather than using it to cut at a point, you use it to slice a wide gash through the path. First, use the Arrow or Shape tool to select the path that you want to cut. Then select the Eraser and drag across the path. It tears through the path and splits it in pieces, like an apple slit with a big, fat knife.

✔ The Eraser tool leaves closed paths closed and leaves open paths open. What a sensible tool.

✔ To specify the width of the opening cut with the Eraser tool, double-click on the eraser icon in the toolbox. Again, you see the Tool Properties dialog box. Enter a new value into the Thickness option box — the default is $1/4$ inch — and press Enter.

When you slice paths with the Knife tool, CorelDraw breaks them into two separate objects. But when you use the Eraser tool, the bits and pieces of the path remain combined into one path in CorelDraw's mind. This means that you can't drag the pieces separately with the Arrow tool. To break the pieces apart, press Ctrl+K or click on the second button in the third row of the Node Edit roll-up as described in the preceding section.

Options you'll use once in a blue moon

I'm tempted to end my discussion of the Node Edit buttons right here. It's not that the rest of the buttons are useless — not all of them, anyway. It's just that they're more specialized. Most beginners and intermediates barely touch these buttons. But the buttons do serve a purpose, so you may as well know about them. Besides, I'm afraid that if I didn't explain them, you might get so curious that you'd resort to reading the Corel manual. And that could be fatal. So in the interest of keeping you alert, informed, and alive, the upcoming list explains the remaining options in the Node Edit roll-up, from most useful to least.

In addition to paths drawn with the Pencil tool, you can apply the Node Edit buttons to nodes and segments in shapes drawn with the Polygon tool. Throughout, CorelDraw maintains the symmetry of the polygon, which can make for some pretty entertaining effects.

Before I get started, I want to explain why so many buttons seem always to be dimmed. In many cases, the button is already in effect. For example, if you select a cusp node, the Cusp button is dimmed because the cusp can't be any cuspier than it already is. Other times, the button isn't applicable. The Align button is dimmed if fewer than two nodes are selected, because you can't align a single node to itself. Well, I guess you could, but what's the point?

✔ The first button in the second row straightens out a curved segment. To use this option, click on a too-curly segment with the Shape tool. A round node-wannabe appears to show that the segment is selected. Click on the button, and the segment becomes straight.

 ✔ The next button in the second row fulfills the opposite function. Click on a straight segment to get the round fetal node and then click on the button to make it a curved segment. Though the segment still looks straight, you can drag the segment with the Shape tool to stretch it.

 ✔ To change a smooth node so that it represents a corner in the path, select the node and click on the Cusp button (third icon, second row). You can then move the control points of the cusp independently of each other.

 ✔ To change a corner to a smooth arc, select the node and click on the Smooth button (fourth icon, second row). CorelDraw locks the control points into alignment so that the transition between neighboring segments is seamless.

 ✔ The fifth button in the second row locks the control points of a node into symmetrical alignment, so that the two levers are always the exact same length. It's a variation on the smooth node that has almost no relevance in today's world. I think Peking Man used it in some sort of greet-the-dawn ritual, but nowadays, forget it.

 ✔ The first icon in the last row wins my vote as the least useful of the Node Edit options. It's supposed to remove extraneous nodes automatically. But think about it for a moment. If CorelDraw were smart enough to eliminate extraneous nodes, it wouldn't have put them in there in the first place. You can rearrange some settings in the Tool Properties dialog box (as explained in the "A little something you really don't need to know" sidebar a few pages back) and get some remarkably disappointing results. But for the most part, this option doesn't do squat.

 ✔ The Stretch and Rotate buttons (numbers three and four in the last row) are marginally useful. You can scale, rotate, flip, and slant individual segments in a path by selecting two or more nodes, clicking on one of these buttons, and dragging a handle. To learn about the standard transformation functions, read Chapter 9. Then come back to these options and try them out.

 ✔ The last button in the roll-up aligns multiple nodes in horizontal or vertical formation. You learn more about alignment in Chapter 6, if you choose to read it. Otherwise, you remain ignorant.

Bouncy paths made of rubber

One option still has a name in the Node Edit roll-up, and that's the Elastic Mode check box. In the past, I've been a tad unfair to this option, making libelous suggestions such as "People who know how to use Elastic Mode are dumber for it." That's true, of course, or I never would have said it. But still, being dumb can be fun, so I may as well tell you how the doggone thing works.

See, when Elastic Mode is on, CorelDraw moves, stretches, and rotates all selected nodes with respect to the node that is farthest away from the node you drag. Even if the far-away node is selected, it remains stationary, while the other nodes stretch away or toward it to varying degrees depending on their proximity. This produces a spongy effect, as if the far-away node is snagged on a nail or something and the rest of the path is made of rubber.

If you turn off Elastic Mode, the selected nodes move, stretch, and rotate a consistent amount, without any rubbery stuff happening. It's less amusing, but it may be more useful if you're trying to achieve a specific effect.

In other words, if you don't like the way a path is behaving, turn off the Elastic Mode check box and see whether that makes things more predictable.

How to Upgrade Simple Shapes

So far, much of this chapter has been devoted to stuff that you can't do to rectangles, ovals, or symmetrical polygons. You can't move the nodes in a rectangle independently of each other, you can't adjust the curvature of a segment in an oval, and you can't drag a single node in a star independently of its symmetrical buddies.

Not, that is, until you convert the simple shapes to free-form paths. To make the conversion, select the shape with the Arrow tool and press Ctrl+Q. That's all there is to it. By pressing Ctrl+Q or choosing <u>A</u>rrange➪Con<u>v</u>ert To Curves, you convert the selected shape to nodes, segments, and control points, just like a path drawn with the Pencil tool. You can then edit the shape to any extent imaginable.

Keep in mind, however, that by converting a simple shape to a path, you ruin all semblance of the shape's original identity. You can no longer use the Shape tool to add rounded corners to a rectangle, change an oval into a pie, or move all the points in a star together, as described in Chapter 4. The Convert To Curves command submits the shape to a state of complete anarchy.

Chapter 6

Celebrating Your Inner Draftsman

o you have problems expressing your feelings? Are you critical of other people's driving? Do you insist on alphabetizing your guests at the dinner table? Do you distrust government, yet at the same time harbor suspicions that Ross Perot is a certifiable loony? If you said yes to any of these — except the bit about Perot — you may be a closet control freak. And you know what? That's okay. Because, doggone it, people like you. A couple of them anyway. Well, maybe *like* is too strong of a word. *Know*, then. They scurry out of the room when you appear because, doggone it, people know you. Isn't that comforting?

This chapter is a call to arms for control freaks, a reawakening of the kindred spirit of the fussbudget. Together, we'll muck around with rulers, guidelines, and other tightly structured features in an attempt to precisely arrange minuscule details that no one notices but that fill you with a secret pride. I speak of the satisfaction that only a job well-worried over can deliver.

I don't want to cure your perfectionism. I want you to rejoice in it! By the way, is that a grease stain on your shirt? Ha, made you look.

You Need to be Disciplined

At least, that's what Madonna would tell you. But I'm talking about a different kind of discipline — namely, the kind provided by the big four CorelDraw control functions:

- *Rulers,* which appear along the top and left sides of the drawing area, serve as visual aids.

- The *grid* is a network of regularly spaced points that attract your cursor and prevent you from drawing slightly crooked lines and other haphazard stuff.

- You can set up custom *guidelines* between grid increments to align objects and generally ensure an orderly environment.

- The *status bar* shows you where your cursor is, the dimensions of shapes, the distance and angle of movements, and a bunch of other stuff I can't tell you right now or else I won't have anything to talk about in the status bar section.

Together, these forces shield you from utter drawing anarchy. Heck, by the time you're done, you'll be a regular artistic Mussolini. Go for it, make those tools run on time!

Rulers with no power

Unlike grids and guidelines, rulers don't constrain your movements or make you draw any better. In fact, they don't *do* much of anything. They just sit there. But rulers can be nice to have around because they show you how big objects are and how much distance is between them. It's like having a compass in the woods: With rulers, you know where you are.

To display the rulers, choose View➪Rulers. As shown in Figure 6-1, one horizontal ruler and one vertical ruler appear along the outskirts of the drawing area. With a little luck and a whole lot of divine intervention, they may even inspire you to create something as fantastic as the Roman Colosseum (Collos.CMX), found in the Travel folder on the fourth of the CorelDraw 6 CD-ROMs.

Here's how to exploit the rulers to their fullest:

- The rulers monitor the location of the cursor using two *tracking lines.* Meanwhile, the status bar displays the numerical coordinates of the cursor, which correspond directly to the tracking lines. In Figure 6-1, for example, the horizontal tracking line appears just to the left of the 5.0 mark, while the status bar displays the coordinate 5.69949.

Rulers   Horizontal tracking line

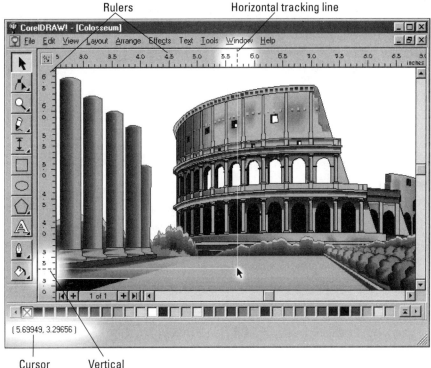

Figure 6-1:
Along with
the status
bar, the
rulers
monitor the
location of
the cursor.

Cursor   Vertical
coordinates   tracking line

✔ All measurements are made from the *zero point*, which is the point where both rulers display the value 0. You can change the location of the zero point by dragging on the *ruler origin box*, which appears at the meeting of the two rulers, as shown in Figure 6-2. The point at which you release becomes the new zero point (see Figure 6-3).

✔ Rulers generally display units in inches. But if you prefer to work in a different measurement system, you can change one or both of the rulers. Choose Layout⇨Grid and Ruler Setup to display the Grid & Ruler Setup dialog box shown in Figure 6-4. To change a ruler, select a different option from one of the pop-up menus in the Units area. The first pop-up menu controls the horizontal ruler; the second controls the vertical ruler.

✔ You can also display the Grid & Ruler Setup dialog box by right-clicking on the horizontal or vertical ruler and then selecting Grid and Ruler Setup from the resulting pop-up menu.

✔ The status bar coordinates always correspond to the units on the horizontal ruler (displayed on the ruler's far right side).

✔ To get rid of the rulers, choose View⇨Rulers again.

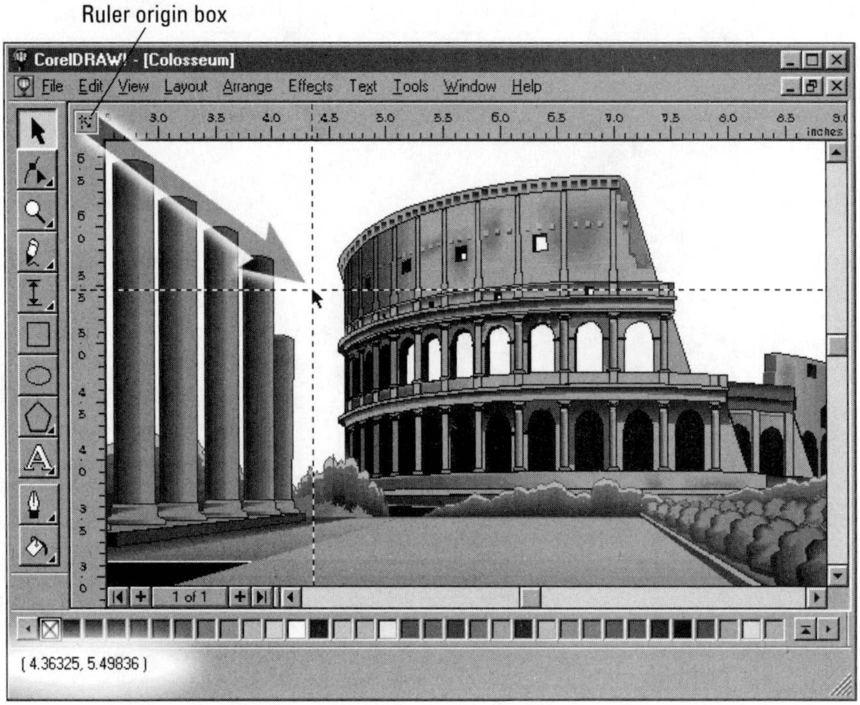

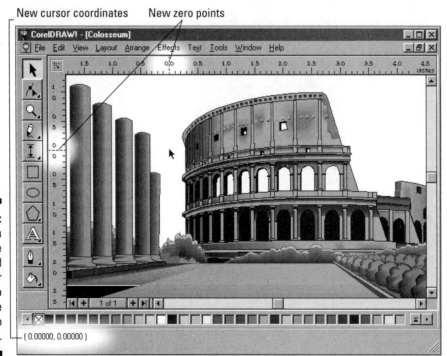

Ruler origin box

Figure 6-2:
Drag from the ruler origin box to move the point from which all measurements are made.

New cursor coordinates   New zero points

Figure 6-3:
When you release, the rulers and status bar update to show the new zero point.

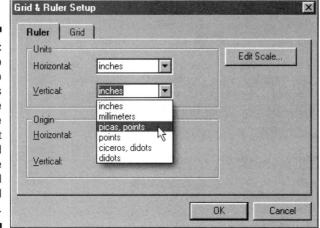

Figure 6-4:
The two
Units pop-up
menus
determine
the
measurement
system used
by the
horizontal
and vertical
rulers.

Go downtown

Imagine a plan for the perfect city center, something like Washington D.C. Every block measures $^1/_{10}$ mile by $^1/_{10}$ mile. No block has an alley. Exactly 11 east-west streets and 11 north-south avenues subdivide every square mile into 100 square blocks.

Oh, sure, it's a little formal. It lacks spontaneity and *joie de vivre,* but you're supposed to be getting work done, not sitting around enjoying the scenery. Besides, it's a grid, just like the one in CorelDRAW.

In Draw, the grid affects the placement of nodes, control points, handles, and so on. So although a free-form path can snake along wherever it pleases, its nodes are constrained to precise grid increments. The same goes for nodes in rectangles, ovals, and blocks of text.

Here's how to set up a grid:

1. **Right-click on one of the rulers and select Grid and Ruler Setup from the pop-up menu**.

   Or double-click on a ruler or choose Layout⇨Grid and Ruler Setup. Either way, you display the Grid & Ruler Setup dialog box.

2. Click on the Grid tab to switch to the second panel of options.

Or press the Tab key until you highlight the Ruler tab and then press the right-arrow key. The Grid panel in Figure 6-5 appears.

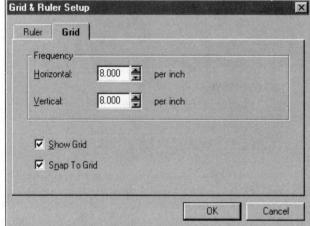

Figure 6-5: Switch to the Grid panel to set up CorelDraw's wondrous grid.

3. Define the distance between grid points by entering values into the Horizontal and Vertical option boxes.

It's here that you specify how many city blocks fit into a mile or inch or whatever. The number of grid points per unit of measure is called the *grid frequency,* just in case you're even remotely interested.

4. Select the Show Grid check box.

This way, you can see the grid points on-screen.

5. Select the Snap To Grid check box.

When this option is active, nodes, control points, and handles gravitate toward grid points. If you don't select this option, you can see the grid, but it doesn't have any effect on how you draw and edit paths. This step is the most important one. Don't skip it.

6. Press Enter.

Or click on OK. The grid points appear in the drawing area, as shown in Figure 6-6.

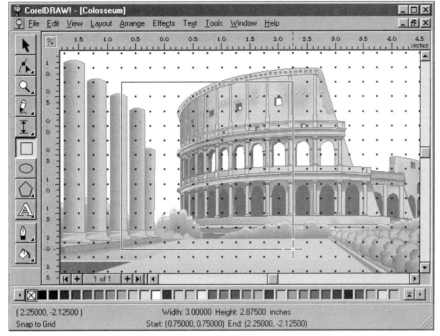

Figure 6-6:
When the
grid is
active, your
cursor
snaps to the
grid points
every time
you draw
and edit
paths.

To try out the grid, draw a rectangle with the Rectangle tool. Your cursor snaps from one grid point to the next, as in Figure 6-6. Incidentally, CorelDraw doesn't always display all grid points. Depending on the grid frequency and zoom ratio, the program may hide some grid points — for example, every other point — to cut down on-screen clutter (as is the case in the figure). But whether or not you can see a grid point, the snapping effect is still in force.

After you establish your grid, you can turn it on and off from the keyboard by pressing Ctrl+Y (or by choosing Layout⇨Snap To Grid).

Let the lines be your guide

If you live in or near a highly-structured city center, you know that it's a mixed blessing. On the plus side, it's great for tourists and new residents who rely on the predictability to get around. For example, anyone fresh off the boat who can count — except, of course, military guys — can find Manhattan's 5th Avenue. On the minus side, a network of streets and avenues can prove stagnant and limiting for commuters and long-time residents. You wish to heck there was a freeway to get up over the traffic or a winding country road to break up the monotony.

Similarly, CorelDraw's grid is great for novices but loses some of its attraction after you become moderately familiar with the program. It's not that you outgrow the need for structure; that's always helpful. What you need is increased flexibility.

That's where guidelines come in. Like the rulers, guidelines are available in horizontal and vertical varieties. Like the grid, they exude gravitational force. But guidelines differ from rulers and the grid in that you can create as many guidelines as you like and place them wherever you want. You can even draw a guide at an angle — a feature new to CorelDraw 6.

✔ To create a guideline, drag from a ruler into the drawing area, as demonstrated in Figure 6-7.

✔ Dragging down from the horizontal ruler produces a horizontal guideline; dragging right from the vertical ruler produces — everybody sing! — a bright red lobster in a green varsity sweater.

Actually, that last action produces a vertical guideline. I just made up the bit about the lobster. No lobsters were made to wear sweaters in the making of this book. One was encouraged to wear a high-school letter jacket, but only briefly. The lobster is now in a recovery program (see Figure 6-8). In fact, he and I are in the same ward.

✔ To move a guideline, drag it. Be careful, though. It's easy to accidentally drag an object when you're trying to drag a guideline (and vice versa).

✔ CorelDraw 6 displays handles at either end of every guide visible on-screen, as you can see in Figure 6-7. To change the angle of a guide, just drag one of these handles. Again, be careful to drag the guide handle and not some object in your drawing.

Guide handles   Vertical guidelines   Horizontal guidelines

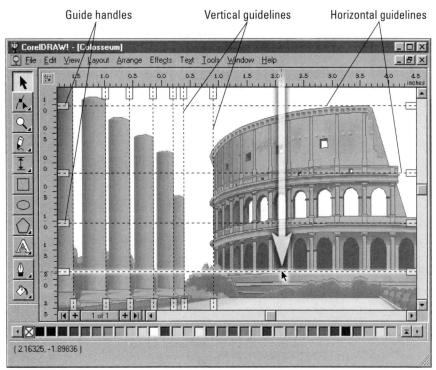

Figure 6-7:
Drag from a
ruler to
create a
guideline.

✔ To delete a horizontal or vertical guide, just drag it back to the ruler it came from. To delete an angled guide, double-click on it to display the Guidelines Setup dialog box and then click on the Slanted tab to change panels. A list of angled guides appears on the left side of the dialog box, complete with techy coordinate data stating the location of some point on the guide and its angle. Use the angle data to figure out which guide is which. Guides with positive angle values slant upward; guides with negative angles slant down. The larger the value, the more the guide slants. Select the guide that you want to delete and then click on the Delete button. If you got the right one, you'll see it disappear in the background. Press Enter to make your change official. If you deleted the wrong guide, press Esc and try again.

✔ You can undo the movement of a guide — just as you can undo any other edit — by pressing Ctrl+Z (or Alt+Backspace).

✔ When the grid is active, the creation and movement of guidelines is constrained by the grid. There's no point to having a guideline that duplicates a line of grid points, so be sure to turn off the grid (Ctrl+Y) so that you can position guidelines freely.

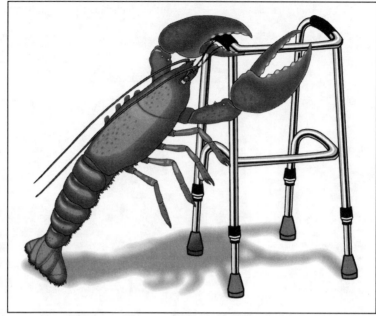

Figure 6-8:
The lobster
demonstrates
his
indomitable
will to
survive.

✔ If both guidelines and the grid are active, a guideline takes precedent over either of its grid-point neighbors. The guideline has a stronger gravitational force, in other words. It's as if Jupiter and Pluto were really close to each other and you were inside the gravitational fields of both planets. Jupiter has the more powerful gravitational force, so you'd fall toward it. Of course, Pluto would follow and come crashing down on your head, but that's strictly a function of planets. The grid is capable of resisting a guideline's attraction.

✔ However, in order for guidelines to attract anything, they must be turned on. Choose Layout⇨Snap To Guidelines to turn the guideline attraction on and off.

The status bar tells all

Like the rulers, the status bar doesn't affect the movement of your cursor. Instead, it provides information on everything you do in CorelDraw. This information is organized into five basic reports, as illustrated in Figure 6-9 and explained in the following list:

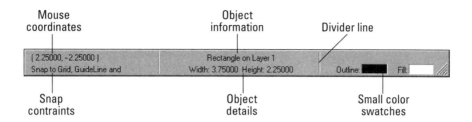

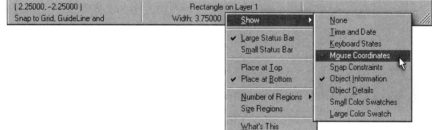

Figure 6-9:
The items in
the status
bar.

✔ Anytime your mouse cursor is inside the drawing area, the status bar lists the horizontal and vertical coordinates of the cursor in the upper-left corner.

✔ The lower-left corner states what snap constraints are in effect — in other words, whether the grid and guides are turned on. When both grid and guides are off, this spot is blank.

✔ The middle reports — labeled *Object information* and *Object details* in Figure 6-9 — vary depending on the operation. If an object is selected, the status bar lists what kind of object it is along with its dimensions and other information. When you're transforming an object — moving, scaling, or rotating it — the status bar reports on the transformation. It tells you the distance of the movement, the percentage of the scaling, and the degree of the rotation.

✔ The lower-right corner of the status bar lists the outline and fill applied to the selected object. If the object is not filled or if an open path is selected, a big X appears in the fill swatch. These reports appear only when an object is selected.

The status bar is divided into three sections by two vertical divider lines. You can allocate more room to one report or another by dragging a divider line to the left or right.

As shown in the lower example in Figure 6-9, you can customize the status bar by right-clicking on one of the reports and selecting an option from the resulting pop-up menu.

- ✔ Change the kind of report that appears in a certain spot by selecting a different item from the Show submenu. For example, to display the time and date in the upper-left corner of the status bar, right-click on the mouse coordinates and select Time and Date from the Show submenu. Experiment to see what other changes you can make.

- ✔ If you're short on screen space, select the Small Status Bar option. Select Large Status Bar to return to the one that's shown in the figure.

- ✔ In previous versions of CorelDraw, the status bar appeared at the top of the interface. If you want to put it back there, select the Place at Top option. And naturally, Place at Bottom puts the status bar back at the bottom of the screen. (I know, I didn't have to tell you that, but my lawyer said that I'd better.)

- ✔ You can also move the status bar by simply dragging it with the regular old left mouse button.

- ✔ The other options in the pop-up menu are a waste of time. Use them only if you're feeling extremely persnickety.

Even something as useful as the status bar can get in your way. If you just want to get the thing out of your face, choose View⇨Status Bar. Choose the command again to redisplay the status bar.

Tell Your Objects Where They Can Go

In Chapters 4 and 5, I explain how to move whole objects and individual nodes by dragging them. But dragging isn't the only means for movement in CorelDraw. You can move objects in prescribed increments, by numerical distances, or in relation to each other.

Incremental shifts

The arrow keys put selected items in motion. Whether you want to move a few nodes selected with the Shape tool or one or more objects selected with the Arrow tool, pressing the arrow keys nudges the items incrementally in the direction of the arrow.

By default, each arrow key moves a selected item ¹/₁₀ inch. However, you can change this to any increment that you want using the Tools⇨Options command. Press Ctrl+J to display the Options dialog box. Then enter a value in the Nudge option box, spotlighted in Figure 6-10. If necessary, select a different unit of measure from the pop-up menu.

If you press and hold the arrow key, the selected node or object scoots across the drawing area until you let up on the key.

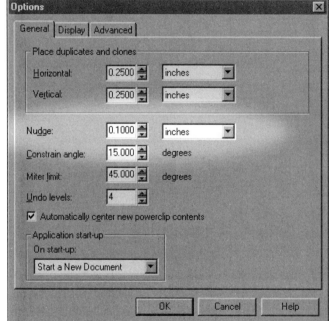

Figure 6-10:
The Nudge value determines the increment by which an arrow key moves a selected node or object.

The big move

To move an object by a numerical distance, press Alt+F7 or choose Arrange⇨Transform⇨Position. The Position roll-up, so handsomely featured in Figure 6-11, bobs to the surface. You can approach moves made with this palette in two ways. You can either move the object relative to its current position or move it to an exact coordinate location.

To move the object a relative distance, enter values into the H and V option boxes. A negative value moves the object leftward or down. A positive value moves the object the other way.

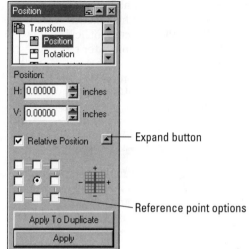

Figure 6-11:
Use the
Position
options in
this roll-up
to move an
object a
numerical
distance or
to a
coordinate
location.

Expand button

Reference point options

Moving an object to a coordinate location is a little trickier:

1. **Click on the Expand button (labeled in Figure 6-11).**

   The roll-up grows to reveal eight check boxes surrounding a single radio button. These boxes are the reference point options.

2. **Turn off the Relative Position check box.**

   You thought that the opposite of *relative* was *in-law,* but it's really *absolute.*

3. **Select a check box or radio button from the reference point options.**

   The check boxes represent the eight handles around the selected object; the radio button represents the object's exact center. So, for example, if you want to position the upper-right corner of an object at a specific location, you would select the upper-right check box. (You can select only one of these check boxes at a time. All of them really ought to be radio buttons. Way to go, Corel.)

4. **Enter the coordinates in the H and V option boxes.**

   The coordinates are measured relative to the rulers' zero point. So if you've positioned the zero point smack dab in the middle of the page, all coordinates are measured from this center. By default, however, the zero point is at the lower-left corner of the page.

   If you're not sure what coordinates you want to use — gee whiz, who *would* know such a thing? — deselect the object, move your cursor to the desired destination, and note the mouse coordinate values in the upper-left corner of the status bar. Then select the object again and enter those very values into the H and V option boxes.

The options in the Position roll-up are applicable to whole objects only. If you select a node with the Shape tool and apply this function, CorelDraw goes ahead and moves the entire object, mostly out of malicious spite. It really is a dumb limitation, but you can't argue with a computer program.

Oh, by the way, the Apply To Duplicate button creates a copy of the object at the new location. Duplication is one of the subjects of Chapter 8.

Fall in line

The last way to move objects is to shift them in relation to each other. Suppose that you drew a series of silhouetted soldiers marching down the road. But you were naturally so busy concentrating on making the shapes look like soldiers against an eerie twilight sky that you entirely neglected to line them up properly. So, instead of marching on a flat road, the soldiers bob up and down. To align their feet along a perfectly horizontal surface, you need to select all the soldier shapes and press Ctrl+A or choose Arrange⇨Align & Distribute.

Shown in Figure 6-12, the Align & Distribute roll-up lets you align objects vertically into columns or horizontally into rows. New to CorelDraw 6, the roll-up also enables you to evenly space objects using the distribution options.

Preview

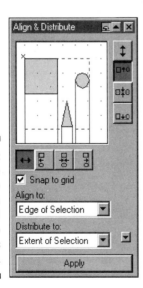

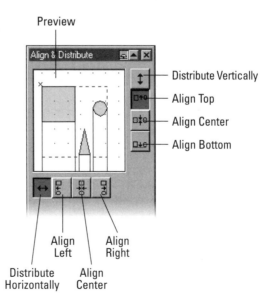

Distribute Vertically

Align Top

Align Center

Align Bottom

Figure 6-12:
Use these
options to
align
selected
objects into
columns
and rows.

Distribute
Horizontal

Align
Left

Align
Center

Align
Right

Distribute
Horizontally

Align
Center

To align or distribute two or more selected objects, click on the icon-happy buttons labeled in the right example of Figure 6-12. The central preview box shows how the selected options affect three sample shapes. You can select only one button at a time from the group of vertical alignment buttons to the right of the preview, as well as one from the group of horizontal alignment buttons below the preview.

In case the preview isn't enough to help you make sense of this roll-up, Figure 6-13 shows each of the vertical alignment options applied in tandem with each of their horizontal counterparts. (The arrows surrounding the Center labels show whether the centering was horizontal or vertical.)

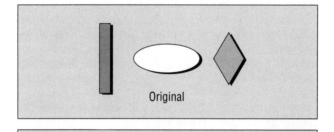

Original

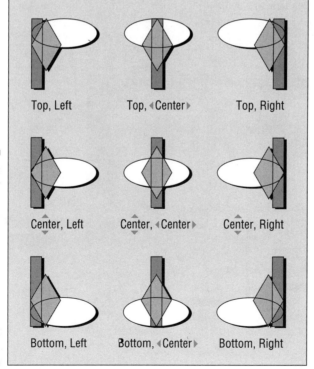

Top, Left   Top, ‹Center›   Top, Right

Center, Left   Center, ‹Center›   Center, Right

Bottom, Left   Bottom, ‹Center›   Bottom, Right

Figure 6-13: Test your spatial reasoning skills! Three simple objects (top) subject to each of the nine possible alignment settings.

You don't have to select an option from both the vertical and horizontal groups. To align the soldiers along the road, for example, you would select the Align Bottom button without selecting any horizontal option. In fact, you more often than not will select only one alignment button from the Align & Distribute roll-up. Otherwise, the shapes bunch up onto each other, as in Figure 6-13.

The following information falls into the gee-whiz-that-certainly-is-interesting camp of Align & Distribute roll-up knowledge.

- ✔ If you select one of the vertical or horizontal buttons but then change your mind, you can deselect it by clicking on it again.

- ✔ Select the Snap to Grid check box to align objects to the nearest grid point according to the vertical and horizontal settings. For example, if you select the Align Top and Align Left buttons, Draw aligns the top-left corner of each selected object to the nearest grid point.

- ✔ For mysterious reasons — I suspect extraterrestrials — the Snap to Grid check box is dimmed until you select a button.

- ✔ Select Center of Page from the Align To pop-up menu to align selected objects with respect to the center of the page. Select Edge of Page to align — that's right — to the edge of the page! See what $19.95 buys you? Eye-popping information, that's what. Do you feel smarter? Because you *look* smarter.

- ✔ When you select Edge of Selection from the Align To pop-up menu, CorelDraw always keeps the last object you selected stationary and moves all the others into alignment with it. If you selected the objects by marqueeing them rather than Shift+clicking, the lowest object remains stationary. Now there's something worth knowing.

- ✔ Select one of the Distribute buttons to evenly space three or more selected objects.

- ✔ When a Distribute button is selected, you can select one of two options from the Distribute To pop-up menu near the bottom of the roll-up. Select the Extent of Selection option to keep the most extreme objects — leftmost and rightmost or topmost and bottommost — stationary and distribute the others between them. Or select Extent of Page to distribute the objects over the entire width or height of the page.

- ✔ If you're really hooked on distribution, you can click on the Expand button to display two more pop-up menus. These menus enable you to even out the space between the objects or even out the space between their edges. It's a fine distinction, but the preview inside the roll-up does a good job of demonstrating the difference. Select an option and see how it works.

- ✔ The options in the Align & Distribute roll-up work only on whole objects. To align nodes selected with the Shape tool, double-click on one of the nodes to display the Node Edit roll-up and then click on the Align button (bottom right). You can't distribute nodes.

Gang Behavior

A moment ago, I asked you to imagine drawing silhouetted soldiers. You probably thought that I was just trying to stimulate your interest by setting a mood. But there was a tiny modicum of method behind my madness, something that's normally entirely absent.

See, you can create a silhouette using a single shape. If, however, each of your soldiers comprised multiple shapes, the Align & Distribute options might present a problem. Figure 6-14, for example, shows a soldier made up of 18 shapes. When I aligned the shapes along the bottom, the soldier fell apart, as in the second example. This happened because CorelDraw aligns the bottom of each and every shape.

To prevent this, you need to make Draw think of all 18 shapes as a single object. To do this, select the shapes and press Ctrl+G or choose Arrange⇨Group. All shapes in the group now behave as a single, collective object.

✔ To align many soldiers that are each composed of many shapes, group the shapes in each soldier — each soldier is its own group, in other words — and then apply one or two options from the Align & Distribute roll-up.

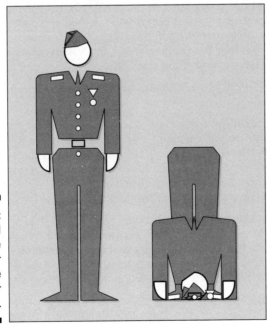

Figure 6-14: It's a sad sight to see a soldier crumble under pressure.

- To bust the group up into its individual shapes, press Ctrl+U (Arrange⇨Ungroup).

- You can include groups in other groups. For example, after grouping the shapes in each soldier, you can group all the soldiers together. If you later want to restore the original shapes, you have to press Ctrl+U once to ungroup the first group. Then you have to select each group within the previous group and ungroup it separately.

- Just because an object is part of a group doesn't mean that you can't edit it. To select a single object inside a group, Ctrl+click on it with the Arrow tool. To adjust the location of nodes and the curvature of segments inside a grouped path, Ctrl+click on the path with the Shape tool.

Your Drawing is a Plate of Flapjacks

Once again, I speak metaphorically. Don't pour maple syrup on the screen or anything. Most condiments *will* damage your computer. My reference to flapjacks has to do with their typical arrangement in stacks. One flapjack is at the bottom of the stack, one flapjack is on top, and each additional flapjack is nestled between two others.

Now pretend that you're looking down at the flapjacks from an aerial view, like a hungry magpie. You can see the butter on the top, several flapjacks beneath that, and a plate at the bottom, as in Figure 6-15. Each flapjack obscures but does not completely hide the flapjack beneath it.

Figure 6-15: Viewing objects in CorelDraw is like looking down on a stack of flapjacks, except not so appetizing.

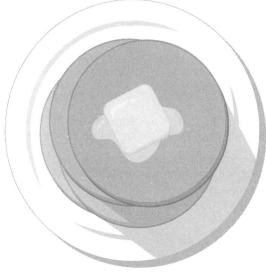

CorelDraw stacks objects in the drawing area in a similar fashion. Every object in your drawing is in front of or behind some other object. When displaying your artwork on-screen or when printing it, Draw starts at the back of the drawing and works its way to the front, one object at a time. If two objects overlap, the frontmost of the two partially obscures the other. This hierarchy of objects is called the *stacking order.*

If you left objects to their own devices, the first object you drew would appear at the back of the drawing, and the most recent object would appear at the front. But you can change the order of any object by selecting it and choosing one of the five commands in the A̲rrange⇨O̲rder submenu.

✔ Press Shift+Page Up (or choose the To Front command) to bring one or more selected objects to the front of the drawing. Figure 6-16 shows the result of selecting the face and hands of the soldier and pressing Shift+Page Up. Having moved to the front of the drawing, the face and hands conceal portions of the shapes that make up the cap and jacket. In the last example of the figure, I selected the jacket and pressed Shift+Page Up again, which covered up the buttons and medal.

✔ Press Shift+Page Down (or choose the To Back command) to send one or more selected objects to the back of the drawing.

✔ Press Ctrl+Page Up to nudge selected objects one step forward. Or, if you prefer, choose the Forward One command.

✔ Press Ctrl+Page Down to nudge selected objects one step backward. If you like choosing things, choose the Back One command.

✔ As your drawing becomes more complicated, you'll want to spend less of your time choosing the commands I've discussed so far and more time using In Front Of and Behind. These commands enable you to stack objects relative to other objects. If you want to place a rat in front of some cheese, for example, select the rat, choose A̲rrange⇨O̲rder⇨I̲n Front Of, and then click on the cheese. To place the cheese and rat behind a cat, select rodent and supper, choose A̲rrange⇨O̲rder⇨B̲ehind, and click on the cat.

✔ Last but not least is the Reverse Order command, which reverses the stacking order of selected objects, as demonstrated in Figure 6-17. You must have at least two objects selected to use this command.

✔ You can access the entire Order submenu of commands — as well as Group and Ungroup for that matter — by right-clicking on a selected object. Right-clicking is an especially convenient way to choose the In Front Of and Behind commands.

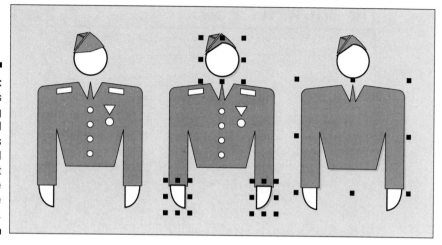

Figure 6-16:
The results of moving the face and hands (middle) and the jacket (right) to the front of the drawing.

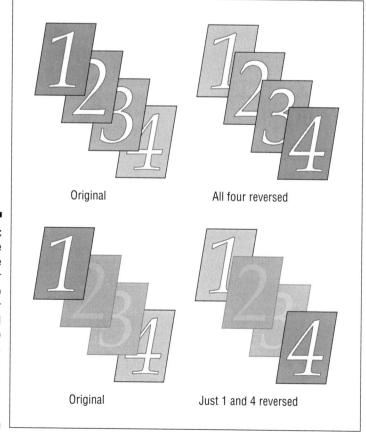

Original

All four reversed

Original

Just 1 and 4 reversed

Figure 6-17:
Applying the Reverse Order command to four selected objects (top) and two selected objects (1 and 4, bottom).

"OK, TECHNICALLY THIS SHOULD WORK. JUDY, TYPE THE WORD, 'GOODYEAR' ALL CAPS, BOLDFACE, AT 700-POINT TYPE SIZE."

Chapter 7
Making Your Shapes Look Like Something

- -

In This Chapter

▶ Filling closed paths with solid colors

▶ Selecting and creating colors

▶ Coming to terms with line widths and points

▶ Applying outlines to open and closed paths

▶ Using the Pen roll-up

▶ Assigning corners and caps

▶ Changing default fill and outline settings

▶ Learning advanced fill options

- -

*I*t was an ashen morning on the blanched desert. The dusty earth was pallid, the cacti were bleached, even the lone coyote was a bit pasty. But worst of all, I myself was entirely without pigmentation.

Suddenly, I spied a flash of color on the horizon. Big, billowy clouds of green, yellow, and a sort of grapey purple were accompanied by the thunder of hoofbeats. It could mean only one thing — the Chromastazi tribe was on the warpath.

Moments later, the swiftest rider emerged from a poofy pink cloud and stopped dead in front of me. Fixing me with his terrible emerald gaze, he drew from his ceremonial paint bucket the biggest, most menacing brush I had ever seen. Before I had time to run, the warrior threw his weapon straight and true. The brush hit me full in the chest, releasing a fountain of colors. As I hit the ground, I couldn't help but notice the sky itself explode with fragments of deepest azure highlighted with streamers of pale blue and crystal white.

"Pale Shape is no more!" went up the savage cry.

Looking down at myself, I hardly believed my eyes. I was no longer transparent. Finally, I knew what it meant to be filled!

— excerpted from *Memoirs of a Pioneerin' Path*, 1875

Fills, Spills, and Chills

Wasn't that thrilling? I remember when I first read that passage in art history class. The student body was so inspired, we spray-painted the professor.

Nowadays, what with these huge wads of computer experience under my belt, I can see the truth of the story. Regardless of how paths look or act, deep down inside, they want to be filled. It's in their nature. Take Figure 7-1, for example. On the left, you see an enhanced version of Shenbop, *primus inter amphibius.* Because all the lines and shapes are transparent, it's nearly impossible to focus on the picture. The Shenbop on the right contains the exact same paths as its transparent neighbor, but the paths are filled, giving the frog form, substance, and a mighty big sense of self-worth.

Figure 7-1:
Several
paths shown
as they
appear
when
transparent
(left) and
when filled
(right).

Fill the void

Newly drawn paths are transparent. To fill the interior of a path with a solid color, do the following:

1. **If a path that you want to fill is open, close it.**

   You can fill closed paths only. Open paths are inherently transparent. You can close a path by dragging from one node to the other with the Pencil tool. Or select the two last nodes in the path and click on either of the Join buttons in the Node Edit roll-up — the third and fifth buttons in the first row — as described in the "How to open, split, close, and join paths" section of Chapter 5.

2. **Select one or more shapes that you want to fill.**

   Using the Arrow tool, draw a marquee around the shapes or click on one shape and then Shift+click on the others.

3. **Select an option from the Fill tool flyout menu or click on a color in the color palette.**

   Click on the Fill tool icon — the one that looks like a paint bucket — to display a flyout menu of fill options. The three icons in the upper-right portion of the flyout menu — spotlighted in the first example of Figure 7-2 — let you fill the selected shapes with no fill (the X icon), white, or black. If a shape has no fill, you can see through its interior to the objects behind it. All other fills are opaque.

   The *color palette* is the strip of color swatches just above the status bar (labeled in the second example in Figure 7-2). The palette contains too many colors to display all at once in a single strip, so you can click on the left and right scroll arrows on either side of the palette to display additional colors. Or click on the up-arrow icon to display a pop-up menu that shows all the colors at once.

The first 11 options in the color palette are shades of gray, which are organized from black to white in 10 percent increments. For example, 50 percent gray is midway between black and white. At the bottom of Figure 7-2, I've clicked on the 30 percent gray swatch. (Notice that the color name — in this case, 30% Black — appears in the status bar when your move the cursor over a shade of gray or color.) All 11 shades are ideal for creating black-and-white artwork.

The color palette wants to be there for you

In this modern world, you don't have to accept the color palette that CorelDraw gives you. You can change the colors, move the palette, and change the way the color swatches look in a variety of terrific ways:

- ✔ To scroll to the beginning or end of the colors in the palette, right-click in the gray area around the swatches — do not right-click on a color itself — to display a pop-up menu of options. Then choose Move to Start or Move to End.

- ✔ To change the colors in the palette to one of CorelDraw's other predefined collections of colors, choose View➪Color Palette. This command displays a submenu of other possible palettes, many of which come from professional color-production companies (if you can believe that such a crazy thing exists).

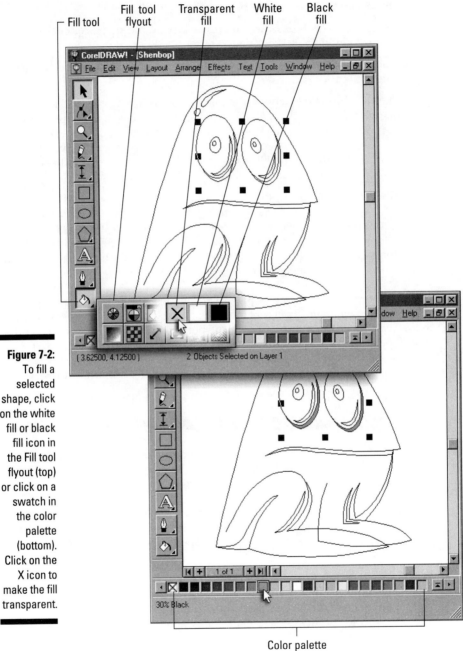

Fill tool

Fill tool flyout

Transparent fill

White fill

Black fill

Color palette

Figure 7-2:
To fill a selected shape, click on the white fill or black fill icon in the Fill tool flyout (top) or click on a swatch in the color palette (bottom). Click on the X icon to make the fill transparent.

✔ Do *not* select View⇨Color Palette⇨Pantone Spot Colors unless you know exactly what you're doing and you have a good reason for using spot colors. (If you don't know what I'm talking about, steer clear of this option.)

✔ To hide the color palette and free up still more screen space, choose View⇨Color Palette⇨None.

✔ Drag a gray area around the color swatches to make the palette float independently of the interface. When the palette is floating, you can resize it by dragging any edge or corner. In Figure 7-3, for example, I've dragged the bottom of the palette to stretch it vertically, which reveals more color swatches.

✔ To re-adhere the floating palette to the interface, drag it onto the status bar or double-click in the palette's title bar.

✔ Just because the palette is not floating doesn't mean that you can't display more than one row of swatches at a time. To see two or more rows, right-click inside the gray area of the palette and select the Customize option. Then enter the number of rows you want to see into the Display option box and press Enter.

Figure 7-3:
Stretch the
floating
palette to
see more
colors at a
time.

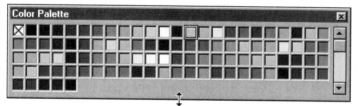

Hasta la fillsta

If you ever want to return a shape to absolute transparency, select the shape, click on the Fill tool icon, and then click on the X icon in the flyout menu. Or, easier still, just click on the X icon in the lower-left corner of the screen, known as the Delete Color button.

Make New Colors in Your Spare Time

If you can't find the color that you want in the color palette, you can create a color of your own. But I warn you, it gets kind of messy. After selecting one or more shapes in your drawing, click on the Fill tool and then click on the second button in the flyout menu, the one that looks like a little roll-up with a Trivial Pursuit piece in it. In response, the Color roll-up graces your screen, as shown in Figure 7-4.

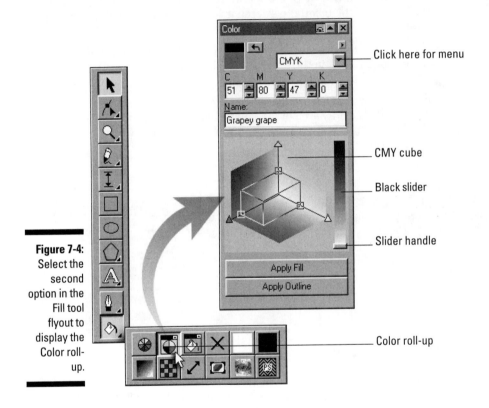

Figure 7-4:
Select the second option in the Fill tool flyout to display the Color roll-up.

Colors are born from other colors

Before I tell you how the Color roll-up works, I have to tell you how colors work. In elementary school or some equally nostalgic institution, you learned how to mix colors using the three *primary colors* — blue, red, and yellow. Commercial printers also make colors by mixing primaries, but the primaries are different.

- Instead of blue, commercial printers use a light green-blue color called cyan.

- In place of red, they use magenta, a pinkish, purplish color.

- Instead of yellow . . . well, actually, they decided to hang on to yellow.

- And because the science of color printing is about as reliable as reading tea leaves, commercial printers throw in black to ensure uniform dark colors.

So there you have it — cyan, magenta, yellow, and black, better known as the CMYK (pronounced *C-M-Y-K,* not *simyk* or *kamick* or *ceemwac*) color model. (Incidentally, printers call black the *key color,* which is why its initial is K.)

Apply your huge expanse of color knowledge

Because too much color theory has been known to drive people stark raving mad, the following items seek to disseminate the abstractions of CMYK into the real world of the Color roll-up.

- Before you do anything, select CMYK from the pop-up menu in the upper-right corner of the roll-up. The menu options represent *color models,* all of which represent different ways of mixing colors to create other colors. But for your purposes, CMYK is the best ticket in town.

- Now you can enter values into the C, M, Y, and K option boxes. Primaries are measured in percentages. The more primary you toss in, the darker the color gets. For example, 100 percent cyan plus 100 percent magenta makes deep blue. If you add either yellow or black, you darken the color. Try entering a few random values of your own to get a feel for things.

- To create a custom shade of gray, enter 0 into the C, M, and Y option boxes and then enter the shade of gray in the K option box. For example, 0 percent is white, 25 percent is light gray, 50 percent is medium gray, 75 percent is dark gray, and 100 percent is black.

✔ If you want to browse through CorelDraw's possible 16 million colors, check out the CMY cube in the middle of the Color roll-up (labeled in Figure 7-4). Click anywhere inside the cube to select a color. If the color you select seems a little bright, try dragging the square handle in the center of the cube away from the color to dull it a little.

✔ To darken a color, drag up on that little handle at the bottom of the black slider. (Both slider and handle are labeled in Figure 7-4.) The higher you drag, the more black you get.

✔ Notice that any change made with the CMY cube or black slider is reflected by the values in the C, M, Y, and K option boxes.

✔ To add the color to the color palette, enter a name into the <u>N</u>ame option box. Then click on the little menu button above the pop-up menu (labeled *Click here for menu* in Figure 7-4) and select the <u>A</u>dd Color to Palette option.

✔ To apply the color to the fill of one or more selected shapes, click on the Apply Fill button.

The Thick and Thin of Outlines

Although you can apply a fill to closed paths only, you can assign an outline to any path, open or closed. Furthermore, whereas a fill has one property — color — an outline has two properties: color and thickness. Known as the *line width,* or, in more gentrified circles, as the *line weight,* the thickness of an outline is traditionally measured in *points,* which are very tiny increments equal to $^1/_{72}$ inch. To put it in perspective, a penny is 4 points thick, a typical pencil is 20 points in diameter, a business card is 254 points wide, a football field measures 259,000 points from one end zone to the other, Mount Everest is 25 million points above sea level, light travels at 850 trillion points per second, presidential elections occur every leap year, and a dozen eggs contain 12 yolks.

Points are a useful system of measurement because most outlines tend to be pretty thin. Nearly all the figures in this book, for example, feature outlines with line widths of 1 point or thinner.

Trace the path

To assign an outline to a path, do this:

1. Select one or more paths.

Always the first step, eh?

2. Select a line width option.

Click on the Pen tool — the one that looks like a pen nib — to display a flyout menu of outline options. The last five options in the bottom row, spotlighted in Figure 7-5, control the thickness of the outline.

3. Select a color for the outline.

You can select from two colors — white or black — in the Pen tool flyout menu. As labeled in Figure 7-5, both options are located in the upper-right corner of the flyout.

If you want to apply another color, right-click on a color in the color palette. Right-clicking changes the color of an outline just as left-clicking changes the color of the fill.

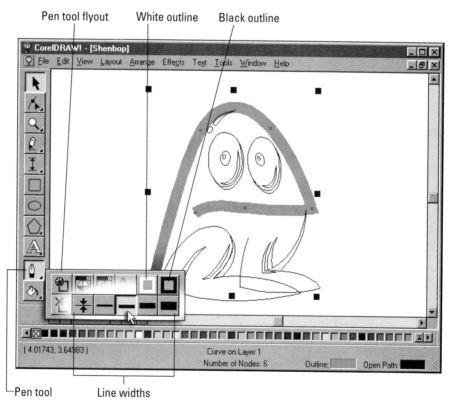

Figure 7-5:
The Pen tool provides access to five line widths as well as black and white color options.

Pen tool flyout   White outline   Black outline

Pen tool   Line widths

How to select a custom outline color

Outline colors work the same as fill colors. If you want to apply a custom color, click on the Color roll-up icon in the Pen tool flyout (labeled in Figure 7-6). The very same roll-up shown back in Figure 7-4 appears.

Useless line widths

Line width, however, is a whole different kettle of fish, or briar patch full of bunnies, or whatever rustic idiom happens to strike your fancy. As shown in Figure 7-6, the Pen tool flyout menu offers access to several predefined line widths and also the more functional Pen roll-up.

Each time you draw a line, the first line width option — appropriately labeled *Ridiculously thin* in Figure 7-6 — is in force. This option generally assigns the thinnest outline that your printer can possibly print. On drawings printed on laser printers and cheaper models, the outline looks okay. But on professional-level typesetters, it can result in a nearly invisible outline that doesn't stand a chance of reproducing.

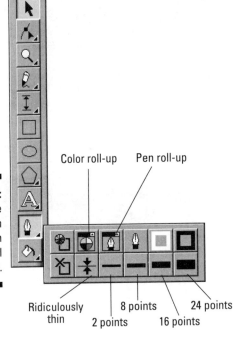

Figure 7-6: The line width options in the Pen tool flyout menu.

Color roll-up   Pen roll-up

Ridiculously thin   2 points   8 points   16 points   24 points

Now, I know that some of you can't imagine that you'll ever in a billion years typeset your artwork. But you may as well prepare your drawings for any event, no matter how remote you think it is. After all, you might go and win one of those Corel $1 million art contests, only to have your drawing professionally printed with ridiculously thin lines. Imagine having to describe the artwork to your grandma with her failing eyesight. "Lordy Lu," she'll cry softly, "if only you had used nice, hefty lines instead of these meager things!" Way to break an old woman's heart.

Figure 7-7 demonstrates three line weight options from the Pen tool flyout menu applied to Shenbop. It's like the story of the three bears or something. The first example is too thin, the result of accepting CorelDraw's default outline. The last example is too fat. Only the middle example qualifies as acceptable.

Figure 7-7:
Being a sensible frog, Shenbop hates the predefined line weights in the Pen tool flyout menu and is highly embarrassed to appear in this figure.

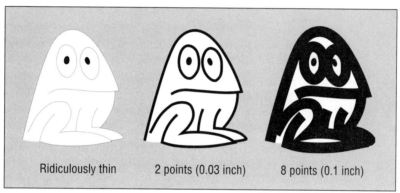

Ridiculously thin   2 points (0.03 inch)   8 points (0.1 inch)

Better line widths

To access other line widths, select the Pen roll-up icon (labeled in Figure 7-6) to display the Pen roll-up shown in Figure 7-8. Alternatively, you can press Shift+F7 to display the roll-up. The Pen roll-up offers several options for changing the outline of a selected path.

✔ Click on the scroll arrows on the right side of the roll-up (labeled *Thicker* and *Thinner* in Figure 7-8) to increase or decrease the line width in $1/100$-inch increments. The area to the left of the scroll arrows displays the line width in inches.

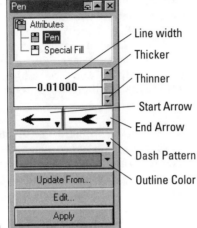

Line width
Thicker
Thinner
Start Arrow
End Arrow
Dash Pattern
Outline Color

Figure 7-8:
The Pen roll-
up lets you
change
outline
attributes.

✔ If the line width is 0.003 inch (0.2 point) or thinner, a cross fills the line width area, as in Figure 7-9. The cross is an indication that your outline is too thin and may not reproduce well.

✔ To change the line width display from inches to points, click on the Edit button. The Outline Pen dialog box appears. Select the Points option from the Width pop-up menu. Then press Enter. From now on, clicking on a scroll arrow changes the line width in 0.7-point increments.

✔ Click on the Start Arrow or End Arrow button (both labeled in Figure 7-8) to display a pop-up menu of arrowhead options, as shown in Figure 7-9. Use the scroll bar on the right side of the menu to access any of 88 arrowheads that can appear at the beginning or end of an open path. (Arrowheads have no effect on closed paths.)

✔ Click on the Dash Pattern button (just below the arrows) to display a pop-up menu of dotted line patterns that you can assign to an open or closed path.

✔ Click on the Outline Color button to select a color for the outline.

✔ Click on the Apply button to apply the settings in the Pen roll-up to the selected paths in the drawing area.

Someone else's outline

In CorelDraw, you can copy the outline from one path and assign it to another. Say that you have two paths, Path A and Path B, known to their friends as Fred and Wilma. To make the outline of Fred look just like the one assigned to Wilma, do the following:

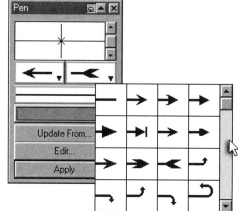

Figure 7-9:
You can
select from
as many
arrowheads
as there are
keys on a
piano.

1. **Select Fred and click on the Update From button in the Pen roll-up**.

   Your cursor changes to a big, fat arrow.

2. **Click on Wilma**.

   The Pen roll-up now displays the outline settings assigned to Wilma.

3. **Click on the Apply button**.

   Now Fred and Wilma look the same, like so many other married couples.

Even better line widths

To recap, the Pen tool flyout menu offers five mostly useless line widths. The Pen roll-up offers an unlimited number of line widths, but only in 0.7-point increments. If you want to access an even wider array of line widths without any weird or artificial constraints, click the Edit button in the Pen roll-up or press F12, which brings up the Outline Pen dialog box, shown in Figure 7-10.

✔ Enter a value from 0.072 to 288 points into the <u>W</u>idth option box. The value is accurate to $^1/_{1000}$ point. That's mighty accurate.

✔ When using inches as your unit of measurement, you can enter any value from 0.001 to 4 inches.

✔ Don't go any thinner than 0.3 point or 0.004 inch. Line widths between 0.3 and 0.5 point are called *hairlines,* because they're about as thick as hairs, depending on how thick your hair is, of course.

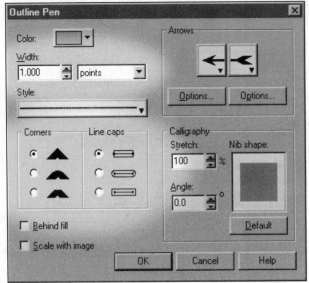

Figure 7-10:
The spotlighted options let you change the thickness of an outline and the appearance of its corners.

Personally, my hair rivals cotton candy for fortitude and manageability. Hairlines look like Corinthian columns compared with my hair. I suspect that my hair wouldn't reproduce well. If I were to photocopy my face, I'd doubtless look like a cue ball.

✔ To change the system of measurement, select an option from the pop-up menu to the right of the option box. In addition to inches and points, the pop-up menu offers millimeters for you worldly, metric types and picas for you newspaper and magazine types.

Corners and caps

In addition to the <u>W</u>idth option, the Outline Pen dialog box offers a couple of other interesting items, which have the spotlight trained on them in Figure 7-10. These options fall into two categories, corners and caps.

Corners determine the appearance of the outline at corner nodes in the path:

✔ First among the Corners radio buttons, the miter corner option ensures sharp corners in a path.

✔ When curved segments slope into each other to form a very acute angle, miter corners can produce weird spikes that make your path look like it's covered with occasional bits of barbed wire. You may go your entire life without encountering this phenomenon, but if you do, select one of the other two Corners radio buttons.

✔ The second radio button is the round corner option, which rounds off the corners in a path. I use this option a lot. It takes the edge off things. A real ice-breaker at parties.

✔ The last option is called the bevel corner because it lops off the end of the corner as if, well, as if the corner were beveled.

Figure 7-11 shows the three corners applied to mere fragments of Shenbop. The outlines appear black. I've represented the paths with thin white outlines so that you can see how path and outline relate. Pretty insightful, huh?

The Line Caps options determine how the outline looks at the beginning and end of an open path. Caps have no effect on closed paths.

✔ The first Line Caps option is the butt cap. Honest, that's what it's called. I'm not trying to be offensive to inspire controversy and sell books. Which is funny, because that's exactly what I was trying to do when I wanted to use the word *butt* in my last book and the editors wouldn't let me. Now they have to. After all, I didn't come up with the term butt cap. Huge corporate forces beyond my control decided on it. I'm sure they giggled while they were at it. They must have been feeling very immature that day.

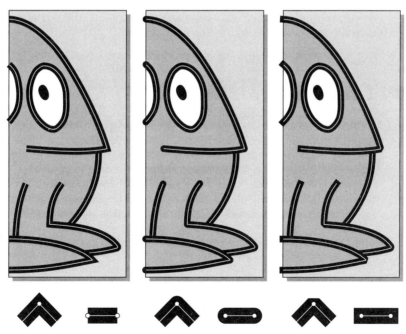

Figure 7-11: CorelDraw's Corners and Line Caps options in practice.

Miter / Butt   Round / Round   Bevel / Square

✔ Just in case you want to know what the butt (snigger) cap option does, it ends the outline exactly at the end of the path. The outline butts up (hee hee) against the node, as it were. (Guffaw!)

✔ The round cap does just that. It extends the outline slightly beyond the end of the path and rounds it off. Like the round corner, the round cap option gives a path a friendlier appearance. Of course, if your path is inherently unfriendly — depicting, say, a slathering Rottweiler chomping on a Chihuahua skull — a mere round cap isn't likely to do much good.

✔ Like the round cap, the square cap extends the outline past the end of a path. But instead of rounding off the outline, it caps it off with a square. This option is useful when you want to prevent a gap between an open path and an adjacent object or when you're simply too embarrassed to use a butt cap, as when drawing for mixed company.

The vanishing outline

To remove the outline of a path, select the path and right-click on the Delete Color button — which looks like an X — in the lower-left corner of the screen.

Generally speaking, you only want to delete the outline of a filled shape. If you delete the outline from a transparent shape or open path, you make it entirely invisible and run the risk of losing the path.

I Don't Like the Default Setting!

If you select an option from the Fill or Pen tool flyout menu or click on the Apply button in the Pen roll-up when no object is selected, CorelDraw assumes that you want to change the default attributes that will affect each and every future path you create. To confirm this assumption, the program displays the rather verbose message shown in Figure 7-12. If you don't want to change the defaults, click on the Cancel button. If you want to change the default settings for all future paths, select the Graphic check box and press Enter.

The Artistic Text and Paragraph Text options affect varieties of CorelDraw text blocks that are discussed in Chapter 10.

Figure 7-12:
This
message
appears
when you
try to apply
a fill or
outline
setting to
nothing
whatsoever.

Fill and Outline Join Forces

If you gave much attention to the fully filled and outlined version of Shenbop shown back in Figure 7-1, you may have noticed something unusual about it. Namely, a few *open* paths, such as the main body and the legs, appear to be filled. The interior of the body covers up the background behind it; the interior of the front leg covers part of the body; and the interior of the hind leg covers part of the front leg. There's no question about it, these paths are filled.

Well, how can that be? After all, I specifically said that you can't fill an open path. I wouldn't lie — my mom won't let me — so there must be something else going on.

The answer is that the body and the legs are actually made up of two paths apiece: one closed path with a fill and no outline, and one open path with an outline and no fill. Figure 7-13 demonstrates how this works. The filled version of the path is stacked behind the outlined version of the path, creating what appears to the uninitiated viewer to be a single shape.

Just for laughs, Figure 7-14 shows the order of the paths used to create Shenbop from back to front. The paths that make up the body and legs are either strictly filled or strictly outlined, providing me with optimum flexibility. In fact, only the whites of the eyes are both filled and outlined. All outlines are 1 point thick. If you're really in the mood for trivia, you'll be interested to know that the border around the figure is 0.5 point thick.

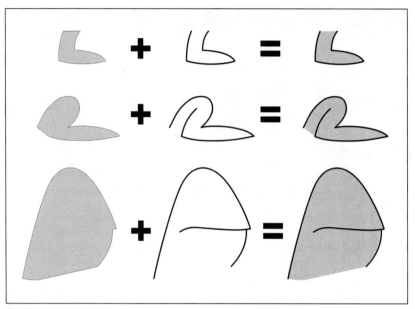

Figure 7-13:
A filled closed path (first column) behind an outlined open path (second column) creates the appearance of a filled open path (last column).

The World of Wacky Fills

If you're one of those people who is sensitive to detail — as an author, I prefer my readers to be more or less oblivious — then you've no doubt noticed that I skipped an option or two along the way. For example, I described the Pen roll-up but made no mention of the Fill roll-up.

Part of the reason for this is that CorelDraw 6 has no Fill roll-up. But it does have a Special Fill roll-up, which is devoted exclusively to advanced fill effects, including gradations, geometric patterns, and textures. Taken to their extremes, each of these effects can prove extremely complicated. So rather than delve into tiresome lists of options and obscure settings, I introduce each effect in the most basic terms possible.

To display the Special Fill roll-up, click on the Fill tool icon to display the flyout menu and then click on the third button in the top row — the one that looks like a little roll-up with a paint bucket in it. As indicated in Figure 7-15, each of the buttons along the top of the Special Fill roll-up duplicates a function in the Fill tool flyout menu. The difference is that the options in the roll-up are easier to use.

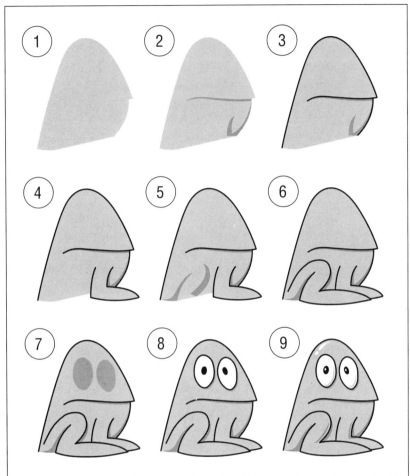

Figure 7-14:
The bits and
pieces of
Shenbop,
from the
back of the
heap to the
front.

The following list explains how to use the options in the Special Fill roll-up. The only exception is the last button, PostScript fill, which is available in the Fill tool flyout menu but is missing from the Special Fill roll-up. As with any fill effect, all the options are applicable exclusively to closed paths.

 ✔ Click on the Fountain Fill button to fill a selected path with a gradual blend from one color to another, called a *gradation* or, in some circles, a *gradient*. Select a beginning color and an end color from the pop-up menus below the gradient preview. Specify the type of gradation by clicking on one of the icons directly above the Update From button. Finally, drag inside the

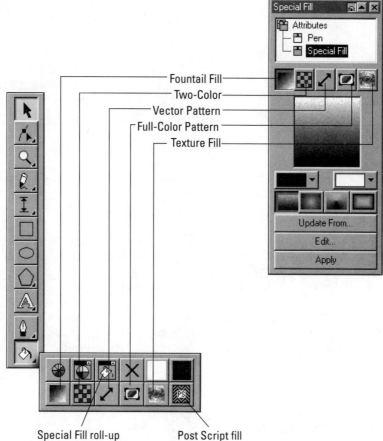

Fountail Fill

Two-Color

Vector Pattern

Full-Color Pattern

Texture Fill

Figure 7-15:
The Fill roll-
up simplifies
many of the
advanced
options in
the Fill tool
flyout menu.

Special Fill roll-up   Post Script fill

gradient preview in the top portion of the roll-up to determine the direction or center of the gradation. To apply the gradation to the selected
shape, you click on the Apply button — which is always the case with
roll-ups.

✔ The Two-Color Pattern button allows you to fill a shape with a pattern of
pixels in either of two colors. Specify the colors by selecting options from
both of the color pop-up menus. To change the pattern, click on the
pattern preview in the top portion of the roll-up to display a pop-up menu
of options. Select the desired pattern and press Enter (or click on OK).

✔ The Vector Pattern button fills a shape with a repeating pattern of object-
oriented graphics. (True nerds call object-oriented graphics *vector-based*
graphics because it makes them sound like they attended their physics
classes. But Webster's describes a vector as "a quantity that has magni-
tude, direction, and sense." And, as we all know, paths have no sense.)

Select an object-oriented pattern by clicking on the preview in the top portion of the roll-up, selecting a pattern from a pop-up menu, and pressing Enter.

✔ The Full-Color Pattern button fills a shape with a pattern of pixels in any of 16 million colors. To change the pattern, click on the pattern preview, select the desired pattern from the resulting pop-up menu, and press Enter.

✔ Textures are naturalistic patterns such as clouds and raindrops. Unlike patterns, textures don't repeat; they just stretch to fill the selected shape. To change the texture, first select a category of textures from the first pop-up menu (just below the texture preview). Then click on the central texture preview, select the desired texture from the resulting pop-up menu, and press Enter. Alternatively, you can select the texture name from the second pop-up menu (above the Update From button), but that's not nearly so fun.

✔ The PostScript Fill button appears only in the Fill tool flyout menu. It lets you apply special object-oriented patterns that are described in complex PostScript code. When you click on the PostScript Fill button, a dialog box filled with a list of patterns appears. Select a pattern and click on the Preview Fill check box to see what it looks like. Press Enter after you select the fill you like. But these fills have a couple of strikes against them. First, PostScript fill patterns don't look right on-screen. Second, you can print them only with high-end laser printers and typesetters that understand PostScript.

Chapter 8

The Fine Art of Cloning

. . . .

In This Chapter

▶ The inside scoop on dinosaur maintenance

▶ News and information about the Windows Clipboard

▶ Why I hate the Clipboard

▶ How to use the Cut, Copy, and Paste commands

▶ What goes on in the minds of people who make up keyboard equivalents

▶ The Duplicate command and its relationship to grouping

▶ A look inside the mind of a true clone

▶ The newest rage in reproduction: drag and drop

. . . .

*W*hat was the big deal with *Jurassic Park?* Oh sure, lawyer-eating dinosaurs — obviously, I'm all for that. And if I were a poison-spitting Dilophosaurus, I can't imagine a tastier treat than a well-fed computer programmer. Those guys spend so much time glued to their chairs, they make veal calves look active. But the cloning bit, how hard can it be? CorelDraw's been able to do it for years. You don't need any mosquito trapped in amber with DNA squirting out its thorax. You give me a Velociraptor, and I'll make as many duplicates as you like.

Mom, Dad, Is There Really a Clipboard?

Like previous versions of Windows, Windows 95 has this thing called the *Clipboard.* You can store one collection of objects on the Clipboard at a time. The Clipboard lets you make copies of these objects and transfer objects between drawings. Three Edit menu commands — Cut, Copy, and Paste — provide access to the Clipboard.

Here's how the three Clipboard commands under the Edit menu work:

✔ The Cut command (Ctrl+X) removes all selected objects from your drawing and places them on the Clipboard. In doing so, the command replaces the Clipboard's previous contents. So if you cut Object A and then cut Object B, Object B knocks Object A off the Clipboard into electronic oblivion.

✔ The Copy command (Ctrl+C) makes a copy of all selected objects in your drawing and places the copy on the Clipboard. Like Cut, this command replaces the Clipboard's previous contents.

✔ The Paste command (Ctrl+V) makes a copy of the contents of the Clipboard and places them in your drawing. Unlike Cut and Copy, the Paste command leaves the contents of the Clipboard unaltered. You can choose the Paste command as many times as you want to make copy after copy after copy.

Snap, crackle, paste

Here's a typical example of how you might use the Clipboard:

1. **Select one or more objects that you want to duplicate.**

   If you have a herd of dinosaurs handy, please select it now. (Incidentally, the drawing in Figure 8-1 comes from the file Tyranno2.CMX, found in the Dinosaur folder on the fourth Corel CD-ROM.)

2. **Choose Edit⇨Copy.**

   Figure 8-1 shows this step in progress. CorelDraw makes a copy of every selected object and places it on the Clipboard. This process sometimes takes a long time, so a message appears telling you that Draw is working on it.

3. **Toodle around.**

   Perform scads of operations. Work for hours and hours. Wait several weeks if you like. Time has no effect on the Clipboard. Just don't touch the Cut or Copy commands, don't exit CorelDraw or Windows 95, and don't turn off your computer.

4. **Have a sandwich.**

   Make me one, too. A BLT, if you have the ingredients.

5. **Choose Edit⇨Paste.**

   Bazoing! (That's a sound effect, in case you didn't recognize it.) CorelDraw makes a copy of the objects on the Clipboard and places them in the drawing area at the exact location where they appeared when you chose the Copy command.

   If you never changed the location of the original objects before you chose Edit⇨Paste, you won't notice any difference in your drawing, because the copied objects sit directly in front of the originals. Drag the copied objects slightly off to the side, and you'll see that you do indeed have two identical versions of your objects, as shown in Figure 8-2.

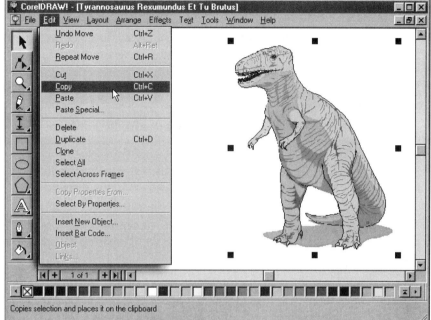

Figure 8-1: To copy a dinosaur, select all the objects that make up the drawing and choose the Copy command.

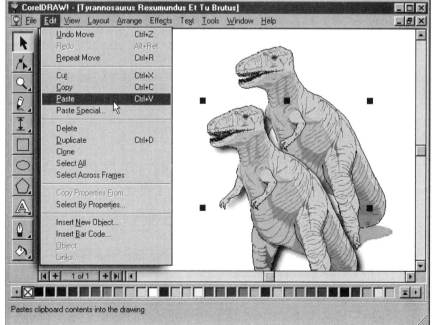

Figure 8-2: The result of choosing the Paste command and offsetting the copied objects from the originals.

Clipboard keyboard capers

Novices generally have problems remembering the keyboard equivalents for the Clipboard commands. Granted, Ctrl+C makes sense for Copy. Ctrl+X is a stretch, but it sort of brings to mind Cut. But where did Ctrl+V for Paste come from?

The answer resides at the bottom-left corner of your keyboard. The keys are Z, X, C, and V. That's Undo (the first command in the Edit menu), Cut, Copy, and Paste.

Then again, if you think of Edit⇨Paste as regurgitating the contents of the Clipboard, Ctrl+V takes on new meaning. Just trying to help.

You can also use these old-style Windows keyboard shortcuts:

 ✔ Shift+Delete for Edit⇨Cut

 ✔ Ctrl+Insert for Edit⇨Copy

 ✔ Shift+Insert for Edit⇨Paste

I can't give you any advice for remembering these keyboard equivalents because, frankly, they're bizarre. Okay, I suppose that because the Delete key deletes objects, it makes sense for Shift+Delete to go one step farther by scooping them up and sending them to the Clipboard. And if Shift+Delete scoops up, I suppose there's a sort of murky logic behind Shift+Insert for Paste, which inserts the objects from the Clipboard into your drawing. But Ctrl+Insert for Copy? Where in the world does that come from? Diseased brains, is my guess. Unfortunately, I can't blame Corel (fun as that might be); Microsoft built these weird keyboard equivalents into an early version of Windows.

In fact, the preferred Z, X, C, and V shortcuts come from the Macintosh platform. As with so many other elements of Windows 95, we have Apple to thank. Or blame. Take your pick.

A few little Clipboard facts

Here are a few random bits of information about the Clipboard that you may want to sock away for future use:

 ✔ The most common purpose for using the Clipboard is to cut or copy objects from one drawing and paste them into another. For example, to create Figure 8-3, I copied the tyrannosaur objects, opened the stegosaur drawing, and pasted the tyrannosaur. The two beasts should be great friends; they have so much in common. One is a tasty, crunchy dinosaur, and the other likes to snack on tasty, crunchy dinosaurs.

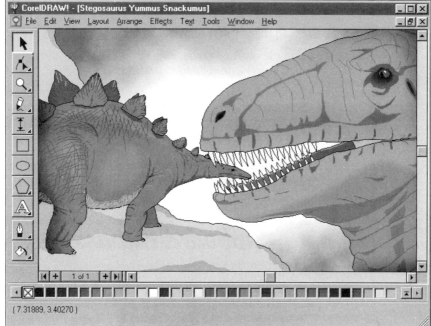

The Clipboard isn't the only way to move objects from one drawing to another, though. You can drag and drop selected objects, as described in the section "Do the Drag and Drop" later in this chapter.

✔ If the current document contains more than one page — as discussed in Chapter 12 — you can use the Clipboard commands to transfer objects from one page to the next.

✔ You can also cut, copy, and paste objects within a single-page drawing. But generally, it's easier to duplicate the objects using the Duplicate or Clone command, as described later in this chapter.

Why I Hate the Clipboard

Well, I don't really hate it. It's a useful feature every once in a while. But the Cut, Copy, and Paste commands have three problems:

✔ Clipboard functions can be very slow, depending on the complexity of your drawing. Copying the tyrannosaur takes . . . well, here, I'll do it right now. I select the graphic, choose the Copy command, and start the old stopwatch. Here comes the message that CorelDraw is copying. It just sits there for a while as if the machine is frozen up. Dum dee dum. Still just sitting there. Maybe I'll twiddle my thumbs a little. Ah, now something's happening. It's wrapping up, almost finished. Done, and in just under 15 seconds! And that's on a Pentium 133, mind you. What a waste of time.

✔ You have to choose two commands to pull off Clipboard actions: first Cut or Copy and then Paste. What a waste of effort.

✔ Every time you choose the Cut or Copy command, the previous contents of the Clipboard go up in smoke. If you want to use the objects on the Clipboard over and over again, you can't go around upsetting them every time you want to duplicate something. What a waste of status quo.

The moral is, you should avoid Clipboard commands whenever possible, which is almost always. The following sections explain how.

The Gleaming Clipboard Bypass

The easiest way to bypass the Clipboard is to choose Edit➪Duplicate or just press Ctrl+D. CorelDraw creates an exact copy of all selected objects and offsets them a quarter inch up and to the right, as demonstrated in Figure 8-4.

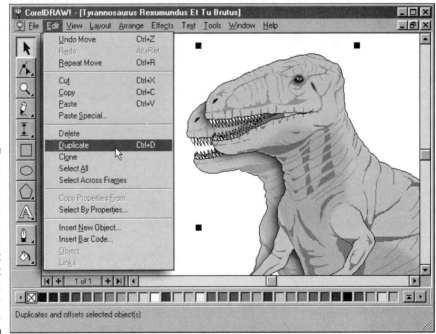

Figure 8-4: Choose the Duplicate command to create a copy of an object without upsetting the Clipboard.

Group before you duplicate

When you duplicate several paths at a time, CorelDraw places each duplicated object directly in front of the respective original object. This means that the paths weave in and out of each other, as demonstrated in Figure 8-5, creating an indecipherable mess. Oh sure, it's great if you're buzzing on caviar and aperitifs at a local gallery and are willing to call anything you spy the highest of all possible art — "Don't you just love it, Madge? It's like *Dino Descending a Staircase!*" — but hardly the thing for the strictly nine-to-five crowd.

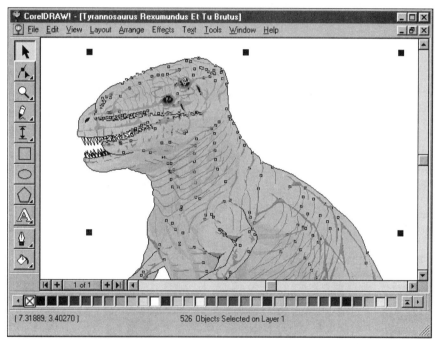

Figure 8-5:
The result of duplicating the T. Rex as 526 independent paths instead of one tidy group.

To remedy this situation, press either of the following key sequences:

Shift+PgUp

Ctrl+Z, Ctrl+G, Ctrl+D

The first option brings the duplicated objects to the front, creating an effect like that shown in Figure 8-4 — assuming that in your panic, you haven't clicked randomly in the drawing area and deselected the paths prior to pressing Shift+PgUp. If you have, you're still okay. The second sequence of keyboard shortcuts steps undoes the damage, groups the original selected objects, and reapplies the Duplicate command.

The Group (Ctrl+G) command is an ideal prerequisite to the Duplicate command. By choosing the Group command, you ensure that all your objects stay together after they are duplicated. Generally speaking, I recommend that anytime you want to duplicate five objects or more, you group them first. If you want to edit the objects, you can always ungroup them afterwards.

Duplication distance

By default, the Duplicate command offsets the copied objects ¹/₄ inch from the originals. You can change the offset by pressing Ctrl+J (or by choosing Tools⇨Options) and editing the values in the first two option boxes, spotlighted in Figure 8-6. Positive values offset the duplicate to the right or up; negative values move it to the left or down.

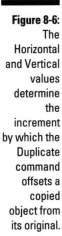

Figure 8-6:
The
Horizontal
and Vertical
values
determine
the
increment
by which the
Duplicate
command
offsets a
copied
object from
its original.

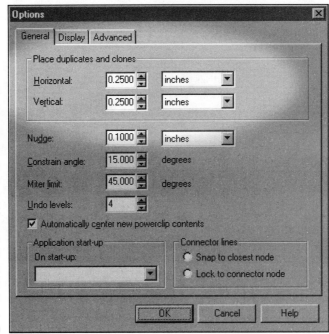

I recommend that you make these values an even multiple of the Nudge value. Better yet, make them the same. This way, if you want to line up the duplicated objects with the originals, all you have to do is press the down- and left-arrow keys.

Duplicate in place

In addition to Ctrl+D, there's another keyboard equivalent for the Duplicate command that no one but me knows about. Well, you'll know about it in a moment. And, of course, it used to be in the manual — back when CorelDraw had a manual. Here goes:

Press the + key on the keypad to duplicate an object without offsetting it. Then drag the duplicate to a new location as desired.

Pretty hot stuff, huh?

They Look Alike, They Act Alike, You Could Lose Your Mind

Imagine what would happen if every time Patty Duke changed her clothes, that identical cousin of hers changed her clothes too. Or if every time Patty missed a question on a test, her cousin entered the same wrong answer. Or if every time Patty locked braces with her boyfriend . . . well, you get the idea. *That's* cloning.

Uh, what's cloning?

Allow me to elucidate. The Clone command creates a true twin of an object. Like the Duplicate command, Edit⇔Clone creates an immediate copy, it by-passes the Clipboard, and it offsets the copy by the amount specified in the Preferences dialog box. But unlike the Duplicate command, the Clone command creates a link between copy and original. Any change made to the original also affects the clone.

Say that I clone the group of objects that make up the T. Rex. After waiting approximately half my life for CorelDraw to complete that operation, I move the cloned group over a little so that I can see what the heck I'm doing. Then, I select the *original* T. Rex and drag one of its corner handles. Instead of scaling just the one tyrannosaur, CorelDraw scales them both. Let's see *Jurassic Park* do that!

Links on the brink

The link between a clone and its original object works in one direction only. For example, if you select a clone and apply a new fill, CorelDraw fills the clone only, as demonstrated in Figure 8-7. But if you select the original and fill it, both original and clone change, as in Figure 8-8.

Furthermore, altering a clone damages the link between cloned and original objects. You can think of the Clone command as providing four links: one that governs the fill of the objects, another that controls the outline, a third that covers all transformations (scaling, rotating, and so on), and a fourth for Clipboard functions. Each of the links is independent of the other three. So even if you apply a different fill to the clone, Draw retains the link between outline, transformations, and Clipboard functions.

Original   Selected clone

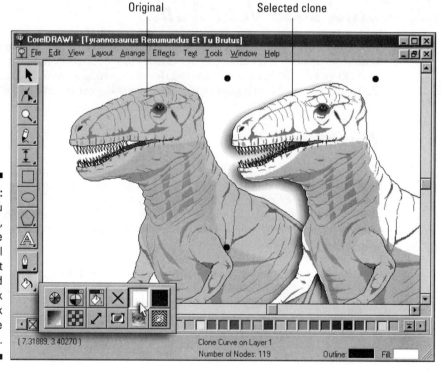

Figure 8-7: When you fill a clone, you leave the original object unaffected and break the fill link between the two objects.

Selected original   Clone

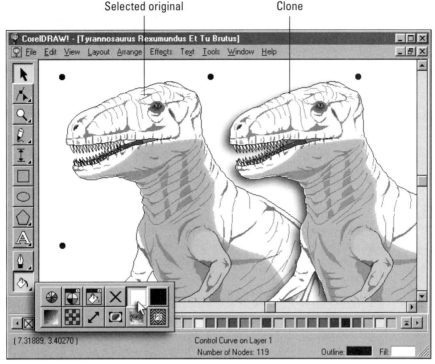

Figure 8-8:
To retain all
links, be
sure to
apply
changes to
the original
object only.

The care and feeding of your clones

Here's some more stuff to know about clones:

✔ You can tell whether you've selected clone or original by keeping an eye on the status bar. When you select a cloned path, for example, the status bar reads *Clone Curve* (as in Figure 8-7). If you select the original path, the status bar says *Control Curve* (as in Figure 8-8). In other words, *Control* = original.

✔ Deleting an object is like cutting it. So if you delete the original, you delete the clone as well. If you delete the clone, clone and all links go away but the original object stays.

✔ Any transformation applied to a clone severs the transformation link completely. If you scale the clone, for example, you also prohibit rotating, skewing, and all the other transformations described in Chapter 9.

✔ If you cut the original object, you cut the clone as well. The same holds true for the Copy command. However, whereas cutting the clone destroys the Clipboard link between original and clone, you can copy a clone as many times as you want with no detrimental effects.

✔ Although grouping and duplicating go hand in hand, grouping limits the functionality of the Clone command. If you want to be able to change the fill and outline of individual objects, for example, you may want to ungroup those objects before choosing Edit⇨Clone. Then press Shift+PgUp to bring the objects to the front of the drawing area and proceed from there.

✔ Of course, you can also select individual objects inside a group by Ctrl+clicking with the Arrow tool. In fact, this is exactly what I did in Figures 8-7 and 8-8 to select the bottom object in the original T-Rex.

✔ If you apply the Group or Ungroup command to cloned objects, you sever all four links between original objects and their clones.

✔ If you clone a group, CorelDraw won't let you ungroup the original object until after you ungroup the clone, which totally wipes out the links. So if you're going to clone a group, be sure that you want it to remain a group.

Some operations do not affect clones. For example, you don't select the clone when you select the original. If you move the original object, the clone remains stationary. And if you change the stacking order of an original object, the clone does nothing much in particular.

Unfortunately, I was unable to discover the answer to one nagging question. If you scratch the original object's tummy, does the clone purr? Or does it bite your head off? Experiment at your own risk.

Do the Drag and Drop

Although the Duplicate and Clone commands outclass the Clipboard in small ways, *drag and drop* really puts it to shame. If you have two drawings open at a time, you can move or copy selected objects by simply dragging them from one drawing and dropping them into the other.

1. **Open two drawings.**

   Make sure that you can see portions of both drawings. You don't want one drawing entirely covering up the other, for example. You can choose Window⇨Tile Horizontally or Window⇨Tile Vertically to split the interface evenly between the two drawings.

2. **Select the objects that you want to move or copy.**

   If you want to copy Object A in Drawing 1, for example, select the Arrow tool, click anywhere in Drawing 1 to make it active, and then click on Object A.

3. Drag the selected objects into the other drawing.

In other words, drag Object A out of Drawing 1 and into Drawing 2. Your cursor changes to an arrow with a dotted page outline.

4. Release the mouse button.

When you release the mouse button, you drop the object into its new environment. Corel deletes the selected objects from the original drawing and moves them to the new drawing. It's just as if you had cut and pasted the objects, except that the Clipboard remains unaffected.

To copy the objects instead of moving them, press and hold the Ctrl key after you start dragging but before releasing the mouse button. A little plus sign appears next to the cursor, as shown in Figure 8-9. Release the mouse button to drop the objects and then release the Ctrl key.

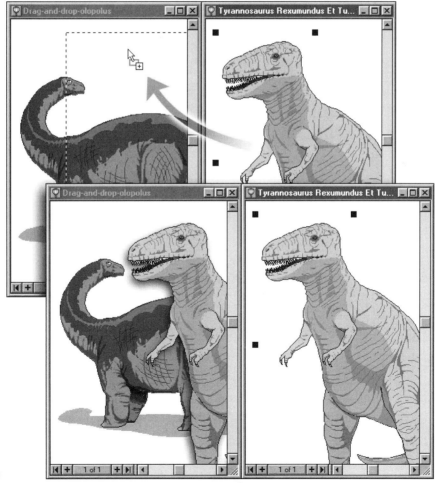

Figure 8-9: By dragging and Ctrl+dropping the tyrannosaur into the brontosaur paddock (top), I copy the carnivore (bottom) without upsetting the contents of the Clipboard.

Chapter 9

The Twisty, Stretchy, Bulgy World of Transformations

*I*n the movie *The Blues Brothers,* original "Saturday Night Live" cast member John Belushi does a series of back flips in a church. You think, "Wow, that's amazing! This guy is so gonzo that despite the fact that he's verging on obesity, high on nonprescription inhalants, and obviously completely out of shape (he spends half the movie breaking out in sweat), he's capable of performing complex floor exercises when sufficiently inspired."

Well, at least that's what *I* thought when I saw the movie in high school. Later, I learned the sad truth that it wasn't *really* John Belushi, but instead a padded stunt man. That fateful day, I promised myself that I would somehow make John's dream of gymnastic excellence come true. (I didn't really do anything of the kind, of course, but stay with me on this one. The whole introduction to this chapter hinges on your temporary suspension of disbelief.)

Today, I make good on that promise. In this chapter, you don't just see John do flips, though he performs quite a nice one in Figure 9-1. You see him undergo a series of elaborate transformations that would cause rational Olympic athletes at the peak of their careers to shrink in terror. By the end of the chapter, you'll swear that the guy is some kind of inhuman shape-shifter who can assume any form at will. Either that, or he's a drawing that I've subjected to CorelDraw's vast array of transformation functions.

GOSSIP

The Belushi caricature comes from a company called Image Club, which offers a huge variety of celebrity and historical caricatures, almost all of which are splendid. (This is in stark contrast to the general-purpose Image Club cartoons, which are pretty awful.)

Figure 9-1:
Belushi
finally does
his own
stunts.

Scaling, Flipping, Rotating, and Skewing

Scaling, flipping, rotating, and skewing are the big four transformations, the ones that have been available to CorelDraw users since our ancestors crafted the first version of the program out of twigs and iron-ore filings in the early 5th century. Just so that you know what I'm talking about — in approximate terms, anyway — here are a few quick definitions:

 ✔ To *scale* (or *stretch*) an object is to make it bigger or smaller. You can scale an object vertically, horizontally, or both.

 ✔ To *flip* an object is to make a mirror image of it, which is why CorelDraw calls this process *mirroring* and other programs call it *reflecting.* In the second example of Figure 9-1, I flipped Mr. Belushi both vertically and horizontally, making the top the bottom, the left side the right side, and vice versa.

✔ To *rotate* an object is to spin it around a central point like a top. Rotations are measured in degrees. A 180-degree rotation turns the object upside-down. A 360-degree rotation returns it right back to where it started.

✔ To *skew* (or *slant*) an object is to incline it to a certain degree. Like rotations, skews are measured in degrees. Just to give you some perspective, a 45-degree skew applied to a rectangle slants the shape so that its sides are perfectly diagonal.

Grouping comes before transforming

It's a good idea to group all objects before you transform them. To transform the Belushi cartoon, for example, I selected all the shapes that made up the drawing by choosing Edit⇨Select All and then pressed Ctrl+G. (You can also choose Arrange⇨Group.) After grouping, you can scale, flip, rotate, and skew with a clear conscience. Grouping prevents you from accidentally missing an object — such as an eye or an ear — while transforming its neighbors.

Scaling and flipping

If you read the "Arrow Tool Tricks" section of Chapter 4, you're already familiar with how to scale and flip an object using the Arrow tool. But just in case you missed that chapter, I'll quickly explain how it works:

1. **Select one or more objects that you want to scale or flip.**

   Eight square handles surround the selected objects.

2. **Drag one of the handles to scale the objects.**

   Drag a corner handle to scale the objects proportionately, so that the ratio between the horizontal and vertical dimensions of each object remains unchanged. Drag the left or right handle to scale the objects horizontally only, as in Figure 9-2. Drag the top or bottom handle to scale the objects in a vertical direction only.

   Shift+drag to scale the object with respect to its center. Ctrl+drag to scale the object by an amount that's an even multiple of 100 percent, such as 200 percent, 300 percent, and so on.

3. **Drag one handle past the opposite handle to flip the objects.**

   In Figure 9-3, for example, I dragged the right handle leftward past the left handle to flip John B. horizontally, exactly as if he were rehearsing an episode of "Samurai Pastry Chef" in front of a mirror . . . except, of course, that he's facing the wrong direction.

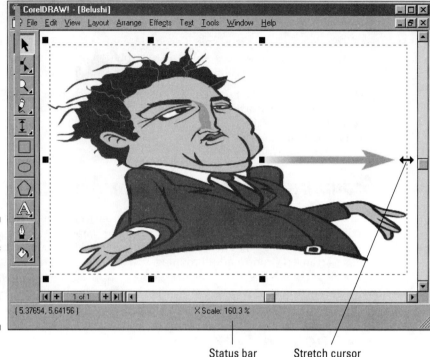

File   Edit   View   Layout   Arrange   Effects   Text   Tools   Window   Help

(5.37654, 5.64156)   X Scale: 160.3 %

Figure 9-2:
The result of
dragging the
side handle
with the
Arrow tool.

Status bar   Stretch cursor

To create an exact mirrored version of the object that is the same size as the
original, Ctrl+drag a handle.

Notice that in both Figures 9-2 and 9-3, the status bar measures the transformation in percentage points. A value below 100 percent indicates a reduction; a
value above 100 percent indicates an enlargement. If the value is followed by
the word *Mirrored* in parentheses, as in Figure 9-3, you have flipped the graphic.

Using the provocative S&M roll-up

You can also scale or flip selected objects by entering numerical values into the
Scale & Mirror roll-up. To do so, choose Arrange⇨Transform⇨Scale and Mirror
or press Alt+F9. In response, the Scale & Mirror roll-up appears, as shown in
Figure 9-4.

The Scale & Mirror roll-up is really part of a group of roll-ups that go by the
combined name of Transform. Scroll to the top of the list just below the title
bar, and you'll see the name Transform above all the others. You can switch to
a different roll-up in the group — such as Rotation or Skew — by clicking on its
name in the list.

Figure 9-3:
By dragging
the right
handle way
the heck
leftward, I
created a
reflection of
Belushi.

Figure 9-4:
Not
recommended
for the weak
of heart, the
infamous
S&M roll-up
makes
objects beg
and scrape.

The options in the Scale & Mirror roll-up stretch your objects just as surely as if they were prisoners on a medieval rack, but without either the mess or the incessant groans of pain.

- ✔ Enter percentage values into one or both of the option boxes to scale the selection.

- ✔ To scale the selection by the same amount both horizontally and vertically, select the Proportional check box.

✔ Click on one of the Mirror buttons or enter a negative value into an option box to flip the objects horizontally or vertically.

✔ Click on the Apply button (or press Enter) to scale or flip the selection.

✔ Click on the Apply To Duplicate button to simultaneously duplicate the selected objects and scale or flip the duplicates. The original objects remain unchanged.

Rotating and skewing

To rotate or skew one or more objects, do this:

1. **Select one or more objects you want to rotate or skew.**

   As always, you see eight square handles.

2. **Click on one of the selected objects a second time.**

   When you do, CorelDraw changes the square handles to a series of double-headed arrows, as shown in Figure 9-5. These arrows are the *rotate and skew handles,* or R&S handles for short. (The curved handles are the

Rotation handle   Skew handle   Center of rotation marker

Figure 9-5: Click on a selection a second time to display the rotate and skew handles and the center of rotation marker.

rotation handles, and the straight handles are the skew handles.) To return to the square stretch and mirror handles, click a third time on a selected object. Each time you click, you toggle between S&M and R&S.

3. **Move the center of rotation marker as desired.**

The circle in the middle of the selection is the *center of rotation marker*, which indicates the point about which the rotation takes place. Make sense? No? Well, think of the marker as a nail in a piece of cardboard. If you spin the cardboard, it whirls around the nail, right? In the same way, a selection rotates around the center of rotation marker. You can move the marker by dragging it.

4. **Drag a rotation handle to rotate the selected objects.**

Drag any of the four corner handles to rotate the selection around the center of rotation marker, as shown in Figure 9-6.

5. **Drag a skew handle to slant the selected objects.**

Drag the top or bottom handle to slant the selected objects horizontally, as in Figure 9-7. To slant the objects vertically, drag one of the two side handles.

Rotate cursor

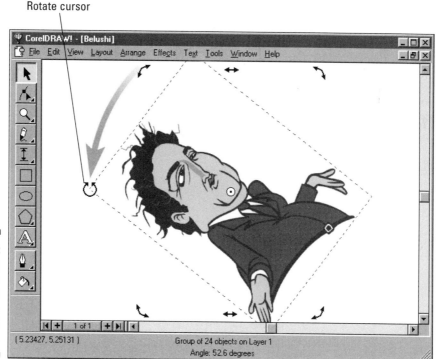

Figure 9-6:
By dragging a rotation handle, I send Mr. Belushi spinning.

As it does when you are scaling and flipping objects, the status bar measures rotations and skews, but in degrees instead of percentage points. When you are rotating an object, a positive value indicates a counterclockwise rotation, as in Figure 9-6; a negative value means the rotation is clockwise.

The same holds true for skewing, but the values don't always make sense. For example, if you drag the top skew handle to the left — which slants the selection backwards — the status bar displays a positive value, just the opposite of what you probably expect. That's why there's very little sense in paying attention to the status bar when you're skewing objects.

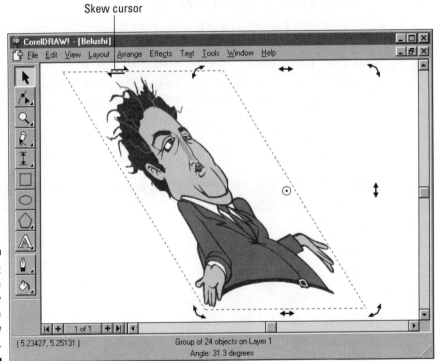

Skew cursor

Figure 9-7:
I slanted the cartoon by dragging the top skew handle.

Transforming by degrees

Keep the following things in mind when you're rotating and skewing objects:

✔ I don't know how much you remember from geometry class, but here's a quick refresher. Think of degrees as being measured on a clock. A clock measures 60 seconds, and a geometric circle comprises 360 degrees. Each clock second is equal to 6 degrees, which means that the hour markers on a clock are each 30 degrees apart. So a ¹/₄ turn — the distance from 12 o'clock to 3 o'clock — is 90 degrees in CorelDraw.

✔ Ctrl+drag a handle to rotate or skew in 15-degree increments. For example, you can rotate a selection by 30 degrees, 45 degrees, and so on. All major turns — ¹/₄ turns, ¹/₈ turns, all the way down to ¹/₂₄ turns — are multiples of 15 degrees.

✔ If you don't like 15 degrees, you can change the angle by pressing Ctrl+J (or choosing Tools⇨Options). When the Options dialog box appears, enter a new value into the Constrain Angle option box. After you press the Enter key, Ctrl+drag a rotation handle to see the effect of your change.

✔ Ctrl+drag the center of rotation marker to align the center point with one of the eight handles. You can also Ctrl+drag to return the marker to the exact center of the selection.

Using the not-so-provocative R&S roll-ups

You can also rotate or skew a selection by entering values into the Rotation and Skew roll-ups, respectively. To rotate a selection, choose Arrange⇨Transform⇨Rotate or press Alt+F8. To slant a selection by the numbers, choose Arrange⇨Transform⇨Skew of press Alt+F11. Figure 9-8 shows the Rotation and Skew roll-ups, which are both part of the Transform group.

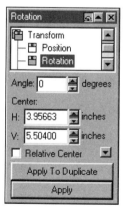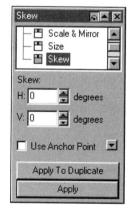

Figure 9-8: The Rotation and Skew roll-ups make objects cartwheel and slide.

Here's how to use the options in the Rotation roll-up:

✔ Enter a degree value into the Angle option box to rotate the selection. Enter a positive value to rotate the objects in a counterclockwise direction; enter a negative value to rotate clockwise. Or, if you prefer, positive is left, negative is right.

✔ Enter values into the Center option boxes to position the center of the rotation. Select the Relative Center check box to position the center marker relative to the center of the selection; turn off the check box to position the marker with respect to the lower-left corner of the page.

✔ When in doubt, just select the Relative Center check box and enter 0 into both Center option boxes. That way, you rotate the selection about exact center. You can't go wrong that way.

And here's what to do with the options in the Skew roll-up:

✔ Enter values into the H and V option boxes to slant the selected objects. CorelDraw permits values between positive and negative 75.

✔ A positive value in the H option box slants the object backward; a negative value slants it forward.

✔ In the V option box, positive is up, and negative is down.

✔ Ignore the Use Anchor Point check box. It enables you to position the center of the skew using some hidden options — you have to click on that little expand button to the right of the check box to get to them. Really, it's not worth the hassle.

Click on the Apply To Duplicate button to duplicate the selected objects and rotate or skew the duplicates at the same time. To rotate or skew the originals, press Enter or click on Apply.

Distortions on Parade

If scale, flip, rotate, and skew were the extent of CorelDraw's transformation capabilities, the program would be a real snoozer. It would be flexible, certainly, but hardly capable of inspiring the fanatic loyalty that accompanies this vast program. The remainder of this chapter covers three amazing transformations you can perform with CorelDraw 6:

✔ Imagine a drawing printed on a sheet of flexible plastic in a rectangular frame. If you were to grab a corner of that plastic and stretch it, the drawing would stretch in that direction. That's what it's like to distort objects in CorelDraw using the Perspective function. Corel calls the function *Perspective* because it simulates the effect of viewing a flat drawing in three-dimensional space.

✔ *Enveloping* is like viewing a drawing's reflection in a fun-house mirror. You can bow the edges of objects inward, outward, or even along the edges of complex paths.

✔ *Extruding* an object gives it real depth by attaching sides to the shape. A square turns into a cube; a circle turns into a cylinder. CorelDraw accentuates the appearance of depth by automatically lighting the extruded shape and rotating it in 3-D space.

TECHNICAL STUFF

Special effects you can ignore

If you take a look at your Effects menu, you'll notice that I ignore one or two commands in this chapter, including Blend, Contour, PowerLine, Lens, Bitmap Color Mask, and PowerClip. I wouldn't blame you if this fact cast a smidgen of doubt on my flawless wisdom. But the truth is, none of these commands are transformations. Most of them aren't even special effects, and a few are just plain goofy. Here's my take on these features:

✔ Effects✿Blend creates intermediate shapes between two selected paths. If you blend between a white square and a black circle, for example, CorelDraw creates a series of shapes that become increasingly circular as they progress from light gray to dark gray. The number-one use for the Blend function is to create custom gradations — it's useful, but hardly an eye-popping special effect. To learn how to create a blend of your own, follow the steps in the "Morph between Two Shapes" section of Chapter 19.

✔ The Contour feature is easily the least useful of CorelDraw's special effects. It fills a path with concentric versions of itself. Theoretically, you can use the Contour function to create gradations that follow the contour of a path, but you generally end up with patterns that look for all the world like shooting targets.

✔ The PowerLine command enables you to draw calligraphic lines that are really closed paths. I don't discuss powerlines in this chapter for the obvious reason that they have nothing to do with transformations. As a matter of fact, I don't discuss the PowerLine function in this book, period. For all its complexities and variations, it ultimately performs less ably and less predictably than a quill dipped in ink. If you want calligraphy, go to Wal-Mart and buy a 95¢ fountain pen.

✔ CorelDraw's Lens function blends the colors of a selected shape with the colors in the shapes below it. You can make an object appear translucent; you can make one shape invert the colors in another; and you can create magnifying-lens effects. These are cool effects, no doubt, but they come at a price. Lens effects almost always increase the time it takes to print a drawing, and they may make a drawing so complicated that you can't get it to print at all.

✔ If Contour is the goofiest command in the Effects menu, Bitmap Color Mask comes in a close second. It lets you bore holes in imported photographs and other pixel-based images. You select a color, and all instances of that color become transparent. If you had a picture of the Death Star against a blue screen, for example, you could make the blue transparent and reveal a drawing full of spaceships below. But because none of us have any pictures of Death Stars against blue screens lying around, you probably won't find yourself using Bitmap Color Mask very often.

✔ PowerClip lets you create stencils. In other words, you can take a bunch of objects and stick them inside another object. The CorelDraw balloon, for example, is a bunch of stripes stuck inside a balloon shape. To use the feature, you just select the objects you want to stick inside another shape, choose Effects✿PowerClip✿Place Inside Container, and then click on the stencil shape. Bingo, in go your objects. But like the Lens function, PowerClip dramatically increases the complexity of a drawing. If you encounter printing errors after using this feature, don't come crying to me.

A Lesson in Perspective

Before I go any farther, I want to caution you against thinking of CorelDraw as a three-dimensional drawing program just because it provides a few wacky effects that simulate 3-D. In a true 3-D program — such as CorelDream 3D — you build a 3-D structure called a *model* that you can walk around and view from any angle imaginable. Then you wrap surface maps around the model, specify the reflectivity of the surfaces, light the model, apply ray tracing, and perform a bunch of other operations that very likely sound Greek to you.

The point is, CorelDraw is solidly rooted in two dimensions. Its tiny supply of 3-D-like effects are pure mockery and flimflam. All in the name of good fun. Something to do on a rainy night. If you want to get a taste for real 3-D, check out Chapter 18.

Viewing your 2-D drawing in 3-D space (sorta)

Now that I've diplomatically sorted out that tender issue, allow me to show you how to distort one or more objects using the Add Perspective command.

1. **Select some random objects.**

2. **Press Ctrl+G or choose Arrange⇨Group.**

   If you don't group the objects, CorelDraw assumes that you want to distort each object individually, which can prove more than a little messy.

3. **Choose Effects⇨Add Perspective.**

   CorelDraw converts the group to a *perspective object* and automatically selects the Shape tool, as shown in Figure 9-9. Perspective objects are a unique kind of object in CorelDraw and require a special editing approach.

4. **Drag on any of the four corner handles.**

   CorelDraw stretches the selection to keep up with your moves.

You can drag handles for as long as you want. Perspective objects are hard to predict at first, so be prepared to spend some time editing. If dragging a handle produces an unwanted effect, just drag the handle back or press Ctrl+Z.

When you finish editing the selection, click on the Arrow tool icon. CorelDraw exits the perspective mode and allows you to perform other operations.

Shape tool   Perspective object

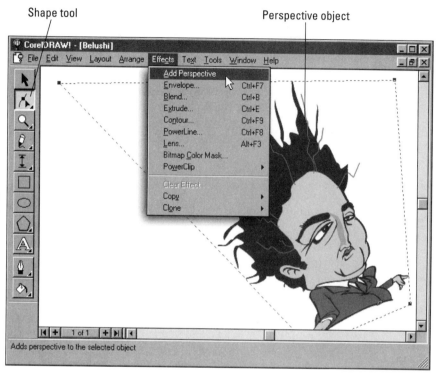

Putting perspective in perspective

Editing a perspective object is pretty straightforward stuff. But just in case, the following list contains a few items to bear in mind along with a few suggested avenues for experimentation.

- Ctrl+drag a handle to drag it in a horizontal or vertical direction.

- Ctrl+Shift+drag a handle to move two handles at once. The handle you drag moves either horizontally or vertically; a neighboring handle moves the same distance in the opposite direction. If you Ctrl+Shift+drag horizontally, the handle to the left or right of the handle you drag also moves. If you Ctrl+Shift+drag vertically, the handle above or below the current handle moves.

- Imagine that the dotted outline that surrounds the perspective object extends forever in all directions. So instead of four straight sides, you had four straight lines extending across your screen. CorelDraw marks the two locations at which each pair of opposite imaginary lines meet — that is, the point at which the left side would meet the right side and the point at which the top side would meet the bottom — with Xs called *vanishing*

points. Unless you're far away from your object, you probably can't see the vanishing points because they're off-screen. But if you zoom out (by pressing F3) or move two opposite sides at an extreme angle to one another (see Figure 9-10), one or both of the vanishing points will come into view.

✔ The reason I even brought up this complicated topic is because you can also drag a vanishing point to further distort the perspective object. Try it to get a feel for how it works.

✔ To restore the dotted outline to a rectangle and take a new stab at a perspective object, choose Effects➪Add Perspective. Note that the object remains in perspective; only the dotted outline changes.

✔ To remove the most recent round of perspective edits from a selected object, choose Effects➪Clear Perspective.

✔ To edit an existing perspective object, just select the Shape tool and click on the object. There's no need to choose the Add Perspective command.

✔ To edit the individual nodes and segments in a perspective object, you have to convert the object back to paths. First press Ctrl+U (Arrange➪Ungroup) to ungroup the object if necessary. Then select the object you want to edit and choose Arrange➪Convert to Curves (Ctrl+Q).

Vanishing point

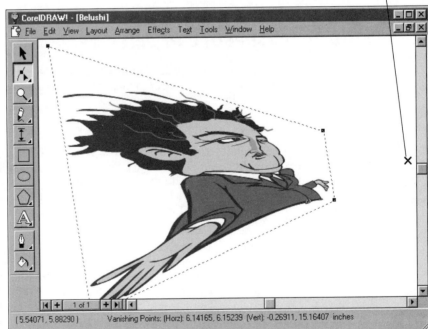

Figure 9-10: The vanishing point represents the location at which two opposite edges of the dotted outline converge.

Envelope of Wonders

CorelDraw's Envelope feature lets you bend and twist objects as if they were imprinted on a piece of Silly Putty. You know how you'd smush a piece of Silly Putty on the comics page of the newspaper and then wrap it around your little brother's face? As for why Corel calls this process enveloping, I can only guess that someone in engineering or development received a pretty gnarly package from UPS.

If you've ever taken a look at CorelDraw's Envelope feature, you probably said something like, "What the . . . ?" or perhaps more appropriately, "Duh." At least, that's what I did. But have faith. If I — king of the short attention span — could learn it, you can too. And believe me, it's worth the effort.

The ultimate distortion

As in previous versions of CorelDraw, the Envelope feature is presented as a roll-up. But in Version 6, the Envelope roll-up is part of the Effects roll-up group. This group includes Blend, Contour, and some of the others I mentioned in the "Special effects you can ignore" sidebar. Not to worry; none of those wacky effects will rear its ugly head unless you click on its name in the list at the top of the roll-up. Even if that unfortunate event occurs, you can just click on the word *Envelope* to return to the Envelope options.

1. **Select those objects.**

   Click and Shift+click with the Arrow tool until your mouse hand goes to sleep.

2. **Group the objects.**

   The Envelope function only works on one object at a time. So if you want to distort several objects, you need to group them by choosing Arrange⇨Group or pressing Ctrl+G.

3. **Press Ctrl+F7 or choose Effects⇨Envelope.**

   CorelDraw displays the Envelope roll up, as shown in Figure 9-11. If you want to free the Envelope roll-up from the Effects roll-up group, just drag the word *Envelope* out of the scrolling list and drop it anywhere on-screen (as I explained in the "Breakaway roll-ups" section at the end of Chapter 2).

4. **Click on the Add New button.**

   It's right there at the top of the roll-up. CorelDraw automatically selects the Shape tool and surrounds the selection with a dotted rectangle that has eight handles — four in the corners and four on the sides.

5. **Select an editing mode.**

   The four icons in the middle of the roll-up represent *envelope editing modes*. For now, it's not important which one you select. I'll explain how each one works in a moment.

6. **Drag the handles to distort the object.**

   The object bends and stretches to keep up with your movements.

7. **Click on the Apply button.**

   Wherever there's a roll-up, there's an Apply button dying to be clicked.

Figure 9-11:
The
Envelope
roll-up lets
you distort
objects as
freely as a
rolling pin
distorts
cookie
dough.

The envelope editing modes

The envelope editing mode icons work like tools. Each one distorts the selected object in a unique and progressively more dramatic way:

✔ In the straight-line mode, CorelDraw maintains a straight side between each of the eight handles, as demonstrated in Figure 9-12. It's rather like the perspective distortion, except for two things: 1) you have some additional handles to play around with and 2) you can move the handles horizontally or vertically only. The left and right side handles move horizontally only; the top and bottom handles move vertically only. The corner handles move both ways.

✔ In the single-arc mode, CorelDraw permits a single arc to form between each pair of handles, as shown in Figure 9-13. Again, you can drag handles horizontally and vertically only. The single-arc mode works best for distorting objects into hourglass and balloon shapes.

Straight-line mode

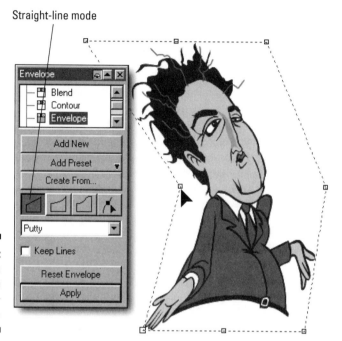

Figure 9-12:
Dragging a
handle in
the straight-
line mode.

Single-arc mode

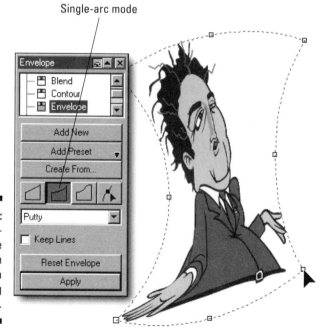

Figure 9-13:
The single-
arc mode
can
produce a
slenderizing
effect.

✔ The double-arc mode allows a wave to form between each handle. As demonstrated in Figure 9-14, you can create rippling distortions, as if you were viewing your object under water. Just as in the straight-line and single-arc modes, you can drag handles horizontally and vertically only.

✔ In the unconstrained mode, the sky's the limit. You can edit the outline exactly as if it were a free-form path drawn with the Pencil tool. You can drag the handles — they're really nodes in this case — any which way you please. To determine the curvature of the segments between handles, CorelDraw provides you with control points, as shown in Figure 9-15.

You can add or subtract nodes using the Node Edit roll-up. Just double-click on one of the handles to make the roll-up appear. You can even select multiple nodes at a time. In short, if you can do it to a Pencil path, you can do it in the unconstrained mode.

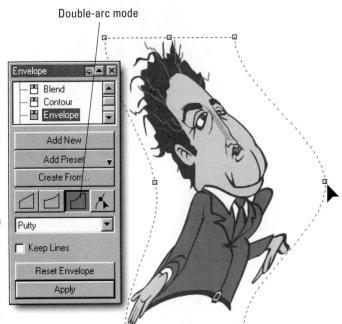

Double-arc mode

Figure 9-14:
You can
create
waves in the
double-arc
mode.

Push the envelope

That's as complicated as enveloping gets. If you don't read another word, you'll be able to distort your drawing so that its own mother wouldn't recognize it. But just in case you're hungry for more, here are a few tricks you may find helpful:

Unconstrained mode

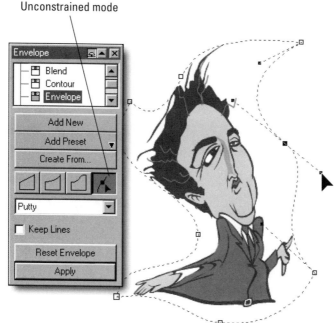

Figure 9-15:
For the distortion aficionado, there's no substitute for the unconstrained mode.

🡒 You can use envelope editing modes in tandem with each other. For example, you might select the straight-line icon and drag one handle and then select the double-arc icon and drag another handle.

🡒 In the unconstrained mode, the Shift and Ctrl keys behave just as they do when you're editing a Pencil path. Shift+click on a node to select it without deselecting other nodes. Ctrl+drag on a node to move it horizontally or vertically.

🡒 In the other modes, Ctrl+drag a handle to move the opposite handle the same distance and direction as the handle you're dragging.

🡒 Shift+drag to move the opposite handle the same distance but in the opposite direction as the handle you're dragging.

🡒 Ctrl+Shift+drag a side handle to move *all* side handles the same distance but in the opposite directions. Ctrl+Shift+drag a corner handle to move all corner handles.

🡒 If you don't feel up to editing the outline on your own, CorelDraw can help you out. Click on the Add Preset button in the Envelope roll-up to display a pop-up menu of outline shapes, as shown in Figure 9-16. Select the outline you want to apply and then click on the Apply button.

🡒 You can cancel an envelope distortion anytime before you click on the Apply button. Just click on the Reset Envelope button or select the Arrow tool.

✔ After you apply a few distortions, the dotted outline may become prohibitively wiggly. To restore the dotted outline to a rectangle and take a new stab at enveloping an object, click again on the Add New button in the Envelope roll-up.

✔ To remove the most recent round of envelope edits from a selected object, choose Effects▷Clear Envelope.

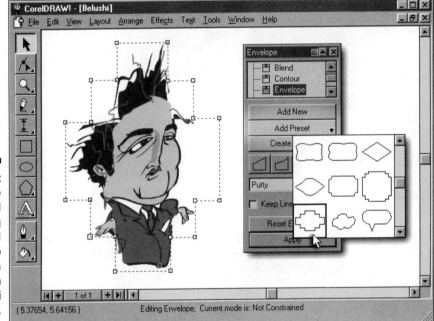

Figure 9-16:
Using the predefined enveloping outlines, I managed to create a southwestern Belushi effect.

Well, Extru-u-ude Me!

In future years, brilliant minds no doubt will argue the merit of discussing extruding — one of CorelDraw's most complex functions — in a... *For Dummies* book. (Yeah, right.) But I figure, what the heck, it's a fun feature, and with enough effort, you may even figure out how to do something useful with it. In the meantime, it's a great way to waste several hours being antisocial and playing with your computer.

Extruding in the real world

First, what is extruding? Simply put, *extrusion* is the act of assigning depth to a 2-D shape by extending its sides into the third dimension. Naturally, that doesn't make any sense, so perhaps an example is in order. Did you ever play with one of those thingies that lets you crank Play-Doh through a stencil to create snaky geometric forms, as illustrated in Figure 9-17? You cut off the snaky bit with a plastic knife and — voilà — you have a 3-D star, polygon, or other useless piece of gook. If this is your idea of a fond childhood memory, you are an extruder. Pasta machines extrude noodles. Sausage makers extrude columns of beef and pork by-products. Warts extrude out of your skin all by themselves. Life is filled with examples of extruding.

Figure 9-17:
Play-Doh
oozing
through a
stencil is an
example of
extrusion.

Extruding in the workplace

For time immemorial, the Extrude roll-up has served as the central head-quarters for CorelDraw's extruding functions. Ever since the Big Bang (or thereabouts), you've been able to access this roll-up by choosing Effects➪Extrude or pressing Ctrl+E.

As with enveloping, CorelDraw can't extrude more than one object at a time. However, unlike enveloping, extruding is *not* applicable to groups. You can extrude a single path — open or closed — or a block of text. Sadly, I'm afraid that rules out any more transformations for John.

To extrude an object, do these things:

1. Press Ctrl+E to bring up the Extrude roll-up.

The roll-up appears in Figure 9-18. Your roll-up is probably part of the Effects roll-up group, which means that you'll see a bunch of stuff at the top of your roll-up that doesn't appear in mine. (I've pulled my Extrude roll-up out of the Effects roll-up group, as explained in the "Breakaway roll-ups" section of Chapter 2.)

2. Select a path.

For now, keep it simple. Select some basic shape like a circle or a star.

3. Click on the Edit button in the Extrude roll-up.

A dotted extrusion outline representing the form of the extruded object appears, as shown in Figure 9-18.

If the Edit button is dimmed, press Ctrl+Q (Arrange⇨Convert To Curves) to convert the object to a free-form path. Now the Edit button is ready to go. It's also worth noting that if you select an object before pressing Ctrl+E — that is, you perform Step 2 before Step 1 — the Extrude roll-up automatically goes into the edit mode. This means that you don't have to click on the Edit button. Just skip to Step 4.

4. Drag on the vanishing point to change the direction of the extrusion.

Labeled in Figure 9-18, the vanishing point represents the point from which the extrusion emanates. If the star were a bullet rushing toward you, the vanishing point would be the gun. Kind of an ugly analogy, I admit, but accurate.

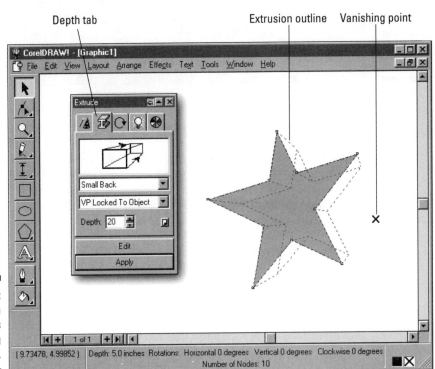

Figure 9-18:
A shape in the process of being extruded.

5. Enter a value in the Depth option box.

This value determines the length of the sides that stretch away from the object toward the vanishing point. If you enter the maximum value, 99, the extrusion outline touches the vanishing point. The minimum value, 1, creates a very shallow extrusion. Figure 9-19 shows some examples.

6. Click on the 3-D rotation tab.

It's the middle tab at the top of the Extrude roll-up.

7. Drag the Corel C to spin the selected object in 3-D space.

In CorelDraw 6, you no longer have to click on arrows to spin the object. You can just drag around inside the roll-up, as demonstrated in Figure 9-20. Give it a try and see how easy it is. The front of the C is red and the back is blue, so you can see right away when you rotate the letter all the way around.

Ctrl+drag to rotate in 45-degree increments. If you want to unrotate the object, click on the X icon.

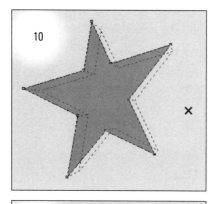

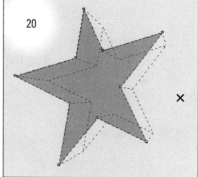

Figure 9-19:
The effect of various Depth values on the extrusion outline.

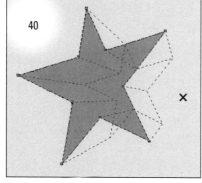

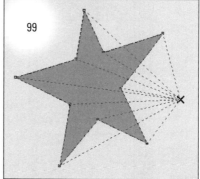

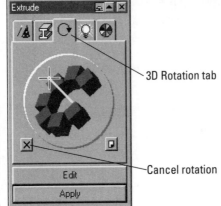

3D Rotation tab

Figure 9-20:
Drag the big
C to rotate
an object in
3-D space.

Cancel rotation

8. **Click on the Lighting tab.**

This tab is labeled in Figure 9-21.

9. **Click on the first light bulb to shine a light on the 3-D object.**

You can shine up to three lights by selecting all three light bulbs.

10. **Drag the light source markers in the cube.**

A number in a circle indicates the location of the light source with respect to the object. Drag one of these markers to any spot in the cube where two gridlines intersect.

Light bulbs

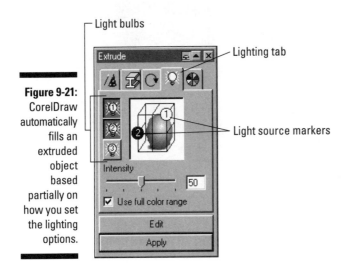

Lighting tab

Figure 9-21:
CorelDraw
automatically
fills an
extruded
object
based
partially on
how you set
the lighting
options.

Light source markers

11. Drag the Intensity slider to increase or decrease the amount of light.

Alternatively, you can enter a value between 0 and 100 into the option box. The lower the number, the dimmer the light.

12. Click on the Object Color tab.

Welcome to the options shown in Figure 9-22.

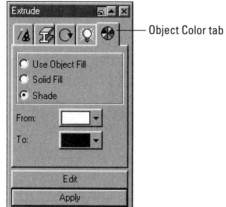

Figure 9-22: Click on the last tab in the roll-up to color the 3-D object.

13. Select the Shade radio button to fill the partially lighted portions of the object with continuous gradations.

There's no reason *not* to select this option. The other two radio buttons produce boring results.

14. Select the desired colors from the From and To pop-up menus.

For the best results, select a light and dark shade of the same color.

15. Click on the Apply button.

CorelDraw automatically draws and fills the object to your specifications. Figure 9-23 shows the star from Figure 9-18 after I rotated it and lit it from the bottom-left corner.

Extruding is a long process, but it's not a particularly complicated one. Even so, you do have the option of wimping out and selecting from CorelDraw's 3-D predefined settings. To access these, click on the 3-D Presets tab, which is the first tab in the roll-up. Then select one of the effects from the pop-up menu below the preview. As Figure 9-24 proudly shows, the preview updates to show you how the effect looks when applied to a sample object. If you like what you see, click on the Apply button.

Figure 9-23:
A three-
dimensional
star created
in a two-
dimensional
drawing
program.

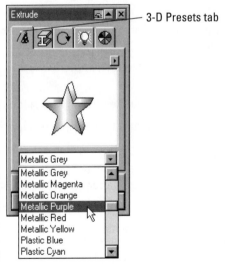

3-D Presets tab

Figure 9-24:
If you don't
feel like
making up
your own
3-D effect,
select
one of
CorelDraw's
prefab
effects.

You can edit a predefined effect after applying it by clicking on the Depth tab —
the one that looks like an I-beam — and following Steps 3 through 15. You know,
click on the Edit button, drag the vanishing point around, and so on.

You can even save your edited effect by returning to the 3-D presets panel and clicking on the Save As button. Enter a name for the effect and press Enter. Your new effect appears in the pop-up menu with all the others. Congratulations, you are now an official 3-D editing fool.

Ripping apart your new 3-D object

After you finish creating and lighting your object, you can break the 3-D object apart and fill it as you please. Just do the following:

1. **Choose Arrange⇨Separate.**

   This step separates the original object from its extruded sides.

2. **Shift+click on the original object with the Arrow tool.**

   This step deselects the object, leaving only the sides selected.

3. **Press Ctrl+U or choose Arrange⇨Ungroup.**

   CorelDraw automatically creates the sides as a group, so you need to ungroup them before you can edit their fills.

After you separate the individual paths that make up the extruded object, you can fill each path independently to create a better looking 3-D drawing.

Part III
Getting the Message Out There (Wherever There Is)

The 5th Wave   By Rich Tennant

"WOW! I DIDN'T EVEN THINK THEY MADE A 2000 DOT PER INCH FONT!"

In this part . . .

*1*f all you could do with CorelDraw was draw, this book would be over by now. But as luck would have it, CorelDraw is equally adept at creating documents such as fliers, newsletters, and those little wrappers that cover your hangers when they come back from the dry cleaners.

Like most desktop publishing programs, CorelDraw lets you enter and edit text, apply special formatting attributes, specify the size and orientation of a page, and print your document to paper. Unlike most publishing programs, however, it also enables you to drag letters independently of each other, create text on a circle, and actually edit the shape of characters of type. Few other pieces of software provide such a wide gamut of publishing capabilities.

At the risk of sounding like the crowned king of hyperbole, there hasn't been a tool like CorelDraw for slapping words on a bit of sliced timber since Johann Gensfleisch — who mostly went about using his mom's maiden name, Gutenberg — decided to smack some letters on a particularly abbreviated version of the Bible.

Chapter 10

The Care and Planting of Text

In This Chapter

▶ Creating artistic text that's truly artistic

▶ Adding text to a text block

▶ Moving, scaling, and rotating text

▶ Creating and editing paragraph text

▶ Pouring characters from one text block to another

▶ Selecting characters with one of the text tools

▶ Converting artistic text to paragraph text and vice versa

▶ Assigning formatting attributes

▶ Getting to know PostScript and TrueType fonts

▶ Correcting the spelling of your text

▶ Looking for synonyms

▶ Inserting symbols

*T*here's more to creating text than whacking your fingers in a hysterical frenzy against the keyboard. Remember all that stuff you learned in typing class? Forget it. Yesterday's news. I, for example, can't type — not a word — yet I write professionally, I format like a champ, and I don't have any wrist problems. Knock on wood . . . aaugh, I knocked too hard! I think I'm going numb!

Ha! Not really! See? My hand's just fine. Seemed so real, though, didn't it? And do you know why? It's not because the text is lucid and gripping. Surely you've figured that out by now. It's because the text *looks good.* The pages in this book appear professional — granted, in a sort of goofy way — so you naturally assume that a professional is behind them, not some crackpot like me. That, my friend, is an example of the miracle of modern computer-book writing.

In the world of corporate communications, text is judged as much by its appearance as its content. Not to put too fine a point on it, text is art. Simply typing in thoughtful and convincing text with a hint of Hippocrene genius is not enough. You also need to know what to do with text after you enter it. And that's what this chapter is all about. (You were beginning to wonder, huh?)

A Furst Luk at Tekst

Unless you already know a thing or two about word processing and desktop publishing, this chapter is going to seem like a trip through the dictionary. You're going to learn so many terms that your brain will very likely swell up and pop. To prepare, you may want to tie a bandanna around your head and set a squeegee near your monitor.

For starters, text is made up of letters, numbers, and various symbols, such as &, %, $, and, my favorite, §, which is meaningless to most of Earth's inhabitants. If § crops up in your documents, it's a sure sign that either a lawyer or an extraterrestrial has been using your machine.

Together, these little text elements are called *characters*. A collection of characters is called a *text block* or, in deference to its path cousins, a *text object*. A text block might contain a single word, a sentence, a paragraph, or an odd collection of §s arranged in the shape of a crop circle.

In CorelDraw, you work with two kinds of text blocks:

- *Artistic text* accommodates logos, headlines, labels, and other short passages of text that require special treatment.

- *Paragraph text* is suited to longer passages, such as full sentences, paragraphs, pithy quotes, encyclopedia entries, epic poems, works of modern fiction, and letters to Grandma.

CorelDraw also offers access to specialized symbols, which — although they're technically not text — you can use as independent objects to highlight text objects or adorn your drawing. Symbols are organized thematically into categories such as animals, furniture, medicine, and semaphore. No smoke signals yet, but I've heard that's in the works.

Pick Up Your Text Tools

You create different kinds of text using different tools, all accessible from the Text tool flyout menu, shown in Figure 10-1. To display the flyout menu, click and hold on the Text tool icon — which may appear as an *A* or as a small page. Then select the desired tool from the menu.

After you select the Artistic Text or Paragraph Text tool from the flyout menu, the selected tool occupies the Text tool slot in the toolbox. This setup means that you can return to the tool without hassling with the flyout menu.

Using the Artistic Text tool

Creating text with the Artistic Text tool is as easy as drawing a rectangle or oval:

1. **Select the Artistic Text tool.**

   If the A icon is available in the toolbox, click on it. If not, select the Artistic Text tool from the flyout menu.

   Better yet, just press F8.

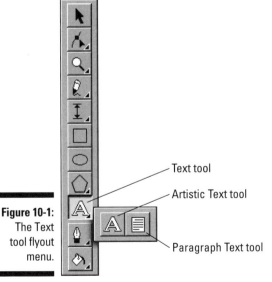

— Text tool

— Artistic Text tool

Figure 10-1:
The Text
tool flyout
menu.

Paragraph Text tool

2. Click in the drawing area at the point where you want the text to begin.

After you click, a vertical line, called the *insertion marker,* appears. The insertion marker indicates the location where new text will appear.

3. Type away.

As you type, the corresponding characters appear on-screen. The insertion marker moves rightward with the addition of each character (see Figure 10-2), indicating the location at which the next character will appear.

4. When you finish, select the Arrow tool.

Or just press Ctrl+spacebar. Eight square handles surround the text, as in the second example of Figure 10-2, to show that it is selected.

Figure 10-2:
Artistic text as it appears when you're entering text (top) and after you select the Arrow tool (bottom).

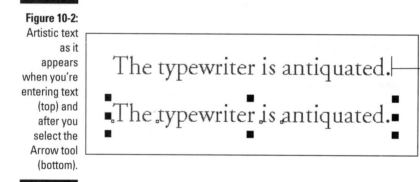

The typewriter is antiquated.⎯⎯ Insertion marker

The typewriter is antiquated.

Nearly every computer program in existence lets you change text after you create it, and CorelDraw is no exception. To add more characters, select the Artistic Text tool (or press F8) and click inside the text block at the location where you want the new characters to appear. In Figure 10-3, for example, I first clicked in front of the *a* in *antiquated* and entered the word *an.* Next, I clicked between the *d* and the period, pressed Enter, and entered *piece of garbage.*

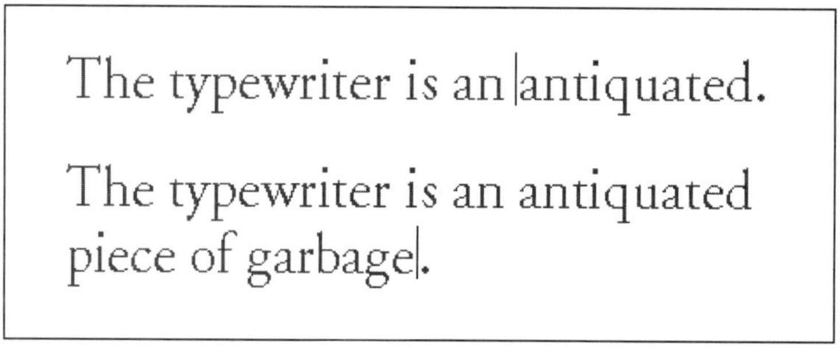

Figure 10-3:
Adding text to an existing text block.

The typewriter is an antiquated.

The typewriter is an antiquated piece of garbage.

Here are a few more ways to enter and edit artistic text:

- Unlike text in a word processor, artistic text does not automatically *wrap* to the next line. In other words, when your text reaches the right edge of the text block, CorelDraw doesn't move the insertion point to the beginning of a new line. You have to manually insert line breaks by pressing the Enter key, just as you have to press the carriage-return key when using a typewriter.

- To move the text block to a new location in the drawing area, drag it with the Arrow tool.

- You can also use the arrow keys to move a text block. Select the text block with the Arrow tool and then press an arrow key to nudge the block to a new location.

- When you drag the handles of an artistic text block with the Arrow tool, you change the size of the characters. Drag a corner handle to scale the characters proportionally.

- Drag the top or bottom handle to make the text tall and skinny, as in Figure 10-4. This kind of text is called *condensed*.

- Drag the left or right handle to make the text short and fat (called *expanded* text).

- Click a second time on a text block to access the rotation and skew handles. These handles work just like those described in Chapter 9, enabling you to create rotated and slanted text.

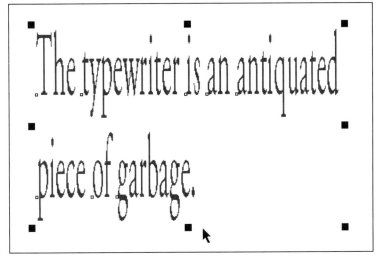

Figure 10-4:
I dragged the bottom handle with the Arrow tool to create condensed text.

Using the Paragraph Text tool

Here's how to use the Paragraph Text tool:

1. Select the Paragraph Text tool.

If the page icon is not available in the toolbox, select the tool from the flyout menu. If that's too much effort — which it is — press Shift+F8.

2. Drag in the drawing area to specify the size of the text block.

You create a rectangular marquee, as shown in Figure 10-5.

3. Bang those keys.

As you work out your aggressions, text will fill up the text block. Unlike artistic text, paragraph text automatically wraps to the next line when it exceeds the right-hand boundary of the text block, as demonstrated in the second example of Figure 10-5.

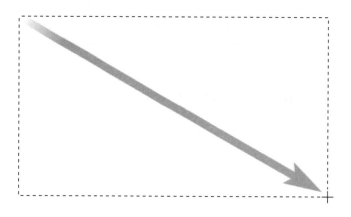

Figure 10-5: Paragraph text automatically wraps to fit inside the text block.

Whan Troyllus met Achylles besyde the clyffhose bar and grylle, Troyllus shoted, "I have come to impal yow. Than, as ye lye monyng, my horse wyll trod on yow untyl ye have gasse."

— Text block

— Old English nonsense

4. When you finish, select the Arrow tool.

Eight square handles surround the text block, just as they do when you create artistic text.

Some of the stuff that I said about artistic text applies to paragraph text as well. For example, you can add more characters to a block of paragraph text by clicking inside the text block with either the Paragraph Text tool or the Artistic Text tool and then typing away. You can move a selected block of paragraph text to a new location by dragging it with the Arrow tool or by pressing one or two arrow keys.

But a couple of operations work very differently:

✔ Dragging a corner handle scales the text block but not the text inside it. CorelDraw reflows the text to fit inside the new text block borders, as demonstrated in Figure 10-6.

✔ Click on the text block twice with the Arrow tool to display the rotate and skew handles. Rotating a paragraph text block rotates the characters inside, just as when you're rotating a block of artistic text. But skewing a paragraph text block slants the text block only, as shown in Figure 10-7. The characters remain upright and flow to fill the borders of the text block.

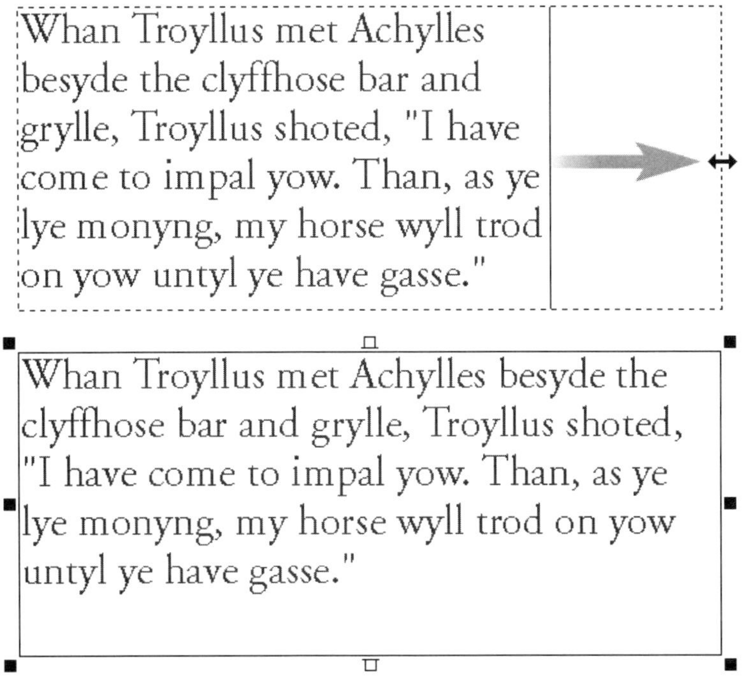

Figure 10-6:
Drag the
handle on a
block of
paragraph
text to
resize the
text block.
The
characters
inside
reflow
automatically
to fit the
new
dimensions.

Whan Troyllus met Achylles besyde the clyffhose bar and grylle, Troyllus shoted, "I have come to impal yow. Than, as ye lye monyng, my horse wyll trod on yow untyl ye have gasse."

Whan Troyllus met Achylles besyde the clyffhose bar and grylle, Troyllus shoted, "I have come to impal yow. Than, as ye lye monyng, my horse wyll trod on yow untyl ye have gasse."

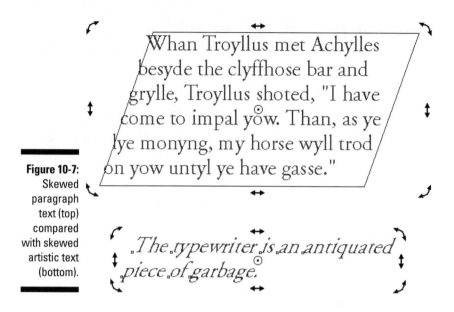

Figure 10-7: Skewed paragraph text (top) compared with skewed artistic text (bottom).

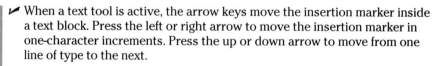

A single paragraph can contain no more than 4,000 characters, which is roughly the equivalent of two pages in this book with no figures. Okay, so maybe George Bernard Shaw would have had problems with this limitation. He and William Faulkner could have moaned about it endlessly in 10,000-character postcards to each other. But I don't think that you'll have any problems.

Navigating among the letters

Whether you're working with artistic or paragraph text, you can specify the location of the insertion marker inside the text by clicking in the text block with either of the text tools. After you position the insertion marker, you can move it around using any of the following techniques:

✔ When a text tool is active, the arrow keys move the insertion marker inside a text block. Press the left or right arrow to move the insertion marker in one-character increments. Press the up or down arrow to move from one line of type to the next.

✔ To move in whole-word increments, press Ctrl plus the left- or right-arrow key.

✔ Press Ctrl and the up-arrow key to move to the beginning of the current paragraph. Press Ctrl and the down-arrow key to move to the end of the paragraph.

- Press the Home key to move the insertion marker to the beginning of the current line. Press End to move to the end of it.

- Ctrl+Home moves the insertion marker to the beginning of the current text block. Ctrl+End moves you to the end of the text block.

How to Flow Text between Multiple Blocks

When you're entering long passages of paragraph text, the text may exceed the boundaries of the text block. Every character you entered still exists, you just can't see it. To view the hidden text, you can do the following:

- Reduce the size of the characters so that they fit better, as described later in this chapter.

- Enlarge the text block by dragging one of the handles.

- Pour the text into a new text block.

That's right, you can *pour* excess text from one text block into another as if it were liquid. Here's how it works:

1. **Drag to create a text block with the Paragraph Text tool.**

2. **Enter far too much text.**

   Type in every page of *Beowolf.* This is your chance to bone up on classical literature.

3. **Select the Arrow tool.**

   Much of the text you entered should not be visible on-screen.

4. **Click on the top or bottom handle of the text block.**

   These handles are called *tabs.* The top tab is empty, to show that the text starts here. The bottom text has a little arrowhead in it to show that there's a bunch of overflow text that doesn't fit inside the text block. You can click on the top tab to pour lines from the beginning of the text block into a new text block. (Lines from the end of the text block shift up to fill the space left behind.) Or you can click on the bottom tab to pour the hidden lines of text into the new text block. In either case, after you click on a tab, your cursor changes to a page icon, as in Figure 10-8.

5. **Drag to create a second text block.**

   Figure 10-8 demonstrates this process. CorelDraw then automatically pours lines of text originally entered into the first text block into this new text block, as shown in Figure 10-9.

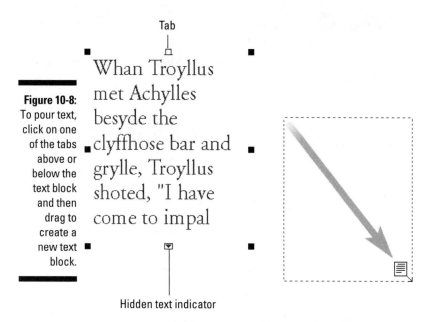

Tab

Whan Troyllus met Achylles besyde the clyffhose bar and grylle, Troyllus shoted, "I have come to impal

Hidden text indicator

Figure 10-8: To pour text, click on one of the tabs above or below the text block and then drag to create a new text block.

Notice that three tiny lines appear inside the bottom tab on the first text block and the top tab on the second. The lines indicate that there's a *link* between the two text blocks.

To experiment with the link, keep stepping:

6. Drag up on the bottom tab on the first text block.

This step leaves less room in the first text block for the text. The overflow text automatically pours into the second text block.

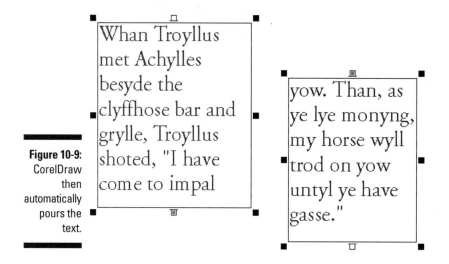

Whan Troyllus met Achylles besyde the clyffhose bar and grylle, Troyllus shoted, "I have come to impal

yow. Than, as ye lye monyng, my horse wyll trod on yow untyl ye have gasse."

Figure 10-9: CorelDraw then automatically pours the text.

7. Press Delete.

CorelDraw deletes the first text block (assuming that the first text block is still selected) but it does not delete the text inside the text block. Instead, the text pours into the second text block.

Pretty keen, huh? As long as at least one text block in the link remains in your drawing, the text remains intact. Now, if you were to delete the second text block, CorelDraw would indeed delete the text because there is no longer anyplace for the text to go.

You can pour text between as many text blocks as you like. Okay, I bet there's some maximum, like 32 or 256 or something, but who cares? You'd be a nut to *want* to pour between that many text blocks! You can even pour your text across multiple pages. (I discuss multiple-page documents in Chapter 12.)

Before You Can Format, You Must Select

To change the appearance of characters in a text block, you assign *formatting attributes* such as typeface, style, size, and a few others that I'll get to later. But before you can do so, you have to select the text.

You can select text in two ways in CorelDraw. You can click on the text block with the Arrow tool, in which case any formatting changes will affect all characters inside the text block. Or you can highlight individual characters and words with either the Artistic Text tool or the Paragraph Text tool. Your changes then affect only the selected characters.

You know what? I'm really sick of saying "either the Artistic Text tool or the Paragraph Text tool." And I'll bet you're just as sick of reading it. When you're doing the stuff I discuss in the rest of this chapter, it doesn't matter which tool you use, so I'm just going to say "a text tool," which means either of the tools; or "the text tools," which means both of them; or "the elbow wrench," which means neither of them.

Selecting with a text tool

Using the text tools is the preferred method for selecting text because it enables you to make selective changes. For example, you can make a single word **bold** or a passage of text *italic.* The following items explain how to use a text tool to select type in any kind of text block:

- ✔ Drag over the characters that you want to select. To show that the characters are selected, CorelDraw *highlights* the characters by setting them against a gray background. Generally, you'll use this technique to select type within a single text block. However, you can drag across type in linked text blocks, as demonstrated in Figure 10-10.

- ✔ Double-click on a word to select the word.

- ✔ Ctrl+click on a word to select the entire sentence.

- ✔ Click to set the insertion marker at one end of the text you want to select. Then Shift+click at the other end of the desired selection. CorelDraw selects all text between the click and Shift+click. For example, to select the highlighted text in Figure 10-10, I could have clicked between the *c* and *h* in *Achilles* and then Shift+clicked between the words *on* and *yow* in the second text block.

- ✔ Press the Shift key in tandem with the left- or right-arrow key to select one character at a time. Press Shift plus the up- or down-arrow key to select whole lines.

- ✔ Press Shift and Ctrl along with the left- or right-arrow key to select whole words at a time.

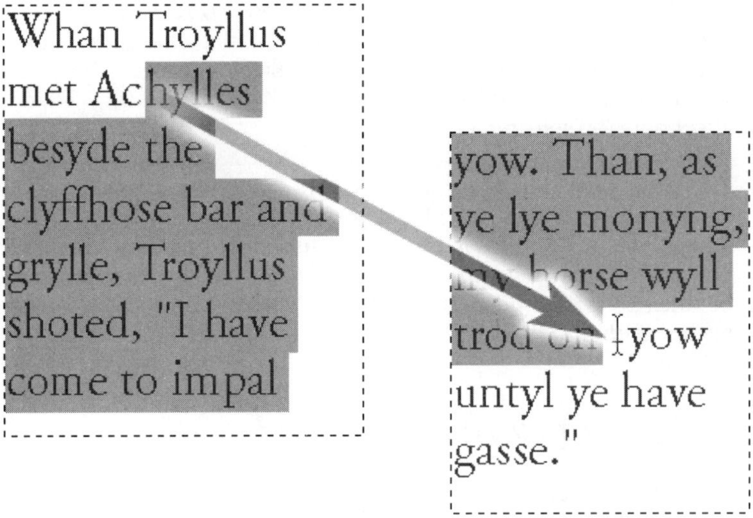

Figure 10-10:
Drag with a text tool to select type in linked text blocks.

Whan Troyllus met Achylles besyde the clyffhose bar and grylle, Troyllus shoted, "I have come to impal yow. Than, as ye lye monyng, my horse wyll trod on yow untyl ye have gasse."

Converting from artistic to paragraph and vice versa

Here's the scenario: You create a block of artistic or paragraph text, but then it occurs to you that you made the wrong choice. No problem. You can easily convert one variety of text to the other by selecting the text with a text tool and transferring it to a new text block via the Clipboard.

To convert paragraph text to artistic text, follow these steps:

1. **With a text tool, select the text you want to convert.**

   You can use either text tool for this purpose.

2. **Press Ctrl+C (or choose Edit⇨Copy).**

   CorelDraw copies the text to the Clipboard.

3. **Press F8 to select the Artistic Text tool.**

4. **Click with the cursor somewhere inside the drawing.**

   Draw creates a new artistic text block.

5. **Press Ctrl+V (or choose Edit⇨Paste).**

   CorelDraw pastes the text into the artistic text block. Now you can perform all those amazing special effects that are only applicable to artistic text, as explained in Chapter 11.

You say you don't want artistic text? You want to be able to create long passages that flow between multiple linked text blocks? Well then, to convert artistic text to paragraph text, take the same steps as before, only opposite-wise:

1. **Use a text tool to select the text you want to convert.**

   Again, you can use either text tool. But don't select the text with the Arrow tool.

2. **Press Ctrl+C.**

   The text hightails it to the Clipboard.

3. **Press Shift+F8 to select the Paragraph Text tool.**

4. **Drag to create a new text block.**

   Or click inside an existing text block to set the location of the insertion marker.

5. **Press Ctrl+V.**

   CorelDraw pastes the heretofore artistic text into the block of paragraph text.

Okay, Now You Can Format

After you select some text to play around with, you're ready to assign formatting attributes. Now, a lot of folks change the typeface and other stuff by using the Character Attributes dialog box, which you get to by pressing Ctrl+T or choosing Text⇨Character. But I'm going to ignore that option because there are better ways. By using the Text toolbar or the Text panel of the Object Properties dialog box — both shown in Figure 10-11 — you can get access to all essential formatting functions without a lot of flopping about or monkeying around, two activities which are below such a rarefied life form as you.

✔ To display the Text toolbar, right-click on the gray area in the toolbox to display a pop-up menu. Then select the Text option.

✔ To display the Text panel of the Object Properties dialog box, right-click on the selected text. After the pop-up menu appears, select the Properties option at the end of the menu. No need to click on the Text tab; CorelDraw is smart enough to display the Text panel without any additional guidance.

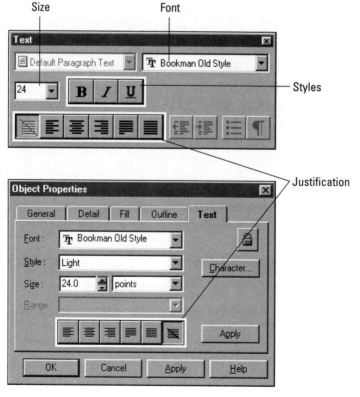

Figure 10-11: Both the Text toolbar (top) and the Text panel of the Object Properties dialog box (bottom) offer all the primo formatting options.

In either toolbar or dialog box, you can change the typeface, type style, type size, and justification. I describe each of these formatting attributes in the following sections.

Selecting a typeface

Changing the typeface is your number-one method for controlling the appearance of your text. Just in case you're wondering what I'm talking about, a *typeface* is a uniquely stylized alphabet. The idea is that an *a* in one typeface looks different from the *a* in another typeface.

Some folks refer to typefaces as *fonts*. Back in the old days — up until as recently as 20 years ago — each letter was printed using a separate chunk of metal, and all the pieces of metal for one typeface were stored in a container called a *font*. (This use of the word, incidentally, is based on the French word *fonte*, which means a casting, as in type casting. It has nothing to do with the baptismal font — you know, one of those basins that holds holy water — which is based on the Latin word *fontis*, which means spring. Dang, this is interesting stuff!)

CorelDraw includes on CD-ROM about 50 quintillion fonts that you can install into Windows (see the appendix for instructions). You can also use any PostScript or TrueType font that you've installed into Windows. If you don't know what PostScript and TrueType are, read the upcoming Technical Stuff sidebar or, better yet, don't worry about it.

To change the font of the selected text, select a typeface from the right-hand pop-up menu in the Text toolbar. Or select a typeface from the Font pop-up menu in the Object Properties dialog box and then click on the Apply button in the bottom-right corner of the Text panel.

If you want to preview what a font will look like before you apply it, do this:

1. **Click on the name of the typeface in either the toolbar or the dialog box.**

   Or click on the down pointing arrowhead to the right of the typeface name. The pop-up menu appears. CorelDraw also displays a preview box to the side of the pop-up menu, as shown in Figure 10-12.

2. **Move the cursor or press the down- and up-arrow keys to scroll through the list.**

   CorelDraw updates the preview box to show the selected typeface.

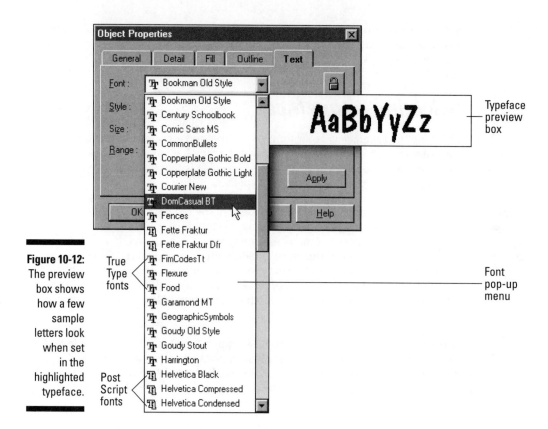

Figure 10-12:
The preview
box shows
how a few
sample
letters look
when set
in the
highlighted
typeface.

True
Type
fonts

Post
Script
fonts

Typeface
preview
box

Font
pop-up
menu

Changing the type style

Most typefaces offer four *type styles:* plain, *italic,* **bold,** and ***bold italic.*** You can
assign one of these styles by selecting the B or I button in the Text toolbar.
(You can also click on the U button to underline the text.) Or select an option
from the Style pop-up menu in the Object Properties dialog box and click on the
Apply button.

The typeface rivalry that isn't worth knowing about

You might not associate something as fundamental as font technology with a brand name, but the truth is, *everything* has a brand name. *Billy Joel* is a registered trademark, for crying out loud. So if your last name is Joel, don't even *think* about naming your kid Billy.

Anyway, the two big brands in the world of digital typography are PostScript and TrueType. Developed by Adobe Systems — the folks who created the well-known image-editing program Photoshop — the *PostScript font format* is the professional printing standard. Hewlett-Packard and several other printer manufacturers offer support for PostScript, as do all major brands of typesetters and other mega-expensive gadgets. Adobe also sells a Windows font manager called ATM (Adobe Type Manager) that lets you print PostScript fonts to non-PostScript printers.

Microsoft and Apple were sick of Adobe having this monopoly in the font market. So they got together and co-developed the *TrueType font format,* which at the time seemed about as likely as the United States and Russia joining forces right after the Bay of Pigs to organize a worldwide polo tournament.

But they pulled it off, and Microsoft has amassed its 17th fortune selling TrueType fonts to eager consumers. Windows 95 offers built-in support for TrueType and can print TrueType fonts to nearly any model of printer. TrueType has been such a success, in fact, that Corel converted its entire 50 quintillion-font library to the TrueType format.

Windows 95 even shows you which kind of font you're about to apply. Two *Ts* before a typeface name in one of the font pop-up menus indicate a TrueType font. An outlined *T1* indicates a PostScript font. (T1 is short for *Type 1,* which is a PostScript font variation.) You can see examples of both types of fonts back in Figure 10-12.

Enlarging or reducing the type size

Remember my discussion of line widths back in Chapter 7? I said that line widths are measured in *points* and that one point is equal to $1/72$ of an inch. Well, type is also measured in points. After all, type is generally pretty dinky. Even monster-big headlines in supermarket tabloids — you know, like "England Frets as Princess Di Dons Unbecoming Swimsuit" or "Aliens Ate My Sweetheart, Then Complained about Taste" — don't get much bigger than an inch tall. For this reason, points are an ideal and time-honored unit of measure among typographers, layout artists, and others who do their best to try to attract your attention to the written word.

Type is measured from the bottommost point on a lowercase *g* to the tippy-topmost peak of a lowercase *b.* (Lowercase letters such as *b, d, k,* and others are generally taller than capital letters.) If you're familiar with typewriter terminology, elite type is 10 points tall — roughly the size of the type you're currently reading — while pica type is 12 points tall.

- ✔ To change the type size, enter any value between 0 (far too small) and 3,000 points (42 inches!) into the left-hand option box in the Text toolbar.

- ✔ Or enter a value into the Size option box in the Object Properties dialog box. If you prefer to use inches or some other nontraditional unit of measure, you can choose it from the pop-up menu to the right of the Size option box. Then click on the Apply button to see how it looks.

Mucking about with the justification

The row of buttons at the bottom of both the Text toolbar and the Text panel of the Object Properties dialog box control the alignment of the lines of type in a text block. This is known as the *justification* — as in, "We need no justification to call this what we please." Starting with the leftmost button in the dialog box and moving to the right, the justification buttons (labeled back in Figure 10-11) work as follows:

- ✔ The Left Justification button aligns the left sides of all lines of text in a text block. The text in this book, for example, is left justified.

- ✔ The Center Justification button centers all lines of type within the text block.

- ✔ The Right Justification button aligns the right sides of all lines of text.

- ✔ The Full Justification button aligns both the left and right sides of the text. As you can see in the last example of Figure 10-13, CorelDraw has to increase the horizontal space between characters and words to make this happen. This option is applicable to paragraph text only.

- ✔ Click on the Forced Justification button to align the left and right edges of *all* lines of type, including the last line. Also applicable exclusively to paragraph text, this option is useful for stretching out a single line of text across the full width of a text block.

- ✔ The No Justification button doesn't work. I know, that's a terrible thing to say, but it's true. Usually, this option produces the same effect as the Left Justification button. But when you get into the more complicated techniques described in the next chapter, it can wreak havoc on your text. The technical support guy I talked to claimed that he's never gotten a call about this option in his career. So not only does it not work, nobody cares about it. Good feature.

Figure 10-13 shows the results of applying the left, center, right, and full justification options. The gray areas in back of the text represent the text blocks.

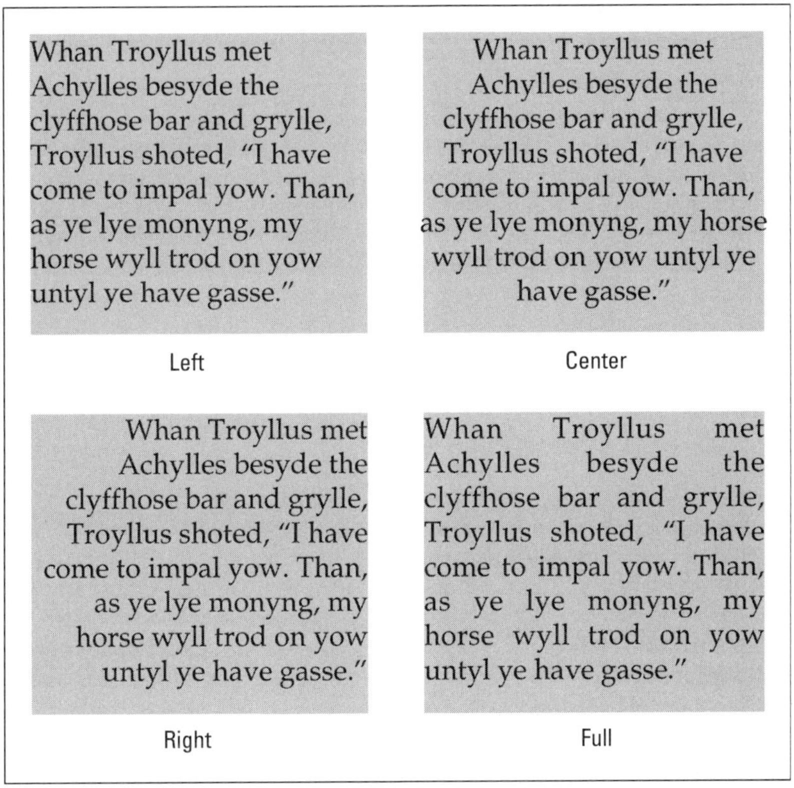

Whan Troyllus met
Achylles besyde the
clyffhose bar and grylle,
Troyllus shoted, "I have
come to impal yow. Than,
as ye lye monyng, my
horse wyll trod on yow
untyl ye have gasse."

Left

Whan Troyllus met
Achylles besyde the
clyffhose bar and grylle,
Troyllus shoted, "I have
come to impal yow. Than,
as ye lye monyng, my horse
wyll trod on yow untyl ye
have gasse."

Center

Whan Troyllus met
Achylles besyde the
clyffhose bar and grylle,
Troyllus shoted, "I have
come to impal yow. Than,
as ye lye monyng, my
horse wyll trod on yow
untyl ye have gasse."

Right

Whan   Troyllus   met
Achylles   besyde   the
clyffhose bar and grylle,
Troyllus shoted, "I have
come to impal yow. Than,
as ye lye monyng, my
horse wyll trod on yow
untyl ye have gasse."

Full

Figure 10-13:
The primary
justification
options
offered by
CorelDraw.

When applied to artistic text, the justification options actually change the location of the text block on the page. If you select the Right Justification button, for example, the right side of the text block scoots over to where the left side of the text block used to be.

Please Check Your Spelling

Granted, CorelDraw isn't a word processor. But that doesn't mean that you want to look stupid because you can't spell *leptodactylous* (which, by the way, means that you have slender toes). For this reason, CorelDraw can check and help you correct your spelling. Okay, so it doesn't know how to spell *leptodactylous* any better than you do. But it does know several thousand common words, and you can teach it to spell *leptodactylous* if you so desire.

Formatting options you have my permission to ignore

In addition to those formatting attributes discussed earlier in this chapter, CorelDraw offers a mess of other formatting options that you may find interesting depending on, well, your level of interest. You can access these options by clicking on the Character, Paragraph, and Columns buttons in the Object Properties dialog box. (The Paragraph and Columns buttons are available only if a paragraph text block is selected, which is why they're not shown in Figure 10-11.)

In very general terms, these options work as follows:

✔ Select a few characters of text and click on the Character button to access options that affect selected characters of text. You can apply underlines and other kinds of lines to characters of text, create superscript or subscript type, or capitalize letters. You can also change the amount of horizontal space between neighboring letters and the amount of vertical space between lines of type. Luckily, you can more conveniently change spacing using the Shape tool, as discussed in the next chapter.

✔ Click on the Paragraph button to be completely overwhelmed by the options in the multiple-panel Paragraph dialog box. The first panel, Spacing, mostly repeats options you can get to by clicking on the Character button. The only unique option in the Spacing panel is the Automatic Hyphenation check box. Select this option, and CorelDraw automatically hyphenates long words so that they better fill the width of a text block. All options affect all text in any selected or partially selected paragraphs.

✔ Switch to the Tabs panel to position tab stops as you would on a typewriter. You need to use these options only if you want to create a table of information — for example, a price list. Switch to the Indents panel to indent text inside a text block.

✔ Switch to the Effects panel to add a symbol to the beginning of a paragraph, which is useful for adding fancy bullets to the beginning of paragraphs in lists (like this one).

✔ Leave the Paragraph dialog box and click on the Columns button to divide the text in the active text block into multiple columns. Believe me, these options produce static results and are more work than they're worth. It's easier to create your own columns by drawing blocks of text, as explained in the "How to Flow Text between Multiple Blocks" section earlier in this chapter.

Correcting your work

Here's how to check the spelling of your document:

1. Choose Text⇨Proofreading⇨Spelling.

Or right-click on a text block with one of the text tools and select Check Spelling from the pop-up menu. Or better still, just press Ctrl+F12.

Whichever method you use, CorelDraw begins checking the words in your document. When it comes to the first bad word, up comes the Spell Checking dialog box, shown in Figure 10-14. The misspelled word appears selected inside the Sentence option box. A series of alternate spellings appear in the Change To list.

2. Select an alternative from the Change To list.

In Figure 10-14, Draw has suggested such humorless replacements as *Wan* and *When.*

If the Change To list does not offer a suitable alternative, you can simply select the offending word inside the Sentence option box and enter your own spelling. Then proceed to Step 3.

3. Click on the Change button.

CorelDraw replaces your misspelled word with the alternative you selected from the scrolling list. The program automatically sets about searching for the next misspelling.

4. Repeat Steps 2 and 3.

Figure 10-14:
CorelDraw
finds many
spelling
problems
in my
historically
authentic
Old English
text.

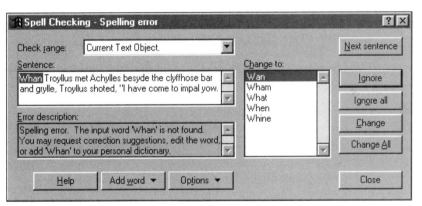

Correcting CorelDraw

The preceding section explains how you use the Spell Checking dialog box if your word is indeed misspelled. But what if your word is correct and CorelDraw is the one with a spelling problem? Take my Old English text, for example. It's 100 percent historically authentic, guaranteed by Lloyd's of London. Yet CorelDraw questions nearly every word. Just goes to show you how much things have changed since the 15th century, or whenever it was that I wrote the text.

Sometimes, you have to teach Draw how to spell. If your word is spelled correctly, you can add it to the dictionary as follows:

1. **Click on the Options button at the bottom of the Spell Checking dialog box.**

   The button responds by displaying a pop-up menu.

2. **Select the Create New Dictionary option.**

   It's right there at the bottom of the pop-up menu.

3. **Enter a name for your dictionary.**

4. **Press Enter to create the dictionary.**

   You only have to perform these first four steps the very first time you teach CorelDraw how to spell. From then on, you can keep adding words to this same dictionary.

5. **Click on the Add Word button.**

   Then select your dictionary from the pop-up menu. Draw adds the word to the dictionary and sets about hunting down the next misspelling.

Using the other spelling options

That takes care of most of the options in the Spell Checking dialog box. But I did miss a few, which are explained in the following list:

✔ If you don't want to correct a word and you don't want to add it to the dictionary — you just want CorelDraw to skip the word and continue checking the rest of the text — click on the Ignore button.

✔ To make Draw ignore all occurrences of a word throughout the current spelling session, click on the Ignore All button.

✔ If you're the type who misspells consistently, click on the Change All button to replace all occurrences of a particular misspelling with the selected correction.

✔ Click on the Next Sentence button to skip a sentence and move on to the next one.

✔ Click on the Close button to stop looking for misspellings and close the dialog box. Then press Enter to get that stupid "Spell Checking is complete" message out of your face. ("I know it's complete, you imbecile program — I'm the one who told you to bag it!")

Shortcut to Typographic Happiness

If you want, you can train CorelDraw to fix your most egregious errors as you make them — without ever once bringing up the Spell Checking dialog box. To use this feature, choose Text⇨Type Assist, which displays the dialog box in Figure 10-15. The five significant options in this dialog box work as follows:

✔ Select the first check box to automatically capitalize any word that follows a period, even if you enter the letter without pressing Shift. I heartily recommend this option.

✔ In the world of professional typography, quote marks curl around the text. But when you enter a quote from your keyboard, you get two boring, straight lines. Those lines aren't quotes, they're ditto marks. To turn your dreadful dittos into beautiful quotes, select the second check box.

✔ Select the third check box to correct any two capital letters in a row. For example, *THe* would become *The.* I don't like this option because it messes with words that are supposed to be formatted in all capital letters. But select it according to your own taste.

✔ If you forget to capitalize the names of days, select the fourth option. Too bad it doesn't correct the names of months and other proper nouns as well.

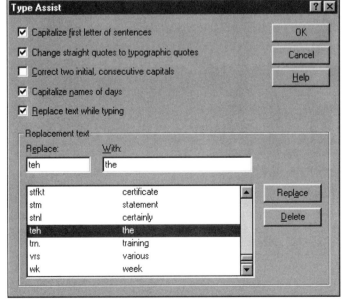

Figure 10-15: Select check boxes to make CorelDraw automatically correct your text as you type it.

✔ The last check box — Replace Text While Typing — replaces abbreviations with spelled-out words. If you type *cont.*, for example, CorelDraw replaces it with *continue*. If you type *3/4*, Draw replaces it with the proper fraction symbol ³/₄.

If you don't like the way CorelDraw replaces abbreviations — you might prefer that it swap *cont.* with the past tense, *continued*, for example — select an abbreviation from the scrolling list, modify the word in the With option box, and click on the Replace button.

You can also make Type Assist correct your spelling. Suppose that you constantly misspell the word *the* as *teh*. Just enter **teh** into the Replace option box, enter **the** into the With option box, and click on the Add button. From then on, CorelDraw corrects your spelling of *teh* on the fly.

Word Vendor

If you're having problems thinking of a word — for example, what's that word... you know, the one that means you have skinny toes? — you can tap into CorelDraw's Thesaurus. You use it like this:

1. **Select the word for which you want a synonym.**

   For example, I selected the word *trod* in the block of Old English prose I presented earlier in this chapter. I decided that *trod* is just too gauche.

2. **Choose Text⇨Thesaurus.**

   The Thesaurus dialog box heaves into view, as shown in Figure 10-16.

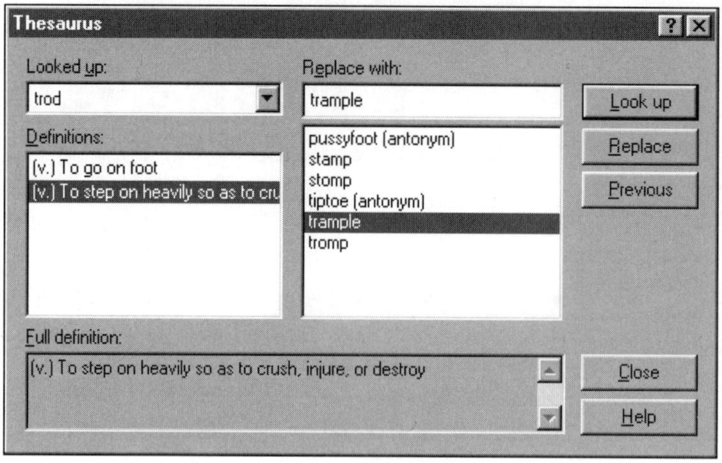

Figure 10-16:
The Thesaurus can make you look like you have half a brain.

Thesaurus	? ✕
Looked up: trod ▼	**Replace with:** trample
	Look up
Definitions: (v.) To go on foot / (v.) To step on heavily so as to cru	pussyfoot (antonym) / stamp / stomp / tiptoe (antonym) / **trample** / tromp
	Replace
	Previous
Full definition: (v.) To step on heavily so as to crush, injure, or destroy	Close
	Help

3. **If the word has multiple meanings, select your meaning from the <u>D</u>efinitions list.**

   I'm thinking of the crush-and-destroy meaning.

4. **Select the desired substitute from the R<u>e</u>place With list.**

   Ah, yes, *trample,* that's much classier.

5. **Click on the <u>R</u>eplace button.**

   CorelDraw closes the dialog box and replaces the selected word.

A Different Kind of Alphabet

The only kind of text I haven't yet described is symbols. Choose <u>T</u>ools⇨Sym<u>b</u>ols or press Ctrl+F11 to display the Symbols roll-up shown in Figure 10-17. This roll-up offers access to a variety of simple pictures that you can use to accent or enhance a drawing. You can even combine symbols to create drawings in and of themselves.

"Little pictures?" you're probably thinking. "Wait a minute. Pictures don't constitute text. What's going on here?" Hey, take it easy. Your problem is that you're used to a Western-style alphabet, in which abstract letters stand for sounds — the same way that a dollar bill stands for a piece of gold approximately the size of a single-celled microorganism. Letters are merely metaphors for real communication.

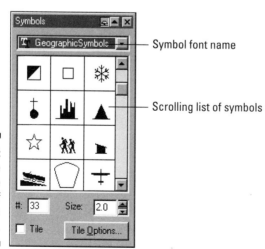

Figure 10-17: Symbols are like alphabets of modern hieroglyphs.

— Symbol font name

— Scrolling list of symbols

But try thinking Eastern. Think hieroglyphics. Think kanji. These are bazillion-character alphabets in which each character represents a word or phrase. Similarly, CorelDraw's symbol library is a big alphabet. If you want to say "chair," for example, show a chair.

To select a symbol, do these things:

1. **Press Ctrl+F11.**

   Or choose Tools⇨Symbols. Behold the Symbols roll-up, front and center.

2. **Select a symbol category from the pop-up menu at the top of the roll-up.**

   The categories are actually fonts that CorelDraw recognizes as containing something other than standard letters, numbers, and punctuation.

3. **Select a symbol from the scrolling list.**

   No need to guess which key to press (as you would if you just applied one of these wacky symbol fonts to a block of text). CorelDraw shows you every single wacky character in the font.

4. **Enter the size of the symbol into the Size option box.**

   The size is measured in the same unit displayed in the rulers, which is most likely inches.

5. **Drag the symbol into the drawing area.**

   No need to mess around with the Tile option. It just repeats the symbol over and over inside a portion of your drawing, like some dreadful electronic wallpaper.

To view more symbols at a time, drag one of the corners of the roll-up.

You can edit symbols in the same way you edit free-form paths, as described in Chapter 5. You can also fill and outline symbols as described in Chapter 7, duplicate symbols as described in Chapter 8, and transform symbols as discussed in Chapter 9. Come to think of it, symbols may be drawings after all.

Chapter 11
Mr. Typographer's Wild Ride

. . . .

. . . .

*I*magine that you're a character of text. An *H*, for example. Or a *P*. It's not important. Be a *S* if you want. So far, you've been riding through CorelDraw's functions on an even keel. Sometimes you wrap to the next line of type, and other times you get poured into a different text block. But ultimately, your life is about as exciting as a traffic jam. There are characters above and below you; you even have a few riding your rear end. It's no fun being a character in a standard text block.

But then one day, you rub shoulders with a street-wise character, like an *E* or an *S* — you know, some character that really gets around — and it tells you about a whole world of possibilities you haven't yet explored. You can play bumper cars, ride loop-de-loop roller coasters, even stretch yourself into completely different shapes and forms. It's one big amusement park for text!

This chapter is your golden admission ticket. Have a blast.

Learning the Rules of the Park

Before I stamp your hand and let you into the park, a word of caution is in order. Just as too many rides on the Tilt-A-Whirl can make you hurl, too many wild effects can leave a block of text looking a little bent out of shape. The trick is to apply text effects conservatively and creatively.

If you're not sure how an effect will go over, show it to a few friends. Ask them to read your text. If they read it easily and hand the page back to you, you know that you hit the mark. If they say, "How did you *make* this?" the effect may be a little overly dramatic, but it's probably still acceptable. If they have trouble reading the text or if they say, "How did you make *this*?" — in the same way they might say, "What did I just *step* in?" — your effect very likely overwhelms the page and is therefore unacceptable.

Then again, I don't want to dampen your spirit of enthusiasm and exploration. Use moderation in all things, including moderation, right? So you make yourself sick on the Tilt-A-Whirl. It's part of growing up. So your first few pages look like run-amuck advertisements for furniture warehouses. It's part of learning the craft.

And if some blue-blood designer looks at your work and exclaims, "Gad, this page! Oh, how it frightens me! Tell me who let you near the computer, and I'll go slap that person briskly!" you can retort, "Well, at least my text has more fun than yours." That's one way to get fired, anyway.

Playing Bumper Cars

You know that you can drag points and handles with the Shape tool. Well, this basic functionality of the Shape tool permeates all facets of CorelDraw, including text. If you select the Shape tool (or press F10) and click on a text block, you see three new varieties of nodes and handles, as shown in Figure 11-1. These nodes and handles appear whether you click on a block of artistic text or paragraph text. They enable you to change the location of individual characters and increase or decrease the amount of space between characters and lines of text.

Selecting and dragging text nodes

Text nodes enable you to change the locations of individual characters in a text block. You can slightly nudge the characters to adjust the amount of horizontal spacing, or you can drag a character several inches away from its text block just to show it who's boss.

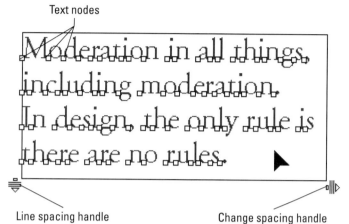

Text nodes

Figure 11-1:
Click on a
text block
with the
Shape tool
to display
these nodes
and
handles.

Line spacing handle   Change spacing handle

✔ Each text node is associated with the character directly on its right. Click on a node to select it and its character. Black nodes are selected; white nodes are not.

✔ To select multiple nodes at a time, drag with the Shape tool to draw a marquee (dotted outline) around the nodes. You can also Shift+click on a text node to add it to the selection.

✔ If you select a few too many nodes in the process of marqueeing, Shift+click on the ones you want to deselect.

✔ Drag a selected text node to reposition all selected characters. In Figure 11-2, for example, I selected every other letter in the word *Moderation* and dragged the selected node associated with the *n*.

Figure 11-2:
Dragging
several
selected
characters
with the
Shape tool
(top) and the
outcome of
the drag
(bottom).

Moderation

Moderation

- ✔ Ctrl+drag nodes to move the letters along the current line of type.

- ✔ Use the arrow keys to nudge selected characters without fussing with your mouse. By default, each keystroke moves the selected characters @bf 1/10 inch. You can change this distance by pressing Ctrl+J (Tools⇨Options) and changing the Nudge value (as explained in the "Incremental shifts" section of Chapter 6).

- ✔ To return a single character to its original position, select its node and choose Text⇨Straighten Text. To undo all changes to an entire text block, select the text with the Arrow tool and choose the Straighten Text command.

Kern, kern, the baffling term

You can drag entire lines to offset lines of type, drag whole words, or just create crazy text blocks by dragging individual characters six ways to Sunday, whatever that means. But the most practical reason for dragging nodes is to adjust the amount of horizontal space between individual characters, a process known as *kerning*.

In Webster's Second Edition — the sacred volume that editors swear by (or should it be "by which editors swear"?) — *kern* is defined as the portion of a letter such as *f* that sticks out from the stem. Those nutty lexicographers say that the term is based on the French word *carne,* which means a projecting angle.

Now, I don't know about you, but where I come from: A) we don't go around assigning words to projecting angles and B) *kern* means to smush two letters closer together so that they look as snug as kernels of corn on the cob. Of course, I don't have any Ivy League degree and I don't wear any fancy hat with a tassel hanging off it, but I'm pretty sure them Webster fellers are full of beans.

Not like *you* care. You're still trying to figure out what I'm talking about. So here goes: Consider the character combination *AV.* It comes up in conversation about as often as the French word *carne,* but it demonstrates a point. The right side of the letter *A* and the left side of the character *V* both slope in the same direction. So when the two letters appear next to each other, a perceptible gap may form, as shown in Figure 11-3. Though the *A* and the *V* in *AVERY* aren't any farther away from each other than the *V* and the *E,* the *E* and the *R,* and so on, they appear more spread out because of their similar slopes.

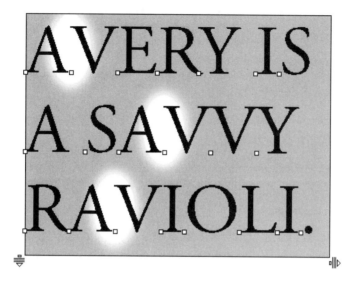

Figure 11-3:
I wish I had a
dime for every
time we
taunted Avery
with this one.

To tighten the spacing, I first chose Tools⇨Options and reduced the Nudge
value to 0.01 inch — a value that's significantly better suited to the art of fine-
tuning text. After pressing Enter to return to the drawing area, I used the Shape
tool to select the *V*s as well as all the letters to the right of the *V*s. Then I
pressed the left-arrow key a couple of times. (Selecting the letters to the right of
the *V*s ensured that I didn't widen the spacing between any *V* and the letter that
follows it.) Figure 11-4 shows the result of kerning the *A*s and *V*s. I also kerned a
few other letters for good measure. (The nodes of these letters are selected in
the figure.)

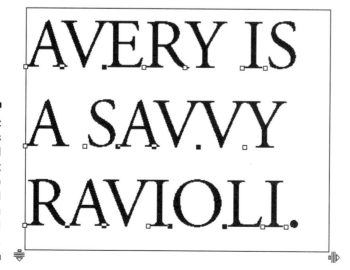

Figure 11-4:
Avery feels
vindicated
now that
those who
would
malign him
have kerned
their ways.

As it turns out, CorelDraw 6 is pretty darn good at kerning certain letter combinations automatically. It handles the classic *AV* combination with as little thought as you and I typically devote to blinking. Even so, I find myself kerning letters just about every time I create them, particularly in headlines and other prominent text blocks. You can trust Draw to do a good job, but only you can make text picture-perfect.

Changing overall spacing

To recap, dragging text nodes changes the space between selected characters only. If you want to evenly adjust the spacing between *all* characters in a text block, you need to drag one of the two spacing handles, labeled back in Figure 11-1.

✔ Drag the character spacing handle (located on the right side of the text block) to change the amount of horizontal space between all characters in the text block, as in the first example of Figure 11-5.

If the message *Snap to Grid* appears in the lower-left corner of the status bar, press Ctrl+Y (or choose Layout⇨Snap to Grid) to turn the grid off. With the grid off, you can drag the spacing handles anywhere you like.

✔ Ctrl+drag the character spacing handle to change the size of the spaces between all words in the text block, as in the second example of Figure 11-5.

Moderation in all
things, including
moderation.
In design, the only

↔— Drag

Figure 11-5:
The results
of dragging
and
Ctrl+dragging
the
character
spacing
handle.

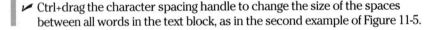

Moderation in all
things, including
moderation.
In design, the only

↔— Ctrl+drag

TIP

✔ Drag the line spacing handle (located on the left side of the text block) to adjust the amount of vertical space between all lines of type, except those that are separated by a carriage return. In other words, lines in the same paragraph are affected, but neighboring lines in different paragraphs are not, as the first example in Figure 11-6 shows.

✔ Ctrl+drag the line spacing handle to change the amount of vertical space between different paragraphs, as in the second example of Figure 11-6. This tip doesn't work with artistic text because there are no paragraphs in artistic text.

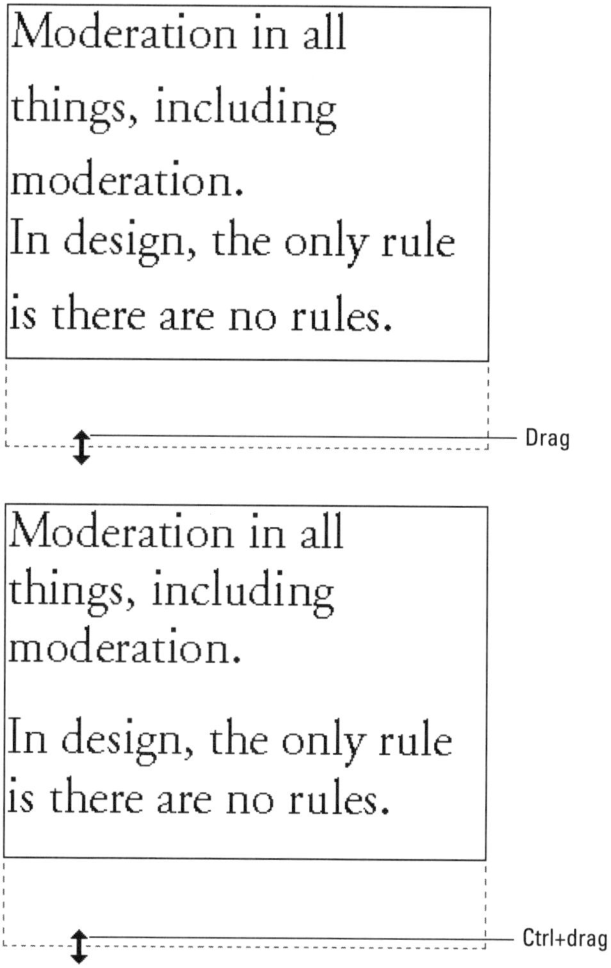

Moderation in all

things, including

moderation.
In design, the only rule

is there are no rules.

— Drag

Moderation in all
things, including
moderation.

Figure 11-6:
Here's what
happens
when you
drag and
Ctrl+drag
the line
spacing
handle.

In design, the only rule
is there are no rules.

— Ctrl+drag

Notice that dragging a spacing handle has no effect on the size of a block of paragraph text. The block itself remains the same size, and the newly spaced characters reflow to fit inside it.

Also, changes you make to a text block affect the characters in that text block only. If the text block is linked to another text block, some reformatted characters may flow into the linked text block, but the characters that originally occupied the linked text block remain unchanged.

Riding the Roller Coaster

CorelDraw calls this feature *fitting text to a path*. But I call it giving your text a ride on the roller coaster. After all, when your text is fit to a path, it appears to be having the time of its life, as Figure 11-7 clearly illustrates.

As shown in the top example of Figure 11-7, text normally sits on an imaginary flat line. This line is called the *baseline*. Not a four-string bass line, more like a home-run baseline. Anyway, you can substitute an oval or free-form path for the baseline like so:

1. Select a block of artistic text with the Arrow tool.

This feature is applicable only to artistic text. You cannot fit paragraph text to a path.

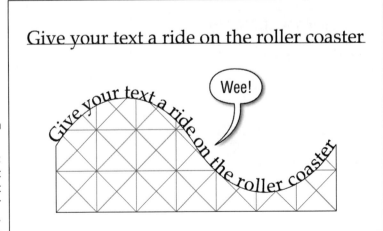

Figure 11-7:
For text, it doesn't get any better than this.

2. Shift+click on a path.

CorelDraw adds the path to the selection. Circles, ovals, and gradually curving paths work best, but any path is acceptable.

3. Choose Te_x_t⇨Fit _T_ext to Path.

Or just press Ctrl+F. The Fit Text To Path roll-up appears. If the selected path is a free-form path, the roll-up looks like the left example in Figure 11-8. If the selected path is a rectangle, oval, or polygon, the roll-up appears as shown on the right side of the figure.

4. Select the desired options.

I describe them all momentarily. For now, you don't need to select anything. You can just accept the default settings and go on.

5. Click on the Apply button.

Watch the baseline adhere to that path. Those little characters are probably losing their lunches (in a good way, of course).

6. If the text doesn't attach to the path the way you had anticipated, select the Place On Other Side check box and again click on the Apply button.

The text switches to the opposite side of the path and flows in the opposite direction.

The Fit Text To Path roll-up offers either three pop-up menus or two pop-up menus and a group of buttons, depending on the kind of path you're using. The options determine the orientation of characters on a path, the vertical alignment of the text, and the horizontal alignment. The following sections explain how they work.

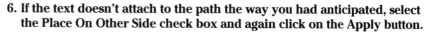

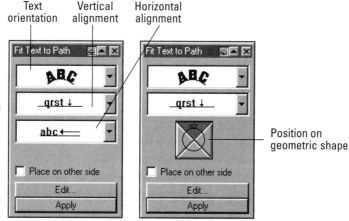

Text orientation   Vertical alignment   Horizontal alignment

Position on geometric shape

Figure 11-8:
Two variations on the Fit Text To Path roll-up.

Orienting text on a path

The first pop-up menu offers you the choice of rotating characters along the path, skewing them horizontally or vertically, or none of the above. Figure 11-9 shows the effects of each of the options on the text from Figure 11-7, in the same order that the options appear in the pop-up menu.

Want my *real* opinion? All right, here goes:

✔ The rotate characters option is the most useful of the four, which is probably why it's the default setting. When in doubt, stick with this option.

✔ The vertical skew option is also very useful, as long as your path doesn't have any super-steep vertical inclines. Along the left and right sides of a circle, for example, characters skew into nothingness.

Figure 11-9:
The effects of the four orientation options, shown in the same order that they appear in the first pop-up menu of the Fit Text To Path roll-up.

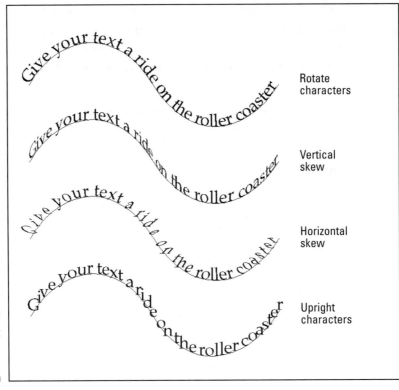

Rotate characters

Vertical skew

Horizontal skew

Upright characters

✔ The horizontal skew option is set up backwards, so that letters skew against the path instead of with it. The *G* at the beginning of the text in Figure 11-9, for example, should skew to the right, into the path — not to the left, away from it. Use this option only if you want to illicit comments like, "Gee, this is weird," or, "Maybe we should go back to typewriters."

✔ The upright characters option is so ugly, it makes the horizontal skew option look like a good idea.

Changing the vertical alignment

The vertical alignment pop-up menu lets you change the vertical positioning of characters with respect to the path. The options work as follows (I've listed them in the order they appear in the menu):

✔ The first option adheres the baseline of the text to the path.

✔ The next option aligns the tops of the tallest characters, called *ascenders* (*b, d, k*) to the path. The text hangs from the path like a money hangs from a tree limb, except that the text doesn't swing back and forth and scratch for ticks.

✔ The third option aligns the bottom of the hangy-down characters, called *descenders* (*g, j, p*) to the path, so that the letters balance like little tight-rope walkers.

✔ The fourth option causes the path to run smack dab through the middle of the text like a gold chain threaded through beaded pearls.

✔ Don't you just love these clever little analogies?

✔ The last option lets you drag the text anywhere you want with respect to the path. After selecting the option, drag the text with the Arrow tool. When you release, CorelDraw redraws the text at its new location, keeping an equal amount of space between the text and path.

Generally, you should stick with the default setting, which adheres text by its baseline. The one time to change this option is when you're creating text on a circle, as I describe in the section after next. (First I have to describe the horizontal alignment options or the section after next won't make sense.)

Changing the horizontal alignment

When you're attaching text to a free-form path, the Fit Text To Path roll-up offers a third pop-up menu that lets you change the horizontal alignment of text.

✔ The first option aligns the first character of text with the first point in the path. This option works like the left justification option in a normal text block.

✔ The second option centers the text on the path, just as the center justification option centers text in a normal text block.

✔ Starting to get the idea?

✔ The last option aligns the last character of text with the last point in the path. It works like — you guessed it — the right justification option in a normal text block.

When you attach text to a geometric object — rectangle, oval, or polygon — CorelDraw replaces the third pop-up menu with a square that contains four inset triangular buttons (see Figure 11-8). The buttons work like radio buttons; that is, you can only select one button at a time. You can either center the text along the top of the object, along the left or right side, or along the bottom.

Creating text on a circle

Want to see the vertical and horizontal alignment options put into use? Well, too bad, because I'm going to show you anyway.

I don't know why, but when folks want to fit text to a path, the path they usually have in mind is a circle. Ironically, however, text on a circle is the least intuitive kind of roller-coaster text you can create. If you simply attach a single text block around the entire circle, half of the text will be upside down. So you have to attach two text blocks to a single circle, one along the top of the circle and another along the bottom. Here's how it works:

1. Draw a circle.

If you need help, see Chapter 4.

2. Create two separate blocks of artistic text.

Select the Artistic Text tool by pressing F8. Click and enter text for the top of the circle and then click at another spot and enter some more text for the bottom. Oh, and keep it short.

3. Select the circle and the first block of text.

Using the Arrow tool, click on the circle and Shift+click on the text that you want to appear along the top of the circle. (From here on, everything is done with the Arrow tool.)

4. Press Ctrl+F to bring up the Fit Text To Path roll-up.

If the roll-up is already displayed, skip this step.

5. Click on the Apply button.

The default settings are fine for now. The text adheres to the top of the circle, as in Figure 11-10.

6. Click in an empty portion of the drawing area with the Arrow tool.

This step deselects everything. You have to do this so that you can select the circle independently in the next step.

7. Select the circle and the second block of text.

Click somewhere along the bottom of the circle to make sure that you select the circle only. (If you click along the top of the circle, you might select the text as well.) Then Shift+click on the second block of text.

8. Click on the bottom triangular button in the Fit Text To Path roll-up.

See the location of the arrow cursor in Figure 11-11.

9. Click on the Apply button.

The second block of text wraps around the bottom of the circle, as shown in Figure 11-11. Unfortunately, the text is upside down. To remedy this . . .

10. Select the Place On Other Side check box and click on the Apply button.

The text now appears as shown in Figure 11-12 — right-side up, but scrunched. To loosen the text up a bit, do Step 11.

11. Select the second option from the vertical alignment pop-up menu.

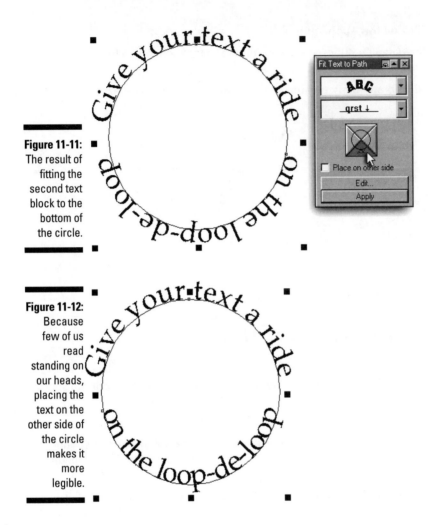

Figure 11-11:
The result of fitting the second text block to the bottom of the circle.

Figure 11-12:
Because few of us read standing on our heads, placing the text on the other side of the circle makes it more legible.

Figure 11-13 shows me in the process of selecting this option, which, as you may remember, aligns the ascenders of the characters to the circle so that the text hangs down.

12. Click on the Apply button.

Your text looks something along the lines of Figure 11-13.

13. Don't do this step.

It's unlucky. If today is Friday, shut the book and don't open it again until you've had it inspected by a psychic.

14. Click in an empty portion of the drawing area with the Arrow tool.

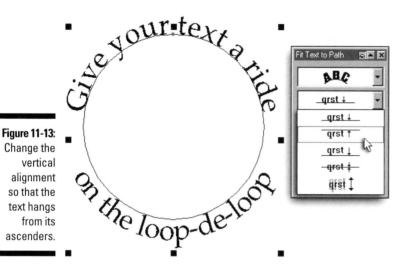

Figure 11-13:
Change the
vertical
alignment
so that the
text hangs
from its
ascenders.

Notice that the top row of type doesn't look like it's quite aligned with the bottom row. To fix this, you need to select the top text block independently of the other text. But first, to prepare for this step, you must deselect everything.

15. **Ctrl+click on a character in the top text block.**

    By Ctrl+clicking, you select the top text block along with the circle but independently of the bottom text block.

16. **Select the third option from the vertical alignment pop-up menu.**

    In Figure 11-14, you can see me selecting this option, which aligns the descenders of the characters to the circle, causing the text to walk the tightrope.

17. **For the billionth time, click on the Apply button.**

    The top text block now aligns correctly with the bottom text block. Figure 11-14 shows text on a circle as it was meant to be.

Editing text on a path

After you fit a block of artistic text to a path, it can be difficult to edit the text with either of the text tools. You *can* do it by carefully moving the text tool cursor around the letters until the cursor changes to an I-beam and then dragging across the text. But this technique requires dexterity and patience.

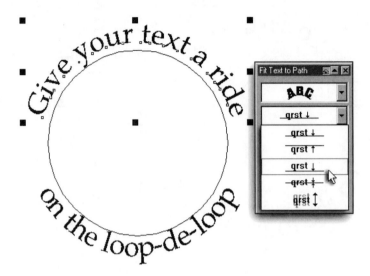

Figure 11-14:
Upper and
lower text
blocks align
perfectly
after I apply
the
descender
option.

The easier technique is to select the text independently of the path. I touched
on this technique in Step 15 of the previous section, but it bears probing in a
little more depth.

TIP

✔ Ctrl+click *on the text* — not on the path — with the Arrow tool to select
the text independently of the path. If you fit two text blocks to a path, as in
the previous example, Ctrl+click on the text twice in a row. (That's twice
in a row on the same text.)

✔ To edit the content of the text, choose Text➪Edit Text or press
Ctrl+Shift+T. CorelDraw displays a dialog box that lets you edit characters
or words. You can even change the typeface, style, and size. Click on the
OK button when you're done. (Don't press Enter; that just inserts a
carriage return.)

✔ To apply new formatting, use the Text palette or right-click on a letter of
text and choose the Properties command to display the Object Properties
dialog box, just as you do when formatting normal text. (I discuss both
palette and dialog box in Chapter 10.)

✔ Click inside the color palette at the bottom of the screen to apply color to
the text. Right-click on a color swatch to apply a color outline around each
letter of text. Click or right-click on the X swatch to delete the fill or
outline, respectively.

✔ Kern the text by selecting text nodes with the Shape tool and then dragging them or using the arrow keys to nudge them. CorelDraw automatically constrains the movement of the text to the contour of the path.

Editing the path

You can change the fill and outline of the path to which the text is attached by selecting the object and using the Fill and Pen options described back in Chapter 7. It's very straightforward — no special tricks involved. In many cases, you'll want to hide the path by selecting the object and right-clicking on the X icon in the lower-left corner of the screen.

 You can also edit the shape of the path using the Shape tool. Just be sure that you click on the path and not the text. For laughs, try dragging the top node of the circle back in Figure 11-14 to cut out a pie wedge. Without missing a beat, CorelDraw fits the text along the contours of the wedge.

Breaking it up

To detach text from a path and return it to the straight and narrow, do the following:

1. **Select the path that has text all over it.**

   Just click on the path with the Arrow tool. No Ctrl+clicking required.

2. **Choose A̲rrange⇨S̲eparate.**

   This step separates the text from the path. However, the text remains all twisty-curly.

3. **Choose Te̲xt⇨S̲traighten Text.**

   The text returns to its plain old self.

Meddling with Type

If you're interested in creating logos or other very special text, you'll want to know about one more command before I close this chapter down. The technique I'm about to describe is applicable only to artistic text.

After selecting a block of artistic text with the Arrow tool, the Shape tool, or one of the text tools, choose A̲rrange⇨Con̲vert To Curves or press Ctrl+Q. CorelDraw converts the outlines of every single character in the text block to free-form paths. An *A,* for example, ceases to be a letter of text and becomes a triangular path with a bar across it.

After you convert the characters to paths, you can edit the paths using the Arrow and Shape tools (described in Chapter 5) exactly as if you drew the characters with the Pencil tool. The top example in Figure 11-15 shows a block of standard, everyday, mild-mannered text. The second example is the same block of text after I converted it to paths and edited the holy heck out of it.

Try this technique out a few times, and you'll soon find that converted characters are as easy to integrate and edit as symbols and other pieces of clip art. Converted text serves as a great jumping off point for creating custom logos and other exciting effects.

Figure 11-15:
A line of artistic text as it appears before (top) and after (bottom) converting it to paths and editing the paths with the Shape tool.

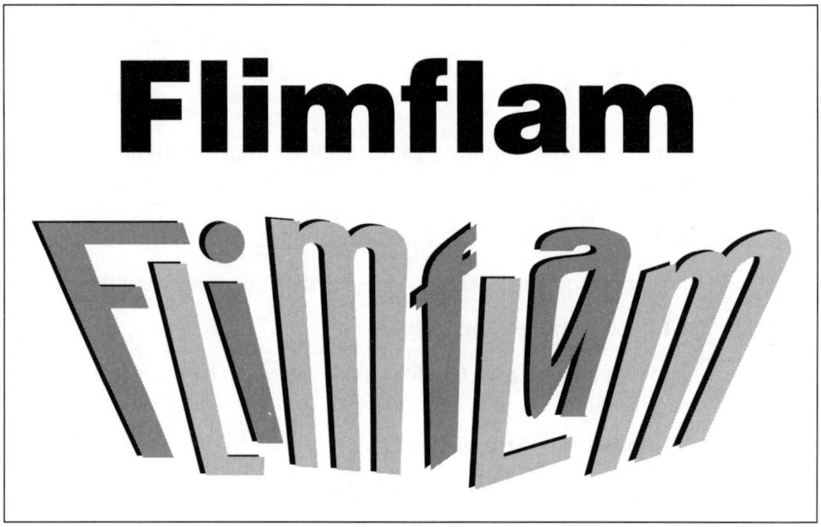

Back up your text before you make it a mess

Prior to converting a block of text to editable paths, you may want to first make a duplicate of the text by pressing Ctrl+D (Edit⇨Duplicate). Doing so will:

✔ Save the original version of the text block in case you really mess up the nodes.

✔ Keep the original handy for quick comparisons.

✔ Provide you with an extra copy of the text in case your boss wants you to change a word or two. (I can hear your boss now. "You just have to press a key, right?")

✔ Make you so happy that you'll spend the rest of your days in a state of ecstatic delirium.

The 5th Wave — By Rich Tennant

"It says,' Seth– Please see us about your idea to wrap newsletter text around company logo. Production.'"

Chapter 12

The Corner of Page and Publish

· ·

In This Chapter

▶ The biting sarcasm of trees

▶ Creating a multipage document

▶ Turning pages

▶ Deleting excess pages

▶ Pouring overflow text from one page onto another

▶ Repeating logos and other objects using the master layer

▶ Hiding master layer objects selectively

▶ Changing the page size

· ·

Desktop publishing has revolutionized the way folks churn up and spit out bits of Oregon forestry, thereby remedying the grossly inefficient way we were churning up the forests back in the 1970s. Happily, we now have more open space in which to park our cars and receive computer-created fliers that we never wanted stuck under our windshield wipers. And now you can be a part of this ever-expanding field.

Okay, that's an overstated bit of sarcasm. With the proliferation of CD-ROMs and World Wide Web pages, computers will very likely lessen our reliance on paper over time. But for now, the printed page remains the medium of choice. Furthermore, although I'd love to get on my high horse and warn you about the evils of printing, I'm obviously in no position to lecture, having myself wasted more pieces of paper than you will probably use in a lifetime. Don't get me wrong — I'm a dedicated recycler. Ecocycle loves me. I use only the cheapest bond paper available, and I print only when I absolutely have to. I don't even own a photocopier. Hey, you want to get off my case or what?

Now that I've insulted folks on both sides of the spotted owl debate, let's get down to business. This chapter and the next are devoted to output. This chapter explains how to set up your pages; Chapter 13 explains how to print them. After you finish these chapters, you'll be fully prepared to create fliers and stick them under windshield wipers with the best of them.

And remember, always use bright pink or dull yellow paper. That way, folks can spot your fliers nine miles from their cars and mentally prepare themselves to snatch the fliers up and wad them into balls at their earliest convenience.

Pages upon Pages

Unless you've read some outside sources or scoped out the Layout menu, you may assume that CorelDraw is good for creating single-page documents only. The perfect program for creating a nice, letter-sized drawing suitable for framing, but that's about it.

Not so. Though primarily a drawing program, CorelDraw lets you add as many pages to a document as you like. (As usual, I'm sure that there's a maximum number of pages, but I'll be darned if I care what it is. I mean, if you're trying to lay out an issue of *National Geographic,* you need a different piece of software. If you have in mind a newsletter, a report, or maybe a short catalog, CorelDraw will suffice.)

Adding new pages to work on

When you create a new drawing (using File⇨New⇨Document, naturally), it starts outs life as a one-page document. To make it a multipage document, you have to add pages manually, like so:

1. Choose Layout⇨Insert Page.

Or simply press either the PgUp or PgDn key. The dialog box shown in Figure 12-1 appears.

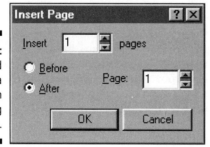

Figure 12-1: You can add pages to a drawing in this dialog box.

2. Enter the number of pages you want to add into the Insert option box.

For example, if you want to create a four-page newsletter, press 3. (You already have one of the pages.)

3. Press Enter.

CorelDraw adds the specified number of pages to your document.

Was that easy or was that easy? (Answer: That was easy.)

Adding pages bit by bit

The rest of the options in the Insert Page dialog box are of use when you find yourself adding pages sporadically rather than in one fell swoop. Suppose that you set up a four-page document and then discover that you need six pages to hold all your wonderful drawings and ideas. Using the Before and After radio buttons together with the Page option, you can tell CorelDraw exactly where to insert the pages. If you want to insert pages between pages 3 and 4, for example, you could do either of the following:

✔ Enter 3 into the Page option and select the After radio button.

✔ Enter 4 into the Page option and select the Before radio button.

Rocket science it ain't. If the pages you want to enter aren't sequential, you have to use the Layout⇨Insert Page command more than once. For example, to insert one page between pages 2 and 3 and two others between pages 3 and 4, you have to choose the Insert Page command twice, once for each sequence.

Thumbing through your pages

After you add pages to your previously single-page drawing, CorelDraw 6 displays a series of page controls near the lower-left corner of the screen, as shown in Figure 12-2. Here's how they work:

✔ Click on the first icon — the left-pointing arrow with a line next to it — to go to the first page in your document.

✔ Click on the left-pointing Page Back button to back up one page — from page 3 to page 2, for example.

✔ Click on the right-pointing Page Forward button to advance one page (for example, from page 2 to page 3).

✔ You can also change pages by pressing the PgUp and PgDn keys. The PgUp key backs up a page, and the PgDn key advances one page.

✔ Click on the Last Page button — the right-pointing arrow with a line next to it — to advance to the last page in the document.

First Page   Page Counter   Last Page

Back Page   Page Forward   Page tabs   Scroll handle

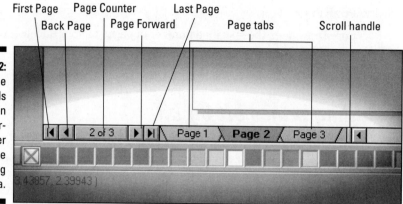

Figure 12-2:
These page
controls
appear in
the lower-
left corner
of the
drawing
area.

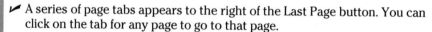

✔ When you're working on the first page in your document, the Page Back button changes to a plus sign. The same thing happens to the Page Forward button when you're on the last page. Click on the plus sign to display the Insert Page dialog box, which is set up to add pages automatically before the first page or after the last page in your document.

✔ Click in the Page Counter area to display the Go To Page dialog box, which enables you to turn to any page you like. Just enter the page number, press Enter, and off you go. (You can also access this dialog box by choosing Layout⇨Go To Page.)

✔ A series of page tabs appears to the right of the Last Page button. You can click on the tab for any page to go to that page.

✔ To increase or decrease the amount of space allotted to the page tabs, drag the scroll handle between the tabs and the scroll bar (the handle's labeled in Figure 12-2).

Removing the excess

If you add too many pages, you can always delete a few of them by choosing Layout⇨Delete Page. A dialog box, shown in all its finery in Figure 12-3, asks you which pages you want to delete. You can delete the single page you're viewing by pressing Enter. Or you can delete a sequential range of pages by selecting the Through to Page check box and entering a page number in the option box to the right.

You cannot delete all pages in the document. That would leave you with no pages at all, and CorelDraw will have none of that.

If you delete a page that you didn't mean to delete, choose Edit⇨Undo Delete Page or press Ctrl+Z (or Alt+Backspace).

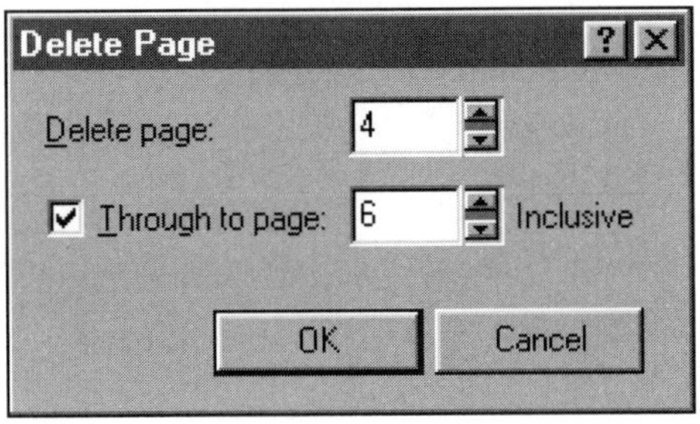

Figure 12-3:
Use this
dialog box to
kiss pages
good-bye.

Flowing text between pages

In Chapter 10, I mentioned that you can pour text across multiple pages. You daring types probably went ahead and tried it out the second you read about it. But a few of you — all right, most of you — are still wondering how that little item works. Give the following a try and you'll see:

1. **Drag with the Paragraph Text tool to create a block of text.**

2. **Enter too much text for the text block.**

3. **Select the Arrow tool and click on the bottom tab in the text block.**

   You get the page cursor.

4. **Press PgDn and then Enter.**

   This step adds a single page after the current page. (It's the same as choosing Layout⇨Insert Page and accepting the default settings.)

5. **Drag with the page cursor on your new page.**

   Your overflow text appears in the new text block.

Isn't that a trip? Despite the fact that the two text blocks are on separate pages, they're linked. If you drag up on the tab in the text block on page 1, excess text flows into the text block on the page 2. Incidentally, linked text blocks don't have to be on sequential pages; they can be several pages apart. You can start a story on page 5 and continue it on page 44. You can even make a separate text block that tells readers, "Continued on page 44." These here are professional page-layout capabilities!

Your Logo on Every Page

If you're serious about creating multipage docs, I have another prescription for you. It's called the *master layer.* No, this isn't a guy who really knows his way around bricks and mortar. This function enables you to put special text and graphic objects on every page of your document without having to place them all individually. For example, if you're creating a company newsletter, you may want to show the name of the newsletter at the bottom of each page and the company logo in the upper-right corner. CorelDraw can handle the chore of inserting the name and logo on every page for you automatically.

Establishing a master layer

If you want CorelDraw to automatically place certain elements on every page of your document, you have to create a master layer and then place the elements on it. Anything that you put on the master layer then appears automatically on all the pages.

The following steps explain how to establish a master layer and put stuff on it:

1. **Choose Layout⇨Layers Manager.**

   Or press Ctrl+F3. Either way, the Layers roll-up shown in Figure 12-4 appears.

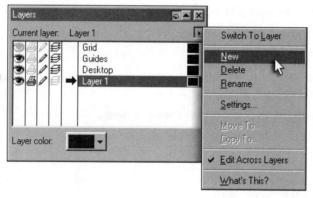

Figure 12-4:
Use the
Layers roll-
up to create
a master
page.

2. **Choose the New command from the roll-up menu.**

   You do this by clicking on the right-pointing arrowhead to display the submenu and then clicking on the New command. CorelDraw adds a new layer — presumably named Layer 2 — to the list in the Layers roll-up.

   You can also right-click anywhere inside the right half of the Layers roll-up and select the New option from the pop-up menu.

3. **Enter a name for the master page layer.**

   Immediately after you create a layer, its name is active, so you can just enter a name from the keyboard. Personally, I like the name Master Page, but you may prefer Herman. Press Enter when you're done.

4. Click on the dimmed Master Page icon to the left of the layer name.

In Figure 12-5, I've zoomed in on this special little icon, spotlighted it, and labeled it so that you won't miss it. Everything you add to this layer will appear on every page in your document.

Master Page icon

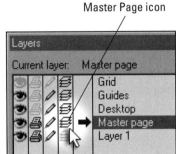

Figure 12-5:
Click on the
Master
Page icon to
make stuff
on the
active layer
visible on all
pages.

5. Add text and graphics to taste.

Create those logos, add those newsletter names, draw those boxes. Add everything that you want to repeat throughout your document. (Incidentally, it doesn't matter what page you're on. A master layer is a master layer throughout every page of the document.)

6. Click in front of Layer 1 in the Layers roll-up.

Or you can double-click on the Layer 1 name. Either way, that little right-pointing arrow jumps from in front of Master Page to in front of Layer 1. This step makes the original layer active again.

7. Drag Layer 1 up a level so that it appears above the Master Page layer.

In all likelihood, you want the text and graphics on the master page to appear in back of the text and graphics you add to a page. By dragging the Layer 1 name up one notch in the list — or alternatively dragging Master Page to the bottom — you change the order of the layers so that the master page rests in back of the active layer.

8. Choose Edit Across Layers from the Layers roll-up menu.

Click again on the right-pointing arrowhead to display the menu — or right-click anywhere inside the right half of the roll-up — and then click on Edit Across Layer. This step turns the command off so that you can only manipulate objects on the current layer, thus protecting the master layer objects.

To see how the master page you just created works, try this: First, draw an oval or something simple on one page of your document. Then press PgDn to go forward a page or PgUp to go back. It doesn't matter which you choose. When you turn to the other page, you'll see all the objects that you added to the master layer. But you won't see the oval you drew on the standard layer.

In most cases, your documents will have only two layers — one for the master page and one for your main document pages. The only reason for having more than two layers is to segregate objects in extremely complex drawings. People who go around drawing human anatomies and blow-outs of car engines — we're talking about folks with the patience of saints — use layers. However, typical novice and intermediate users have little reason to explore layers — except for creating a master page, of course — and they're all the merrier for it. *I* almost never use layers, and I'm an *expert*. At least, that's what my wife tells me every time I take the trash out to the curb. And she's not just saying it either; you can sense that she really means it.

In any case, to find out a little more about layers — not much, mind you, but a little — read the first section of Chapter 21.

Hiding master layer objects on page 1

As a general rule of thumb, you don't display master layer objects on the first page of a multipage document. For example, what's the point of listing the name of the newsletter at the bottom of the first page? The name is already listed at the top of that page in big bold type. Very likely, the company logo is a part of the newsletter title, so there's no reason to repeat it, either.

To hide master layer objects on one page only, do this:

1. Turn to the first page.

Or, if you don't want to see the master layer objects on some other page, turn to it.

2. Right-click on the name of your master layer in the Layers roll-up and then select the Settings command.

You can also select the name of your master layer and choose Settings from the roll-up menu, but right-clicking is easier. The Master Page Settings dialog box appears, as in Figure 12-6.

3. Deselect the Visible check box.

This step hides the master layer objects.

4. Select the Apply Layer Changes to the Current Page Only check box.

This step allows you to change the settings for the current page only.

5. Press Enter.

CorelDraw closes the dialog box and returns you to the drawing area. All master layer objects have now disappeared from view. However, the objects remain visible on all other pages.

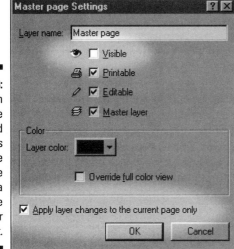

Figure 12-6:
Click on each of the spotlighted check boxes to hide the master-page objects for a single page of your document.

I Need a Bigger Page!

In the United States, most folks use letter-sized paper. That's 8 ½ inches wide by 11 inches tall, in case you've never worked in a stationery store or set foot in an office-supply warehouse. In other countries, page sizes vary. But no matter what — at least, I don't know of any exceptions — CorelDraw is set up for the most likely scenario. If you're using the most common page size in your neck of the woods and you like your pages upright, you don't have to worry about the command I'm about to describe.

But what if you're doing something slightly different? Maybe you're creating a document that will be printed on legal-sized paper, a longer page size designed for lawyers to scribble their many §s on. Or maybe you're planning to print on letter-sized paper but you want to flip the page on its side. In these and other cases, you need to choose Layout⇨Page Setup to display the Page Setup dialog box shown in Figure 12-7.

Use the options in this dialog box as follows:

 ✔ To change the size of the pages in the document, select a predefined page size option from the Paper pop-up menu.

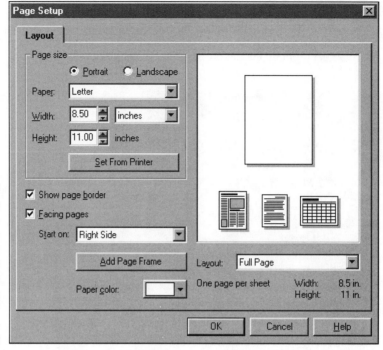

Figure 12-7:
The Page
Setup dialog
box lets you
change the
size of the
pages in
your
document.

↙ If you're unsure how large one of the predefined page sizes is, just select it. CorelDraw automatically displays the dimensions of the selected page size in the Width and Height option boxes.

↙ If you just want to set the page size to match the size of the paper loaded into your printer, click on the Set From Printer button.

↙ If none of these page sizes strikes your fancy, enter your own dimensions into the Width and Height option boxes.

↙ Select the Landscape radio button to lay the page on its side. Select Portrait to stand it up again.

↙ Select the Facing Pages check box to display two facing pages in the drawing area at once. For example, when you open up a four-page newsletter, page 2 and page 3 face each other. The even-numbered page (page 2) is on the left, and the odd-numbered page (page 3) is on the right. If you want to see these pages as your reader will see them, select the Facing Pages option.

↙ Don't even bother with the rest of the options. Unless you're creating three-fold fliers on bright pink paper, with ugly borders around each page, they're a complete waste of time.

Chapter 13

Those Poor, Helpless Trees

. . . .

In This Chapter

▶ Preparing your drawing to be printed

▶ Orienting your drawing on the printed page

▶ Selecting a paper size

▶ Printing every page of a document

▶ Printing multiple copies

▶ Printing a specific range of pages

▶ Scaling the drawing on the printed page

▶ Tiling poster-sized artwork onto several pages

▶ Using the page preview options

▶ Creating color separations

. . . .

*A*dvising a perfect stranger like you how to use your printer is like trying to diagnose a car problem without ever seeing the car, without knowing the make and model, without having driven more than, say, ten models in my entire life, and without even knowing what sort of symptoms your car's exhibiting. Printers come in so many different types and present so many potential printing hazards that I can't possibly give information designed specifically for your machine.

In other words, I'm completely in the dark. I'm the blind leading the blind. Sure, I can tell you how to print from CorelDraw — in fact, that's exactly what I'm going to do in this chapter — but every word that I write assumes that:

✔ Your printer is plugged in.

✔ Your printer is turned on and in working order.

✔ The printer is properly connected to your computer.

✔ Windows 95 is aware of your printer's existence.

✔ Your printer is stocked with ribbon, ink, toner, paper, film, or whatever else is required in the way of raw materials.

Oh, and one other thing. Make sure that you *have* a printer. I've known people to try to print with no printer in the building.

If you barely know the location of the printer, let alone anything else about the God-forsaken thing, assume for now that everything is A-OK and follow along with the text in this chapter. If you run into a snag, something is probably awry with your printer or its connection to your computer. As a friend of mine likes to tell me, "When in danger or in doubt, run in circles, scream and shout." If you shout loudly enough, someone may come to your rescue and fix your problem.

A helpful reader has advised me that the "scream and shout" quote originates "from none other than the greatest science fiction writer of all time, Robert Anson Heinlein." I'll take his word for it.

The Printing Process

The overall printing process includes these steps:

1. Turn on your printer.

If you're in an office setting and the printer is far from your desk, shout down the hall or across the vast expanse of cubicles to see whether it's turned on. I suggest, "Is the printer on, you bonehead?!" If the person near the printer responds with anything but, "Aye-aye," speak to your supervisor immediately.

2. Press Ctrl+S or choose File⇨Save.

Although this step is only a precaution, it's always a good idea to save your document immediately before you print it, because the print process is one of those ideal opportunities for your computer to crash. You computer gleans a unique kind of satisfaction from delivering pristine pages from the printer and then locking up at the last minute, all the while knowing that the document on disk is several hours behind schedule. If you weren't the brunt of the joke, you'd probably think that it was amusing, too.

3. Press Ctrl+P or choose File⇨Print.

A dialog box appears, enabling you to specify the pages that you want to print, request multiple copies, scale the size of the printed drawing, and mess around with a horde of other options.

4. Click on the Properties button.

Up comes another dialog box that lets you make sure that you're printing to the correct printer and that the page doesn't print on its side.

5. Press Enter twice.

And they're off! The page or pages start spewing out of your printer faster than you can recite the first 17 pages of *Beowolf*.

It's magic, really. Through the modern miracle of computing, you've taken what is for all practical purposes a completely imaginary drawing — a dream known only to you and your machine — and converted it into a tangible sheet of hard copy. Don't be surprised when you show your work to a few fellow amateurs and they kick you out of their club for good. That's the price of progress.

Making Sure That Everything's Ready to Go

Before you tell CorelDraw to print your drawing, it's a good idea to make sure that everything's ready to go. It's like checking to see that you have your keys with you as you exit your house. It's by no means an essential step; just as you probably have your keys, everything is probably already in order to print. But it's a good idea that may help you avoid some grief later on.

Selecting a printer

When you press Ctrl+P (or choose File⇨Print), CorelDraw displays the Print dialog box. The dialog box offer lots of options, but for now, the only ones you need to care about are the Name pop-up menu and the Properties button, emphasized in Figure 13-1. (The entire Print dialog box appears in Figure 13-4.)

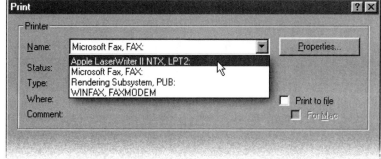

Figure 13-1:
Select a printer and then click on the Properties button.

Select the type of printer that's connected to your PC from the Name pop-up menu. If you generally print all your documents from the same printer, the proper printer should already be displayed.

If your computer has a fax/modem, you can print your drawing to a fax machine hundreds or thousands of miles away. Just choose Microsoft Fax from the Name pop-up menu. Then press Enter. Windows 95 walks you through the process of sending a fax, asking you for a fax number, recipient, subject, and all that other fax stuff.

Changing paper size and orientation

Next, click on the Properties button to display a dialog box like the one shown in Figure 13-2. Though your dialog box may look different from the one pictured here, it should provide three or four areas of interest:

✔ Select the correct paper size from the Paper Size list at the top of the dialog box. Ideally, the paper size should match the page size you selected in the Page Setup dialog box (described just pages ago, in Chapter 12). Unless you have some special kind of paper loaded in the paper tray, you probably want letter-sized paper.

✔ Not available in many Setup dialog boxes, the Layout options let you group multiple pages from your drawing onto a single printed page. For example, you could select the 4 Up radio button to print four pages from your drawing on a single page, each reduced to ¹/₄ its normal size. This option is useful for getting a sense of what your pages look like without wasting a lot of paper and printing time.

✔ Select a radio button from the Orientation area to make sure that your drawing lines up correctly on the printed page. If your drawing is taller than it is wide, select Portrait. If not, select Landscape.

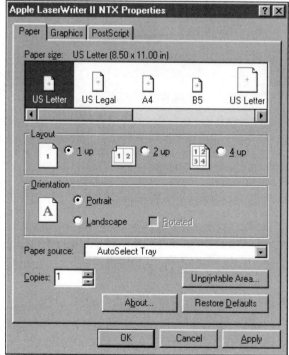

Figure 13-2:
This dialog box lets you check to make sure that everything's in order.

✔ Specify where the paper is coming from by selecting an option from the Paper Source pop-up menu. Some office printers have more than one paper tray. If you want to print on letterhead or some other kind of special paper, select the Manual Feed option. Then shout to the printer guy, "Shove a piece of letterhead into the manual feed slot, would you?"

You may also find a Copies option box, which lets you print more than one copy of each page in your drawing. Ignore this option for now. An identical, more convenient version of the option resides in the standard Print dialog box, as explained in the upcoming "Printing multiple copies" section.

Printing Those Pages

When you press Enter, CorelDraw returns you to the Print dialog box, displayed in its entirety in Figure 13-3. Naturally, I could tell you how every single one of these options work. But for the moment, I'll assume that you're more interested in getting the job done than learning about printing on an option-by-option basis. To this end, the following sections outline some common printing scenarios. Later on, I describe a few of the most important printing options on their own.

Figure 13-3:
The Print dialog box lets you specify which pages you want to print and how many copies of each page you want.

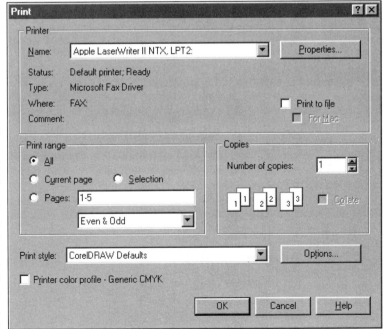

Printing the entire document

To print your entire document — whether it's a single-page drawing or a multipage document — do the following:

1. **Shout at the printer guy to make sure that everything's all ready to go.**

   Or just make sure that the printer is turned on yourself.

2. **Press Ctrl+P or choose File⇨Print.**

   The Print dialog box appears.

3. **Press Enter or click on OK.**

   CorelDraw initiates the printing process.

As CorelDraw works on printing your drawing, it displays a little message box, telling you what it's up to. A progress bar shows how close the printer is to printing your artwork. If you think of something you missed — for example, "Aagh, I forgot to draw in the toenails!" — and you're interested in saving a bit of tree, not to mention a bit of time, click on the Cancel button or press Esc. CorelDraw obediently closes the message and returns you to your drawing.

Printing multiple copies

Generally, the tried and true method for producing multiple copies of a drawing, newsletter, or other document is to print a single copy and then photocopy it or trundle it off to a commercial printer. The latter option offers the benefit of a wide variety of paper stocks and the satisfaction of truly solid inks, compared with the malaise of toner and spotty ink cartridges supplied by computer printers. Even a fly-by-night, cut-rate commercial printer delivers better results than a photocopier.

However, if you don't have time for a commercial printer and the office photocopier is out of whack as usual, you can print multiple copies directly from CorelDraw:

1. **Make sure that the printer is turned on and stocked with enough paper.**

   A full paper tray is a happy paper tray.

2. **Press Ctrl+P or choose File⇨Print.**

   There's that Print dialog box again.

3. **Enter the number of pages you want to print in the Number of Copies option box.**

   You can go as high as 999 copies, a sufficient number of copies to send most printers to the repair shop.

4. **Select the Collate check box to group all pages in a document together.**

When Collate is turned off, CorelDraw prints all copies of page 1, followed by all copies of page 2, and so on. When the option is checked, Draw prints the first copy of each page in the document, then the second copy, then the third, and so on. The helpful little graphic to the left of the check box even changes to demonstrate what you can expect.

5. **Press Enter.**

If you're planning to go off and have some coffee and a croissant while your 126 copies print, you may want to warn your officemates that the printer will be tied up for a while, not so much for their benefit as for your own. I used to work at a service bureau, so I know what coworkers do when someone goes off and leaves a long print job running. They walk over to your machine and click on the Cancel button. When you arrive back an hour later, confident that the pages are finished, you find three copies waiting on your desk with a Post-it note that says, "Quit hogging the printer!"

In an office environment, every long print job requires a sentinel. At least have someone keep an eye on your machine while you're gone.

Printing a few pages here and there

When working on a multipage document, you won't always want to print every single page. One time, you may just want to see what page 2 looks like. The next, you'll want to reprint page 6 after fixing a typo. Still another time, you'll have to print a new copy of page 3 after the first one jams in the printer. To print certain pages only, follow these steps:

1. **Is the printer turned on?**

Check and see.

2. **Is your head screwed on straight?**

Always a good thing to check.

3. **Press Ctrl+P.**

You've been through this enough times to use the keyboard equivalent and quit relying on the Print command.

4. **Click on the Current Page radio button to print the single page displayed on-screen.**

If you want to print a range of pages, select the value in the Pages option box (or press Tab). Then type in the pages separated by a dash. For example, to print pages 1, 2, and 3, enter *1-3* into the Pages option box.

> You can also print nonsequential pages separated by commas. To print pages 1, 2, 3, 5, 7, 8, and 9, for example, you enter *1-3,5,7-9*.

5. Press Enter.

Still More Printing Options

If your only interest in printing is to get the pages out, you've read everything you need to know. But if you want to store up some extra printing knowledge for a rainy day, you might like to know what the following options do:

- ✔ Click on the Selection radio button to print only those objects in the drawing that are selected. (If no object was selected when you chose the Print command, this option is dimmed.)

- ✔ Click on the Options button in the lower-right portion of the Print dialog box to display the insanely crowded Print Options dialog box, shown in Figure 13-4. For the sake of clarity, I spotlighted the most important options, which let you change the size of the drawing with respect to the printed page. (These options don't affect the actual size of the objects in the drawing area, mind you; they affect output only.)

- ✔ Select the Preview Image check box to see the drawing inside the *page preview area* (labeled in Figure 13-4). The page preview area is the subject of the next section.

- ✔ Enter values in the Top and Left option boxes to specify the location of the drawing as measured from the top-left corner of the printed page.

- ✔ Enter a value into the Width option box to change the width of the drawing. By default, CorelDraw resizes the drawing proportionally, automatically adjusting the Height value according to your changes to the Width value. This is why the Height value is dimmed.

- ✔ To resize the drawing disproportionately, turn off the Maintain Aspect Ratio check box. The Height value becomes available so that you can edit it independently of the Width value.

- ✔ Enter values into the % option boxes to the right of Width and Height to enlarge or reduce the printed size of the drawing by a percentage value.

- ✔ To center the drawing on the printed page, select the Center check box.

- ✔ Select the Fit to Page check box to reduce the size of the drawing so that it just fits onto a sheet of printed paper. This option is especially useful when you're printing poster-sized drawings on printers that only handle letter-sized paper.

Page preview area

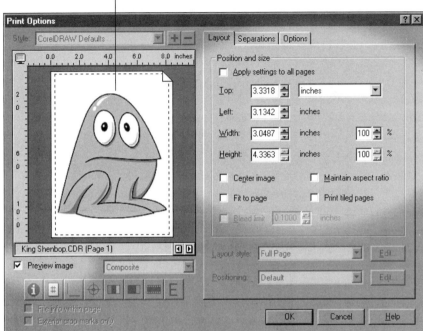

Figure 13-4:
Use the
options in
the Print
Options
dialog box
to change
the size at
which your
drawing
prints.

✔ If you want to print a large drawing on small paper without reducing the drawing, you can cut it up into paper-sized chunks by selecting the Print Tiled Pages check box. For example, when printing an 11 × 17-inch drawing on a standard laser printer, the Print Tiled Pages option divides the drawing up into four pieces and prints each piece on a separate page.

✔ Man, is this stuff dry or what? Reading about printing options is like having sand in your mouth. Makes you want to spit. Ptwu, ptwu.

✔ Luckily, it's much easier to change the printed size of a drawing using the page preview area than to mess around with many of the options I've mentioned so far. Read on to find out how.

Using the page preview area

In Figure 13-5, I've isolated the page preview area from the Print Options dialog box and labeled its parts. The parts work as follows:

✔ Drag one of the corner scale handles to proportionally increase or decrease the printed size of the drawing.

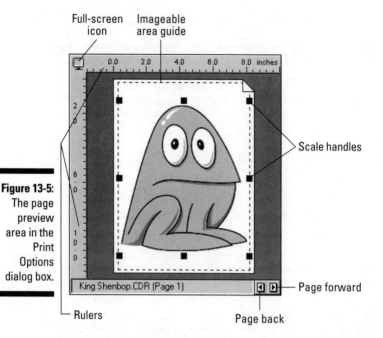

Full-screen icon

Imageable area guide

Scale handles

Page forward

Page back

Rulers

King Shenbop.CDR (Page 1)

Figure 13-5:
The page preview area in the Print Options dialog box.

✔ If the Maintain Aspect Ratio check box is turned off, Draw displays handles at the top and bottom of the graphic as well as on the left and right sides. Drag one of these handles to stretch the drawing without regard for the original proportions.

✔ Drag the graphic inside the scale handles to change the placement of the drawing on the printed page.

✔ The *imageable area guide* outlines the area in which your printer can print objects. Except for typesetters and other fabulously expensive high-end printers, all printers have a dead zone around the outside of the page on which they cannot print. (Fax machines and old-style dot-matrix printers can print all the way from the top of the page to the bottom, but have dead zones along the sides.)

✔ If you select the Print Tiled Pages check box, you can enlarge the drawing to take up multiple pages. As you drag to make the drawing larger, Draw adds more and more pages. If you make the drawing smaller, Draw automatically deletes pages. You can't move the drawing on the pages, but you can scale it to any size you like.

✔ The rulers provide points of reference when you're scaling your drawing. They even display tracking lines so that you can monitor the location of your cursor.

✔ Click on the page back arrow to preview the previous page. Click on the page forward icon to preview the next page. These icons are applicable to multipage documents only.

✔ Click on the full-screen icon in the upper-left corner of the rulers to enlarge the page preview area to fill the entire screen. Click on the icon again to shrink the preview area to normal size.

Printing full-color artwork

So far, I've covered and ignored roughly equal halves of CorelDraw's printing options. For reasons that I've already discussed, I intend to leave it that way. But you should know about one other option, especially if you intend to print color drawings: the Print Separations check box.

Before I go any further, some background information is in order. You can print a color drawing in two ways. You can either print your drawing on a color printer, or you can separate the colors in a drawing onto individual pages. Each method has its benefits and its drawbacks:

✔ Printing on a color printer is easy, and you get what you expect. The colors on the printed page more or less match the colors on-screen. Unfortunately, a commercial printer can't reproduce from a color printout. Oh sure, you can make color photocopies, but professional printing presses can only print one color at a time.

✔ If you want to commercially reproduce your artwork, you have to tell CorelDraw to print *color separations,* one for each of the primaries cyan, magenta, yellow, and black (introduced in the section "Colors are born from other colors" in Chapter 7).

To print color separations in CorelDraw 6, do the following:

1. Press Ctrl+P.

Look out, it's the Print dialog box.

2. Click on the Options button inside the Print dialog box.

Up comes the same Print Options dialog box that I showed you back in Figure 13-4.

3. Click on the Separations tab in the right half of the dialog box.

The tab is near the top, right between Layout and Options. This step switches you to the Separations panel.

4. Select the Print Separations check box.

It's the first check box in the panel.

5. Click on OK to close the Print Options dialog box.

6. Click on OK in the Print dialog box to initiate the print process.

CorelDraw automatically prints a separate page for each of the four primary colors.

Each page looks like a standard black-and-white printout, but don't let that worry you. When you take the pages to your commercial printer, a technician will photographically transfer your printouts to sheets of metal called *plates*. Each plate is inked with cyan, magenta, yellow, or black ink.

The technician prints all the pages with the cyan plate first, then runs the pages by the magenta plate, then the yellow plate, and finally the black plate. The inks mix together to form a rainbow of greens, violets, oranges, and other colors. For example, the four separations shown in Figure 13-6 combine to create a green Shenbop sitting on a royal purple lily pad. (Use your imagination — this is, after all, a black-and-white book.)

Cyan

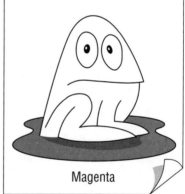

Magenta

Figure 13-6: The color separations required to print a full-color Shenbop.

Yellow

Black

Part IV
Corel's Other Amazing Programs

The 5th Wave   By Rich Tennant

"YOU'VE PLUGGED YOUR MOUSE INTO THE
ELECTRIC SHAVER OUTLET AGAIN."

In this part . . .

*I*n the hundreds of kind letters and reader-response cards received about earlier versions of this book, the number-one request has been to include more information on Photo-Paint. Well, your wish is my command. I've completely cleaned out this part of the book and replaced Chapters 15 through 18 with three full chapters on Photo-Paint and one on CorelDraw 6's newest program, Dream 3D. As before, Chapter 14 concentrates on swapping artwork between CorelDraw and Photo-Paint. But even the majority of that chapter has been rewritten to document new ways to share stuff under Windows 95.

Chapters 15 through 17 provide a condensed guide to editing photographs on a computer. After introducing the Photo-Paint interface, I move on to such topics as opening images from Corel's extensive photo library; painting inside images using traditional tools such as pencils and airbrushes; erasing mistakes; applying effects; and cloning portions of the image to cover up blemishes and add in stuff that wasn't there in the first place. I also cover Photo-Paint's selection tools in alarming detail and explain the best way to sharpen the focus of an image and correct contrast and brightness. Instead of encouraging you to waste time with Photo-Paint's 50 different ways to sharpen and correct images, I teach you how to use the two commands that do far and away the most good.

Chapter 18 takes you on a brief and gentle tour through what is undoubtedly Corel's most complex program, Dream 3D. Arguably Corel's most exciting and challenging addition in years, Dream 3D takes you to the next frontier in computer graphics — three-dimensional drawing. I show you how to import 3-D objects, how to move and rotate them in 3-D space, how to apply surface textures, and how to save the finished drawing as a photographic image. With remarkably little effort, you'll be rendering 3-D artwork, a practice so rarefied that fewer than 10 percent of all computer artists have ever attempted it.

Chapter 14

Programs in the Night, Exchanging Data

. . . .

In This Chapter

▶ How to put something you created in Program A into Program B

▶ A variety of OLE that has nothing to do with matadors

▶ South-of-the-border birthday celebrations

▶ A step-by-step discussion of embedding objects

▶ What to do if dragging and dropping doesn't work

▶ How to link objects to disk files

▶ When all else fails, import

. . . .

*P*rogress and technology bring with them an element of terror. Machines help us work more productively and with less effort, but lurking in the background is an unmistakable promise: You're barely keeping up as it is. The next bit of technology is going to leave you in the dust.

At least that's the way it seems sometimes. And believe me, I'm every bit as susceptible to it as you are. Every time I turn around, there's some new piece of software or hardware that's bound and determined to make me feel like I've been covering the computer industry for five minutes.

So when I tell you that the stuff in this chapter is a piece of cake, you can trust me — despite the fact that it discusses such nightmarish-sounding terms as *embedding* and *OLE*. Unlike those other wacko technological breakthroughs, this one isn't going to give you any problems. I promise. In fact, it's going to solve a problem that's probably been plaguing you ever since you opened up that massive CorelDraw 6 package: How do you take something that you created in one program and put it into a document that you created in another program?

OLE Must Be Pretty Bad to Deserve that Windup

Well, all right, *object linking and embedding* — *OLE* (pronounced *olé*) for short — does have a certain eerie sound to it. But that's just to amuse the computer zealots who aren't happy unless they know at least a dozen 15-syllable phrases that are guaranteed to shock their like-minded friends into frenzied states of information-age envy.

For the rest of us, OLE should be called *birthday party*. Program A gives Program B a gift of text, graphics, or other digital stuff. Program B remembers who gave it what so that if any changes or alterations need to be done, Program B can call on Program A to make the changes. Okay, it's an idealized birthday party — if your Uncle Elmer gave you a jacket that didn't fit, he'd give you the receipt instead of returning it himself — but let's just say that computer programs have better manners than that. When a program gives a gift, it guarantees the gift for life.

The reason I'm telling you about OLE is because it links all of Corel's diverse and independent programs and enables them to work together like . . . well, I think you've had enough analogies for one day. If CorelPhoto-Paint gives an object to CorelDraw, you can revisit CorelPhoto-Paint and edit the object by just double-clicking on the object in CorelDraw. It's like one big, happy family. Oops, that's an analogy, isn't it?

Take OLE by the Horns

One thing you need to remember about OLE is that there's no command, or file, or option, or anything else called OLE. It's an invisible function built into Windows 95 that paves the way for a variety of commands and options that I'll describe shortly, the same way natural selection paves the way for fish to walk on their fins and protozoa to attain higher educations. (Man, these analogies are going downhill.)

Now, you and I could explore every nook and cranny of OLE — and eventually we *will* explore a few of them — but the best way to really understand how it works is to try it out.

The following steps explain how to open something in CorelPhoto-Paint and transfer it into a CorelDraw drawing by way of the age-old custom of drag and drop. You can then make changes to the image using Photo-Paint's tools and commands while remaining inside CorelDraw. Will wonders never cease?

Placing an object or image from one program into another in this fashion is known as *embedding*. (And you thought embedding was what your kids did when they smushed chocolate chips into the sofa.) It's called embedding because Windows 95 implants additional information about the object, such as which program created it and how to call up the program when it's time to edit the object.

1. **Make sure that CorelDraw is running.**

   If it isn't, start the program as described back in Chapter 2.

2. **Run CorelPhoto-Paint.**

   Use the Windows 95 Startup menu in the lower-left corner of the screen. You know, choose Startup⇨Programs⇨Corel Applications⇨CorelPhoto-Paint. In a few moments, the Photo-Paint interface springs to life, filled with a bewildering array of new menus and tools.

3. **Inside CorelPhoto-Paint, open an image.**

   As in CorelDraw, you open a file on disk by choosing File⇨Open or by pressing Ctrl+O and selecting a file inside the ensuing dialog box. In Figure 14-1, I opened the Teddy file included in the Objects folder, which is inside the Photopnt folder on the third CD-ROM.

Rectangle Mask tool

Figure 14-1: The Teddy image as it appears when opened inside CorelPhoto-Paint.

If you likewise open the Teddy image or one of the others in the Objects folder, you can skip to Step 7. Corel has already done the intermediate steps for you by converting the images in the Objects folder into independent objects. If you open some other image, you have to convert the image into an object for yourself, as the next steps explain.

If you open an image off a CD, Photo-Paint may respond with a stupid message about how you can't use the Save command. (After all, you can't save to a CD, so you have to use the Save As command instead.) Press Enter to tell Photo-Paint to quit its belly-aching.

4. **Select the Lasso tool.**

   Press and hold on the Rectangular Mask tool's icon in the toolbox, which is the dotted rectangle immediately below the Arrow tool (as labeled in Figure 14-1). After the flyout menu appears, select the Lasso Mask tool. That's the fourth icon from the left, the one that looks just like a lasso.

5. **Drag around the image to select it.**

   Encircle the portion of the image that you want to add to your drawing. After you draw the selection boundary, double-click with the tool. Photo-Paint surrounds the image with a dotted selection outline to show that it's selected.

6. **Choose <u>O</u>bject⇨<u>C</u>reate From Mask.**

   This is a weird but necessary step. In order to transfer an image from Photo-Paint into Draw, you have to first convert it into an independent object. The Create From Mask command does just that. It also automatically selects the Arrow tool, which is precisely the tool you want selected. Now skip to Step 8.

7. **Click on the image to select it.**

   You folks who performed Step 6 don't need to do this, which is why I told you to skip to Step 8. But you folks who skipped here from Step 3 need to specify the object that you want to select. Photo-Paint displays eight square handles around the object, just as if it were selected in Draw.

8. **Scale the Photo-Paint screen so that you can see the Draw screen in the background.**

   The easiest way to embed a Photo-Paint object into Draw is to drag the image from one program and drop it into the other. You have to be able to see at least a little of the drawing area inside Draw to make the drop.

9. **Drag the selected image out of the Photo-Paint window and Ctrl+drop it into Draw.**

   Figure 14-2 shows the act in progress. This is essentially the same technique I explained in the "Do the Drag and Drop" section of Chapter 8 — only now you're dragging and dropping between different programs. By

Photo-Paint   Draw

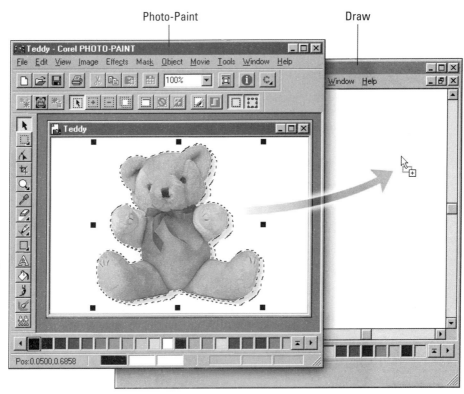

Figure 14-2:
Dragging
an image
from Photo-
Paint and
Ctrl+dropping
it into Draw.

pressing the Ctrl key midway into the drag and holding it until after you
release the mouse button, you create a duplicate of the image. If you don't
press Ctrl, you delete the original image from Photo-Paint and move it into
Draw.

10. Click on the CorelDraw title bar.

This step brings the Draw program to the front of the screen. As Figure
14-3 demonstrates, object-oriented drawings — such as Shenbop — can
exist side-by-side with their image counterparts — such as Teddy — even
though the two were created in separate programs. Just wanted you to
see that.

You may want to magnify the embedded image by clicking on it once or
twice with the Zoom tool. Thanks to a little thing called *resolution* —
explained in the "Dots per inch" section of Chapter 15 — an image may
appear much smaller in Draw than it did in Photo-Paint. So don't hesitate
to zoom in.

Photo-Paint   Draw

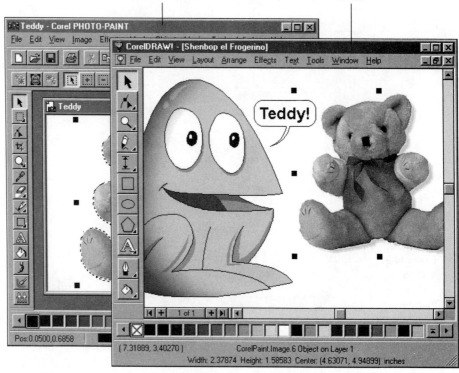

Figure 14-3:
Your
drawing
may not
react as
enthusi-
astically to
embedding
as mine
does.

11. Switch back to CorelPhoto-Paint.

The easiest way is to click on the Photo-Paint title bar.

12. Press Alt+F4.

You don't need Photo-Paint any more, so choose File⇨Exit to quit the Photo-Paint program. When a message appears asking whether you want to save the image, click on the No button. Windows 95 automatically returns you to CorelDraw.

13. Save your drawing.

Then close it. Do whatever you want. You can even exit CorelDraw, exit Windows 95, turn off your computer, and wait several weeks before performing the next step. It doesn't matter. When you're ready to go on, restart CorelDraw and open the drawing that contains the embedded image.

14. Suppose that you want to edit the image.

I don't know if *supposing* actually qualifies as an active step, but it's essential to this exercise. In my case, I wanted to make the teddy bear stick out its tongue to demonstrate its fear and loathing of cartoon frogs.

15. Double-click on the image inside Draw.

Or choose that wackiest of commands, Edit⇨CorelPaint.Image.6 Object⇨Edit. My, that's user friendly. CorelDraw sends a message to Windows 95 requesting that it locate and run Photo-Paint. Windows 95, being a good-natured soul, obliges. But instead of starting as a separate program, as in the old days, Photo-Paint's tools and menus take over the CorelDraw interface. This way, you can edit the image while still viewing the rest of the drawing in the background. As illustrated in Figure 14-4, I was able to edit the teddy bear while keeping an eye on Shenbop. This process is called *in-place editing*.

16. Isn't this awesome?

You have to admire the way these programs communicate with each other. Pretty soon, they'll eliminate the need for users entirely, and we humans can go lie in hammocks and sip mint juleps for the rest of our days.

17. Edit the image as desired.

If you're interested, I describe how to use Photo-Paint's painting tools in Chapters 15 through 17. For now, just select the Paint tool (labeled in Figure 14-4) and doodle away. I added big eyes and a sticky-outy tongue to make my bear express displeasure with his predicament.

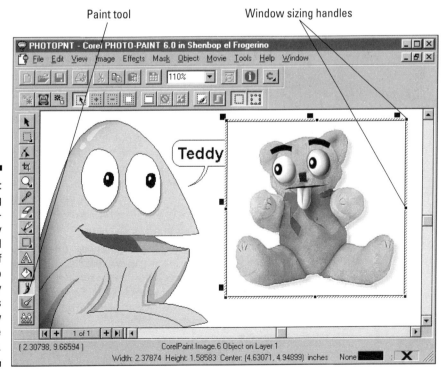

Figure 14-4: Using Photo-Paint's many tools to add a look of disgust to the teddy bear helps out my Draw scene considerably.

After you double-click on your image, it may appear surrounded by a special set of scroll bars, which let you view hidden portions of the image. You can also scale the size of the image window by dragging the little sizing handles — not the big handles, but the tiny ones labeled in Figure 14-4.

18. When you finish editing, click outside the image.

When you click outside the window, Windows 95 quits Photo-Paint, hides its tools and menus, and returns you to the standard CorelDraw interface.

As an alternative to dragging and dropping, you can embed an image by copying it in Photo-Paint and pasting it into CorelDraw. In the preceding steps, press Ctrl+C in place of Step 8, switch to CorelDraw in Step 9, and press Ctrl+V in Step 10. Otherwise, the process works the same.

You now know how to take an object created in one Corel program and embed it into another. You also know how to edit an embedded object. As long as you got the previous exercise to work, you don't have to read another page in this chapter. Just repeat the exercise every time you want to trade information between Photo-Paint and Draw.

However, if you encountered an out-of-memory error when trying to run Photo-Paint and Draw at the same time or you don't have enough screen space to make Step 9 work, read on for your alternatives.

More Ways for CorelDraw to Receive Gifts

Altogether, you can introduce objects into CorelDraw in three ways:

- ✔ You can embed the objects, as demonstrated in the preceding section.

- ✔ As I mentioned at the beginning of this chapter, OLE stands for *object linking and embedding.* I've discussed embedding, but not the other half, *linking.* You link an object by loading it from disk into CorelDraw, much as if you were opening a drawing. CorelDraw maintains a link between the object and the disk file. If you later change the disk file, the object updates automatically. (Incidentally, this kind of linking has nothing to do with the linked text blocks I discuss in Chapter 10.)

- ✔ *Importing* an object is like giving a gift anonymously. CorelDraw has no idea where the object came from, nor can it call on another program to edit the image. As with linking, you load the file from disk into CorelDraw. But that's it. No automatic updates, no quick editing techniques, no nothing. If you later change the object using a different program, you have to import it from scratch in order to update the object in CorelDraw.

- ✔ The beauty of importing is that it has nothing to do with OLE, so it works even when embedding and linking give you fits.

Linking, the semi-smart technique

You can link objects for use in CorelDraw in two ways:

- You can copy an object in Photo-Paint or some other program and then choose Edit⇨Paste Special inside CorelDraw to establish a link. Unfortunately, this approach provides less functionality than simply choosing the standard Paste command — which embeds the object, remember? At the same time, this approach requires you to run two programs simultaneously, which invites the same old memory errors mentioned earlier. To sum it up in laymen's terms, this approach is dopey.

- The second and much smarter way to link an object is to load it directly from disk using Edit⇨Insert New Object, as described in the following steps.

The following is a typical linking scenario:

1. **Create an image in CorelPhoto-Paint.**

   When you're finished, save it to disk. Then quit Photo-Paint by pressing Alt+F4 or choosing File⇨Exit.

2. **Start CorelDraw.**

   This way, you don't have two programs running at once, clogging up the works.

3. **Choose Edit⇨Insert New Object.**

   The dialog box shown in Figure 14-5 appears.

4. **Select the Create from File radio button.**

   You'll find it on the left side of the dialog box.

5. **Click on the Browse button and locate the file you created in Photo-Paint.**

   The Browse button brings up a standard open-up-a-file dialog box (just like the Import dialog box described in Chapter 3). When you locate the Photo-Paint file you want to add to your drawing, double-click on it to return to the Insert New Object dialog box.

6. **Select the Link check box.**

   If you don't select Link, CorelDraw embeds the file, which can give you the same old problems you had when editing an embedded image earlier in this chapter.

7. **Click on OK.**

   Or press Tab, Enter. CorelDraw works away for a few moments and then displays the image in the drawing area.

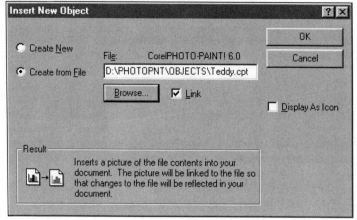

Figure 14-5:
Use these
options to
create a link
between
your
drawing and
an image
saved on
disk.

8. Save the drawing.

Then quit CorelDraw by pressing Alt+F4.

9. Start CorelPhoto-Paint.

10. Open the image you just got through linking and edit it.

Go nuts.

11. Press Alt+F4 to exit Photo-Paint.

12. Start CorelDraw again.

Hoo boy, these steps sure are exciting.

13. Open the drawing you saved in Step 8.

CorelDraw displays a message to demonstrate that it is updating all linked objects in the drawing. When the drawing appears, the linked objects are displayed with all edits intact.

14. Save the drawing.

Just to make it official.

Importing, the last ditch effort

If nothing else works and you don't feel like tearing out your hair (or the hair of the computer expert in your office), you can import an image created in Photo-Paint into CorelDraw. Remember, with importing you don't retain any link to the originating program — if you want to update the object, you have to open it in Photo-Paint, edit it, and then re-import it into Draw.

Here's how to import:

1. **Create an image in CorelPhoto-Paint or some other program.**

   Don't forget to save it to disk.

2. **Quit the program.**

   Just press Alt+F4.

3. **Start CorelDraw.**

4. **Press Ctrl+I.**

   Or choose File⇨Import. Draw responds by displaying the Import dialog box, which I discuss at length in Chapter 3.

5. **Locate the image file you want to import.**

   When you locate the file, click on it to select it.

6. **Press Enter or click on the Import button.**

   Or double-click on the file you want to import. CorelDraw displays the imported image in the drawing area.

There you have it: Three ways to introduce objects created in Photo-Paint into CorelDraw. Now, don't think that you *have* to import Photo-Paint images into Draw. You can open an image in Photo-Paint, edit it in Photo-Paint, print it from Photo-Paint, and never deal with Draw throughout the entire process. Like any of CorelDraw's other 50 gazillion functions, OLE and the Import command are merely at your disposal when and if you need them.

The 5th Wave
By Rich Tennant

"WELL'P — THERE GOES THE AMBIANCE."

Chapter 15
Everyone Say "Hello" to CorelPhoto-Paint

- -

In This Chapter

▶ Fooling gullible consumers like you

▶ Starting CorelPhoto-Paint

▶ Introducing the Photo-Paint interface

▶ Getting rid of nonessential interface garbage

▶ Opening images from CD-ROM

▶ Zooming and scrolling

▶ Creating a new image

▶ Understanding resolution and color

▶ Saving, printing, and closing images

- -

*I*n the world of print advertising, nearly everything you see is a distortion of reality. Food products are lacquered with hair spray, the performance of major appliances is simulated, prefab clothing is custom tailored to fit the actors. As your mom warned you, you can believe only half of what you see, none of what you hear, and the exact opposite of what you see and hear in ads.

But what goes on in front of the camera is nothing compared with what happens after the film enters the mind of the computer. Rumor has it, for example, that every major movie poster is a veritable collage of body parts and other elements. The body you see almost never belongs to the actor whose head is pasted on top of it. In most cases, there's nothing *wrong* with the actor's body; it's simply more convenient to have an extra strike some poster pose and later slap one of the hundred or so head shots of the actor onto the body.

CorelPhoto-Paint is the sort of program you might use to slap well-known heads on obscure bodies. Although it's not necessarily as capable as the mega-expensive image-editing systems used by professionals, Photo-Paint performs more than adequately for the price. You can open an image stored on disk and edit it in your computer. Draw a mustache on Aunt Patty, put Grandma Ida's eyebrows on Grandpa Neil's face, or distort little baby Melvin until he looks like Mighty Joe Young. The possibilities are absolutely limitless.

Blasting Off with Photo-Paint

You start Photo-Paint by choosing Start⇨Programs⇨Corel Applications⇨CorelPhoto-Paint. (For a quick refresher on starting programs inside Windows 95, read the first few pages of Chapter 2.)

After Photo-Paint starts, you see the Photo-Paint interface, which looks something like the one shown in Figure 15-1. Don't worry if your interface doesn't look *exactly* like mine. For one thing, Photo-Paint doesn't automatically open frog and hawk images when you start the program. And the roll-up may appear in a different location. But the interface shown in the figure is more or less what you can expect to see.

Here's paint in yer eye!

Hopefully, you recognize a few old friends from CorelDraw when you look at Figure 15-1. Photo-Paint offers a title bar, a menu bar, a whole bunch of tools, a color palette, and a status bar, all of which perform like their counterparts in CorelDraw.

But just to make sure that you don't lose anything in the translation — or, perhaps more appropriate, to ensure that the translation doesn't lose you — the following list should help jog your memory:

✔ You choose commands from menus by clicking on a name in the menu bar and then clicking on a command name in the ensuing menu. You can alternatively press the Alt key followed by the underlined letters in both the menu and command names.

✔ Or feel free to try out the keyboard shortcuts listed to the right of the command names in the menus. Common commands — such as File⇨Open and Edit⇨Copy — have the same shortcuts as they do in Draw — in this case, Ctrl+O and Ctrl+C.

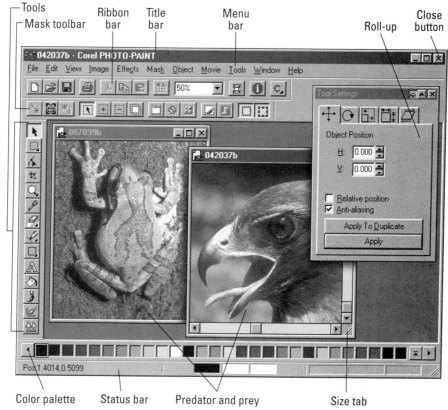

Figure 15-1:
The crowded Photo-Paint interface makes Draw's interface look rather stark and simplistic by comparison.

Tools
Mask toolbar
Ribbon bar
Title bar
Menu bar
Roll-up
Close button

Color palette   Status bar   Predator and prey   Size tab

TIP

✔ The icons in the two bars below the menu bar — the ribbon bar and the Mask toolbar (both labeled in Figure 15-1) — duplicate functions already found in the menus. To find out what an icon does, let your cursor hover over the icon. Photo-Paint responds by displaying a little yellow label.

✔ Any tool that includes a small triangle in its lower-right corner offers a flyout menu of alternative tools. For example, if you hold down the mouse button on the Rectangular Mask tool — second tool down — Photo-Paint displays the flyout menu shown in Figure 15-2. Click on an icon in the flyout to switch to a related tool.

✔ You can move the toolbox to a different location by dragging the gray area around the tools. You can also move the ribbon bar and Mask toolbar in the same way. To return toolbox, ribbon bar, or Mask toolbar to its original position, double-click on its title bar.

✔ The Tool Settings roll-up, which appears in Figure 15-1, appears on-screen by default. It changes according to the tool you select and enables you to change the performance of the tool.

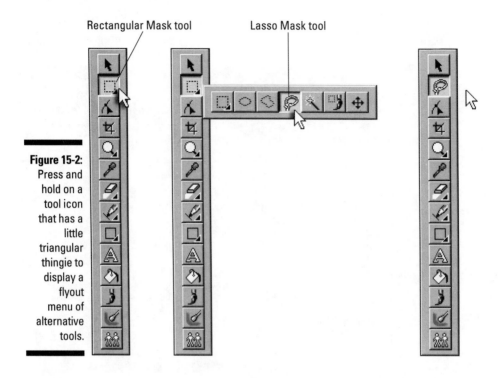

Rectangular Mask tool   Lasso Mask tool

Figure 15-2:
Press and
hold on a
tool icon
that has a
little
triangular
thingie to
display a
flyout
menu of
alternative
tools.

Don't hide the Tool Settings roll-up; it's very useful. If it gets in your way, you can click on the up-pointing arrow icon in the upper-right corner of the roll-up to roll it up. Click on the icon again to redisplay the roll-up's contents.

If you accidentally close the Tool Settings roll-up, press Ctrl+F8 or choose View⇨Roll-Ups⇨Tool Settings.

✔ When in doubt, right-click on something to display a pop-up menu. You can uncover all kinds of useful Photo-Paint functions by right-clicking on tools, roll-ups, or the image itself. Generally, the functions in the pop-up menus duplicate commands found in the standard menus, but they can still come in handy.

Strip away the extraneous junk

One thing I have to say about the new Photo-Paint 6 interface is that it's *way* too crowded. The number of icons in the ribbon bar and Mask toolbar has more than doubled since Version 5, and all the icons — including the tool icons — have shrunk so much that you have to use a magnifying glass to see them. It's confusing, chaotic, and downright claustrophobic.

Luckily, you can change things. As I mentioned in the "Ribbon bar" section of Chapter 2, I hate ribbon bars. They take up space, their icons are scrunched and unrecognizable, and they duplicate commands that are already readily available in the menus.

If you disagree — you prefer clicking on the little suckers to choosing commands or pressing keyboard shortcuts — then by all means, leave the ribbon bars on-screen. But if you want to free up screen space and create a generally friendlier environment, do as I do:

1. **Press Ctrl+T or choose <u>V</u>iew⇨<u>T</u>oolbars.**

   Or right-click on the gray space around the tools to bring up a pop-up menu and then choose the Toolbars option. In either case, the Toolbars dialog box emerges.

2. **Turn off the Standard and Mask/Object check boxes.**

   You're telling Photo-Paint to make the two ribbon bars along the top of the screen go away.

3. **Select <u>M</u>edium from the Size radio buttons.**

   This step increases the size of the tool icons.

4. **Press Enter.**

   Or click on OK. You now have bigger tool icons and no ribbon bars.

   If you're using a 17-inch monitor or larger, everything should look great. You can skip the rest of the steps. But if you have a 14-inch screen, a couple of tools are hidden by the color palette and status bar, as demonstrated in Figure 15-3. If this happens to you, perform Step 5.

5. **Drag the tools onto the menu bar.**

   I know it sounds weird, but this is how you move the tools to the top of the screen. Start by dragging some portion of the gray area around the tool icons. A rectangle moves along with your cursor to show that you're moving the toolbox. Drag onto the menu bar — as demonstrated in Figure 15-3 — and release. The tools adhere to the bottom of the menu bar in a horizontal row, as shown in Figure 15-4.

Now isn't that better? Figure 15-4 is significantly less cluttered and more intelligible than Figure 15-1, and yet you have access to just as many features as you ever did.

Because I've specifically created the figures in this book to show you what you'd see on a 14-inch monitor, the tools in most future figures appear in a horizontal row, as in Figure 15-4. This doesn't affect how Photo-Paint works — you can still do everything I instruct you to do regardless of where your tools are. It's just something to keep in mind.

Figure 15-3:
You can
move the
toolbox to
the top of
the screen
by dragging
it.

Hidden tools

Figure 15-4:
The cleaner,
less
confusing
Photo-Paint
interface.

Opening Frogs, Hawks, and Other Critters

Although you can create an image from scratch in Photo-Paint, it's more likely that you'll be using the program to edit existing images, such as a photograph on disk or on CD-ROM. In my case, I wanted to add a dangerous-looking snake image to my already scary frog-and-hawk scene.

To open an image file, you choose File⇨Open or press Ctrl+O. Photo-Paint displays the Open an Image dialog box, as shown in Figure 15-5. To find a veritable treasure trove of photographic images, insert the third CD-ROM included with your CorelDraw 6 package. Open the Images folder on the CD and then open the Photos folder. Inside are more than 20 folders filled with as many as 100 photographs apiece.

Figure 15-5:
Though
Corel's
image files
have
nonsense
numerical
names, you
can take a
peek at
them by
turning on
the Preview
check box.

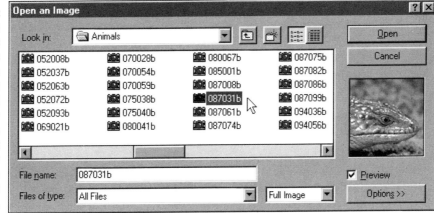

Unfortunately, the image files have unintelligible names such as 053011b. (These images were originally scanned as special Kodak Photo CD files, which accounts for the random naming system.) If you turn on the Preview check box, though, Photo-Paint shows you a tiny preview of what the photograph looks like when you click on the image file. If you want a good snake image, open the Animals folder and select the file named 087031b, as in Figure 15-5.

Photo-Paint can open images saved in any of the most popular image formats, including TIFF, PCX, JPEG, and Photo CD. For the lowdown on file formats, read Chapter 22, "Ten File Formats and Their Functions."

After you select the file you want to open, press Enter or click on the Open button. When you open an image off a CD-ROM, Photo-Paint displays a message telling you that the Save command is disabled. Because you can't save to a CD, Photo-Paint doesn't let you use the Save command at all. Instead, you have to use File⇒Save As. Just press Enter to hide the message and get on with your life.

The image opens up inside its own independent window, as in Figure 15-6. Now you can edit it till you're blue in the face.

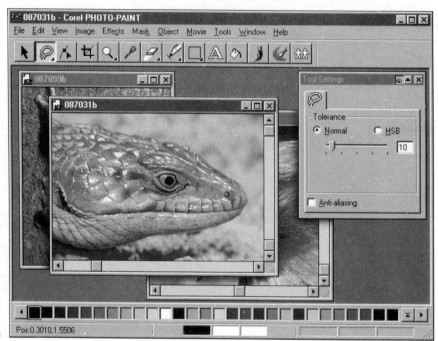

Figure 15-6:
Each image appears in its own independent window.

Making the Rounds

When you first open an image, Photo-Paint displays it as large as it can while still showing the entire image on-screen. But that doesn't necessarily mean that you can see every single pixel in the image. If you want to see one image pixel for every on-screen pixel, choose View⇒Zoom 100%. Or just press Ctrl+1. (Too bad CorelDraw doesn't offer this convenient shortcut.)

The most accurate way to see an image is pixel for pixel. Otherwise, Photo-Paint has to redraw the image slightly to make the image pixels match the screen pixels. This redrawing is only temporary — Photo-Paint doesn't change any pixel in the actual file unless you tell it to — but the screen image may give you a slightly wrong impression of how the image will print. Of course, you have to view the image at smaller sizes sometimes, but it's good to return to the 100 percent view whenever possible.

To make the image fill the screen, click on the Maximize button, labeled in Figure 15-7. Photo-Paint hides all other open images so that you can concentrate on the one you're editing. You can still view another open image by choosing its name from the bottom of the Window menu. To return an image to an independent floating window, click on the Restore button (which takes the place of the Maximize button), also labeled in Figure 15-7.

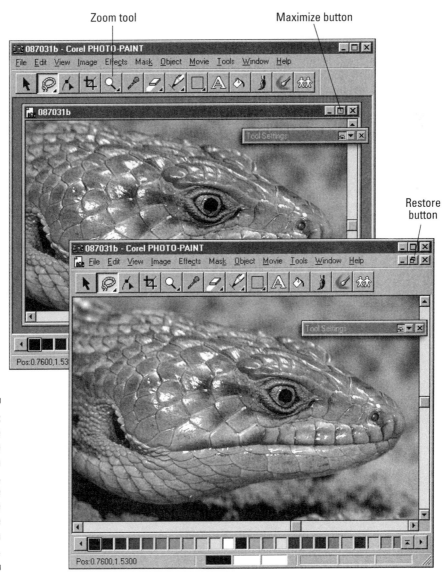

Zoom tool

Maximize button

Restore button

Figure 15-7: Click on the Maximize button (labeled, top) to make the image fill the screen (bottom).

Here are a few other ways to zoom and scroll around inside an image:

- ✔ Select the Zoom tool — the one that looks like a magnifying glass — and click in the image to magnify the image to twice its present size.

- ✔ Right-click or Shift+click with the tool to reduce the image to half its present on-screen size.

- ✔ Or use the same shortcut keys you use in CorelDraw: Press F2 to magnify the image; press F3 to reduce it.

- ✔ To fit the image on-screen so that you can see the entire photograph at once, press F4.

- ✔ You can also choose specific view sizes — anything from 25 to 1600 percent — from the View⇨Zoom submenu.

- ✔ To view the image at the same size it will print, choose View⇨Zoom 1:1. (Keep in mind that this setting is different than View⇨Zoom 100%, which shows one image pixel for every screen pixel, generally making the image appear larger than it will print.)

- ✔ You can also drag with the Zoom tool to create a marquee. Photo-Paint then magnifies the area inside the marquee to fill the entire screen.

- ✔ By default, Photo-Paint does not change the size of the window when you zoom in or out of the image. You have to manually resize the window by dragging the tab in the lower-right corner, where the scroll bars meet (labeled *size tab* back in Figure 15-1).

To make Photo-Paint automatically resize the window as you magnify or reduce the image, do this: Press Ctrl+J (or choose Tools⇨Options) to display the Options dialog box. Then select the Automatic View Resize check box and press Enter. Now press F3 a couple of times. Photo-Paint reduces the window as it reduces your photograph.

- ✔ If the image is bigger than the window, you can drag the scroll boxes in the scroll bars to reveal hidden portions of the photograph. Or you can click on the scroll arrows.

- ✔ You can even scroll by pressing the arrow keys. Each press is equivalent to clicking a scroll arrow once.

- ✔ But better yet, select the Hand tool from the Zoom tool flyout menu and then drag the image with respect to the window. This Hand tool moves the image as you drag; as you may recall, CorelDraw waits to scroll the drawing until after you release the mouse button.

If you don't care for the commands and tools I've mentioned so far and you have plenty of room on-screen, you may want to keep the Navigator roll-up handy. To display the roll-up, press Ctrl+F6 or choose View⇨Roll-Ups⇨Navigator. As labeled in Figure 15-8, the roll-up features a preview of the entire image with a row of icons along the bottom.

✔ A rectangle in the preview outlines the portion of the image visible on-screen. Drag the rectangle to scroll the image.

✔ The first three icons work just like commands in the View menu. (In fact, I've labeled the icons in Figure 15-8 according to their respective commands.) Click on the first icon to see every pixel in the image. Click on the second icon to see the entire image at once. Click on the third icon to view the image at the size at which it will print.

✔ Click on the Zoom In button to magnify the image by a factor of 2. Click on the Zoom Out button to reduce the image by the same amount. It's just like pressing the F2 and F3 keys, respectively.

Image preview

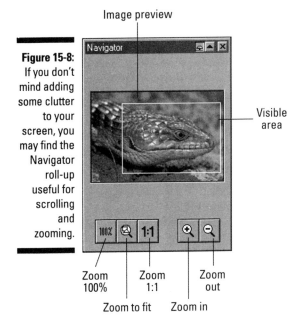

Figure 15-8:
If you don't mind adding some clutter to your screen, you may find the Navigator roll-up useful for scrolling and zooming.

Visible area

Zoom 100%   Zoom 1:1   Zoom out

Zoom to fit   Zoom in

Forging Ahead into the Void

If you'd rather not work from an existing image — as you do every time you press Ctrl+O — you can create an empty canvas and paint a new image from scratch. If the thought of doing so appeals to you, I can only assume that you're the type who's willing to forge ahead utterly on your own into the barren wasteland of the blank page. You're a pioneer — perhaps a little short on common sense, but full of confidence and bravery.

To create a new image, press Ctrl+N or choose File⊅New. Photo-Paint displays the dialog box shown in Figure 15-9. I've darkened the two lowest check boxes in the dialog box to show how completely irrelevant they are to creating a new image. The remaining options require you to make three decisions:

1. How large an image do you want to create?

2. What is the resolution?

3. How many colors do you want to play with?

You don't need any help with image size; just enter the desired width and height of the image into the Width and Height option boxes. (You can also select a preset image size from the Size pop-up menu, but you probably won't want to. These sizes are designed specifically for creating on-screen images for multimedia presentations.)

However, resolution and color open up whole new cans of worms, which is why I take a little extra time to explain them in the following sections.

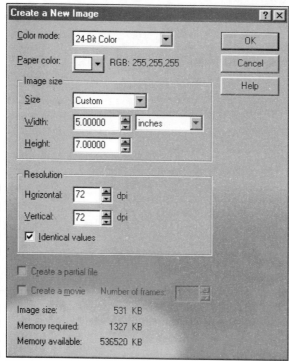

Figure 15-9:
This dialog box lets you specify the size, resolution, and number of colors in a new image.

Dots per inch

Remember Chapter 1? I know that it was a long time ago, but you may want to take a moment and reread the "CorelPhoto-Paint" section. It tells about acquiring images and covers a few other items you may have found yourself wondering about — not the least of which is how images work.

To quickly recap: Unlike CorelDraw drawings, in which objects are defined using complex mathematical equations, Photo-Paint images are made up of tiny colored dots called *pixels*. The number of pixels in an inch is called the *resolution*. So if you create an image that measures 4 inches by 5 inches with a resolution of 72 dots per inch — or *dpi* (pronounced d-p-i) for short — Photo-Paint creates an image that's 288 pixels wide ($4 \times 72 = 288$) by 360 pixels tall ($5 \times 72 = 360$).

You specify a resolution by entering a new value in the Horizontal option box. As long as the Identical Values option is checked, you don't need to change the Vertical value; Photo-Paint automatically makes sure that both values are the same.

Do not turn the Identical Values check box off. Many printers cannot handle different horizontal and vertical resolutions. And besides, turning off the option can make for some pretty ugly results. This is one of those options Corel throws in just to trip you up.

Select your crayons

So far, I've managed to ignore the first option in the Create a New Image dialog box, which requires you to specify the number of colors you want to be able to display on-screen at once. It's as if your mom required you to select a box of crayons before you sat down to color. Photo-Paint's Color Mode pop-up menu lets you select one of six boxes of crayons.

- The first option, Black and White, provides only two crayons, a black one and a white one. That's all you get.

- The second option is Grayscale, which offers 256 shades of gray, ranging from white to black.

- The next option, 16 Color, contains 16 crayons. But the interesting thing about this box is that you can swap crayons after you begin working on your image. If you don't like the default shade of red, for example, you can change it to one of 16 million other possible color variations at any time. Just choose Image➪Color Table, double-click on the red color swatch, and adjust the color as desired. If any pixels in your image are colored in red, Photo-Paint updates them to the new color.

- The 256 Color option is similar to 16 Color, except that you have 16 times as many colors in your crayon box. But just as you can with the 16 Color option, you can change a single crayon in the box at any time by choosing Image⇨Color Table.

- The 24-Bit Color option gives you access to all 16 million colors at once. This option provides the most versatility, but it comes at a price. A 16 million-color image takes up three times as much room on disk as the same image in 256 colors. (All the photographs on the third CorelDraw CD-ROM are 24-Bit Color images.)

- Don't worry about the 32-Bit CMYK option. It's specifically designed for painting CMYK images that you want to print to color separations (as described in the "Printing full-color artwork" section of Chapter 13). But you can print *any* color image to color separations, so the 32-Bit CMYK option makes your image more complicated without any real benefit.

What resolution do I use?

I wish that I could just tell you the perfect resolution to use and send you on your way. But even professionals who create images day in and day out can't agree on a perfect setting. Although I can't tell you exactly what resolution to use, I can give you some guidelines, however.

First, a little background: Higher resolutions result in better looking images because there are more pixels to fool your eyes into thinking that they're seeing a regular photograph. Lower resolutions result in less focused images with occasionally jagged outlines.

However, high-resolution images also take up more space on disk and make Photo-Paint work harder and print slower. Low-resolution images are speedy to edit and print.

Therefore, use as low a resolution value as you can get away with:

- If you just want to print the image on a laser printer and tack it up to your wall, a value between 90 and 120 should suffice.

- If you're creating an image to include in a company newsletter, bump the resolution up to somewhere between 120 and 180. All the images printed in this book fall into this range. All the full-screen images — such as Figures 15-1 and 15-7 — were printed at 140 dpi.

- If you plan on printing a full-color image for the cover of a catalog or some other spiffy publication, try a value between 180 and 300.

Try printing some test images between the extremes listed above and see how they look. You may even want to consult with a commercial printer whose opinion you trust. There's a lot of confusion in this area — and you'll very likely get different answers depending on who you ask — so let me close with the only hard and fast rule: There is no wrong resolution value. What works for you is what counts.

Growing and growing

The lower-left corner of the Create a New Picture dialog box — spotlighted in Figure 15-9 — tells you how much of your computer's memory your image will consume. The Memory Required value can't exceed the Memory Available value. If it does, Photo-Paint complains that it's out of memory and refuses to create your picture.

Keep this in mind when creating a new image,

because your Width, Height, Resolution, and Color Mode choices all contribute to the size of the image in memory. If you do run into a memory limitation problem, try lowering the Resolution values. If that doesn't work, change the Color Mode option from 24-Bit Color to Grayscale or 256 Color. And if the problem persists, lower the Width and Height values.

For the best results, select the Grayscale option to create images that you want to print on a black-and-white printer or select 24-Bit Color to create full-color artwork. Frankly, the other options aren't particularly useful.

Oh, and by the way, you can also change the color of the new canvas by selecting a color from the Paper Color pop-up menu. In general, however, I recommend that you leave the canvas white. After all, a white background ensures bright and vivid colors; any other background will mix with and therefore dim colors that you apply with some of the painting tools. Call me crazy, but I usually prefer to apply color with the painting tools as I go along instead of imposing a color on my artwork right from the start.

Changing the Resolution and Color of Photographs

Now that I've explained what's going on with resolution and color, I should mention that these amazing properties don't merely affect new images; they also affect photographs that you open from CD-ROM or disk. For example, if you open an image from the third CorelDraw CD, its resolution is 96 dpi and it contains millions of colors.

To change the resolution of an image, do the following:

1. **Choose Image⇨Resample.**

   Up comes the Resolution dialog box, which lists the width and height of the image, along with two resolution values, much the same as the Create a New Image dialog box.

2. Select the Maintain Original Size check box.

This step is extremely important! If you do not turn this option on, you run the risk of adding or deleting pixels, which you most certainly do not want to do.

3. Make sure that Maintain Aspect Ratio is checked.

This option is probably already selected, but it's worth a quick check to make sure.

4. Change the Horizontal value.

Thanks to Step 3, you don't have to worry about the Vertical value. Photo-Paint changes that automatically.

5. Press Enter.

Or click on OK.

To change the number of colors in an image, choose a command from the Image⇔Convert To submenu. For example, if you wanted to prepare one of the Corel photographs for inclusion in a black-and-white publication, you would remove the colors from the photograph by choosing Image⇔Convert To⇔Grayscale (8-Bit). In fact, that is exactly what I did to the frog, hawk, and snake photographs contained in this chapter.

When's the last time you read a book that not only taught you an entire universe of valuable information but also served as an constant example of the lessons? "Created with Photo-Paint for Photo-Paint users. That's right, folks, this is the kind of carefully crafted quality readers have come to expect from *CorelDRAW! For Dummies.*" But wait, there's more. If you act now . . . oh, I forgot, I don't have to sell you this book. You're already saddled with it.

Saving, Printing, and Closing Your Work of Art

Whether you create an image from scratch or open a photograph from disk, there are three operations you simply cannot avoid. Resist though you might, you absolutely have to save your changes, print the image, and, of course, close it. Generally speaking, these basic operations work very much like they do in CorelDraw, but there are a few differences. Just for the record, here's how they work:

✔ To save an image, press Ctrl+S or choose File⇔Save. Remember, if you save early and save often, the brain you save could be your own.

✔ To save an image opened off a CD-ROM, you have to choose File⇨Save As. Photo-Paint displays the Save an Image to Disk dialog box. Here you can decide where to save the image on disk and what name you'd like to use. Because you're using Windows 95, your file names can be virtually as long as you want (up to 256 characters).

✔ You may also want to change the file format by choosing an option from the Save as Type pop-up menu. By far the best option is TIFF Bitmap. TIFF is a standard among standards, supported by more programs than just about any other image format. (For more information about file formats, see Chapter 22.)

The second best format is JPEG Bitmap, which alters the pixels in the image in order to save disk space. After you press Enter, a second dialog box appears proffering some technical-looking options. Ignore all the options except the Quality Factor slider bar. Make sure that the value to the right of the slider is 10 or smaller. I'll say that again — 10 or *smaller*. (Higher values do major damage to the image — much more than I consider acceptable.) If the value is larger than 10, enter 10 into the option box and press Enter. Otherwise, just press Enter.

For more info on file formats, read Chapter 22, which introduces you to the top 10 formats you need to know.

✔ Press Ctrl+P or choose File⇨Print to display the Print dialog box. These options work precisely as described in Chapter 13, which covers all the printing news that's fit to print.

✔ To close the image in the foreground window, press Ctrl+F4, choose File⇨Close, or click on the Close button in the upper-right corner of the image window (the one with an X on it). If you haven't saved your most recent round of changes, Photo-Paint asks whether you'd like to save the changes or chalk them up as a waste of time.

✔ Press Alt+F4, choose File⇨Exit, or click on the Close button above the menu bar to get out of Dodge. If you've modified any open image since it was last saved, Photo-Paint asks you whether — perchance — you might like to save the image to disk. After you answer this question for each and every altered image, you exit the Photo-Paint program and return to the Windows 95 desktop (or some other program you may be running).

Chapter 16
Spare the Tool, Spoil the Pixel

In This Chapter

▶ The new Photo-Paint 6 toolbox

▶ Specifying the foreground, background, and fill colors

▶ Erasing and undoing big heaps of mistakes

▶ Avoiding the outline tools

▶ Creating rectangles and other basic shapes

▶ Filling colored areas with other colors

▶ Using Photo-Paint's 15 amazing Paint tool brushes

▶ Applying special effects

▶ Cloning little bits and pieces of your photograph

▶ Erasing back to the saved version of an image

*P*hoto-Paint 6 is one of those rare software upgrades in which less is more. Version 5 supplied a whopping 51 tools, too many tools for its own good — which, coincidentally used to be a headline in this book. The new Photo-Paint cuts the number down to 27. That's fewer tools than Photo-Paint offered when Corel released the first version — Photo-Paint 3 — more than three years ago. For you, this translates to a more straightforward program. For me, it means a perfectly good headline down the tubes.

The prime factor driving the consolidation of Photo-Paint's tools is the enhanced Tool Settings roll-up, which lets you alter the way the selected tool works. As shown in Figure 16-1, the options in this essential roll-up change depending on which tool is selected. When the Zoom tool is selected, for example, the roll-up contains a single, inconsequential check box. But when you select the Paint tool (labeled in Figure 16-1), the roll-up springs to life with three panels of options — considerably more than in previous versions. The options enable you to adjust the tool's performance with an astounding and sometimes excessive amount of precision.

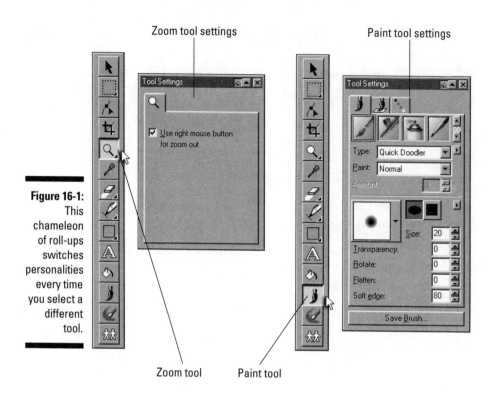

Zoom tool settings

Paint tool settings

Zoom tool

Paint tool

Figure 16-1: This chameleon of roll-ups switches personalities every time you select a different tool.

So although this version of Photo-Paint offers fewer tools, the tools do more. Instead of selecting from six different painting tools — as in Version 5 — you select one Paint tool and modify its performance in the Tool Settings roll-up. Less on-screen gook, more functionality — that's Photo-Paint 6's motto.

In the sections that follow, I touch on all of Photo-Paint's painting and effects tools. That excludes the first five tools in the toolbox (surrounded by gray boxes in Figure 16-2) as well as the Text tool (also surrounded by gray). You may recall that I explained the Zoom and Hand tools in characteristically crystal-clear fashion in the previous chapter. And you have my word that I'll cover the other tools — known collectively as selection or mask tools — in Chapter 17. (That goes for the Text tool, too.)

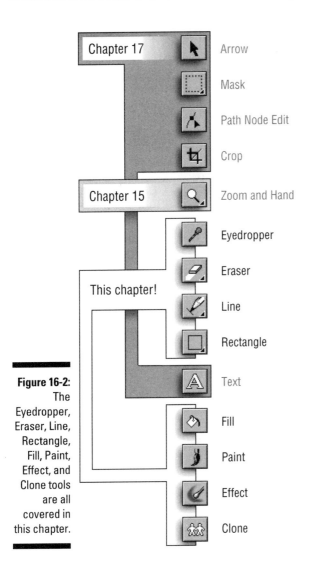

Figure 16-2:
The
Eyedropper,
Eraser, Line,
Rectangle,
Fill, Paint,
Effect, and
Clone tools
are all
covered in
this chapter.

That still leaves a slim majority of the tools — the two groups outlined with white boxes in the figure — open for discussion in this chapter. Some explanations are rather brief — as in, "stay away from this tool, it's no good" — and others are more extensive. When you finish reading, you should have a clear grasp on how the tools function, which ones you want to use on a more or less regular basis, and which ones you can safely ignore.

Loading Your Tools with Color

Before you can apply any color to your image, you have to specify which color you want to use. As you do in CorelDraw, you select colors from the color palette at the bottom of the screen. Photo-Paint keeps track of three colors at a time — the foreground color, the background color, and the fill color. All three are displayed in the center portion of the status bar, as labeled in Figure 16-3.

✔ The Line and Paint tools both draw in the foreground color (which Corel calls the *paint color*). Photo-Paint also applies the foreground color to the outlines of simple shapes — such as those drawn with the Rectangle tool — and to characters created with the Text tool.

You can select a new foreground color by clicking on one of the swatches in the color palette.

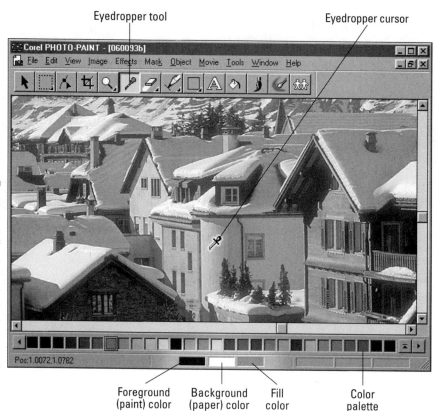

Eyedropper tool   Eyedropper cursor

Figure 16-3:
The three colors in the middle of the status bar repre-sent the foreground, background, and fill colors.

Foreground (paint) color   Background (paper) color   Fill color   Color palette

✔ The background color (which Corel calls the *paper color*) is used by the Eraser tool. Also, if you select an area and press Delete, Photo-Paint fills the selection with the background color.

To switch to a different background color, Ctrl+click on a swatch in the color palette.

✔ The Fill tool uses the fill color. Photo-Paint also uses this color to fill simple shapes created with the Rectangle, Oval, and Polygon tools.

Change the fill color by right-clicking or Shift+clicking on a swatch in the color palette.

Lifting Colors Right Off the Canvas

When editing photographic images, you may find it helpful to match the foreground, background, or fill color to an exact color in the image. Doing so helps to hide your edits by maintaining color consistency with the original image. Sometimes, you want your effects to scream, "Look at me, I'm an electronic manipulation created in Photo-Paint!" But other times, you'd just as soon they didn't. When you're looking for subtlety, look to the Eyedropper tool.

The Eyedropper tool enables you to select colors from the image itself and then turn around and apply these colors using other tools. It's as if you're siphoning color out of your photograph using a turkey baster or some other extracting device. Well, it's kind of like that anyway. The only difference is that you don't delete any color from the photograph. Oh, and unlike a turkey baster, the top of the Eyedropper won't fall off in the dishwasher and melt on the heating unit.

✔ After arming yourself with the Eyedropper, click on a color in the image to select a new foreground color.

✔ Ctrl+click on a color in the photograph to replace the background color.

✔ Right-click or Shift+click on a color to replace the fill color.

✔ Double-click on the Eyedropper icon in the toolbox or press Ctrl+F2 to display the Color roll-up, which lets you define a custom color. This roll-up works just like its counterpart in CorelDraw, which I describe in the "Making New Colors in Your Spare Time" section of Chapter 7.

Erasing and Undoing Your Way Back to the Good Old Days

In real life, an eraser gives you the opportunity to retract a pencil stroke. But it doesn't do a very comprehensive job — you can still see some pencil remnants — and you can't use the eraser to undo other kinds of strokes, such as pen strokes, paint strokes, and big globs of black tar.

Photo-Paint handily addresses this problem by offering not one, but three erasers that erase everything under the sun. They still leave room for improvement — as I gleefully explain in the next section — but they're a heck of a lot better than those greasy little Pink Pearl fragments that littered the pencil tray in your desk at school (you know, right next to the Hot Wheels that always got confiscated sooner or later).

Version 6 also offers a new Undo List command that enables you to undo multiple operations. The implementation isn't quite as convenient as in CorelDraw, but it can come in extremely handy, as explained later in this section.

Scrubbing away those stubborn stains

Photo-Paint provides three different kinds of erasers, one of which is useful, another that isn't useful at all, and a third that's just plain weird. Ironically, the eraser that appears in the toolbox by default is the least useful tool of the bunch. (Okay, that's standard operating procedure for Corel, but it's ironic to normal folk like you and me.) To get to the more practical erasers, press and hold on the Eraser tool icon to display a flyout menu of additional tools, as labeled in Figure 16-4.

Much as you value my personal opinion on every little facet of Photo-Paint, there's always the chance that you'd like to investigate the erasers on your own before deciding which one you prefer. So here's how they work:

  ✔ Drag with the Local Undo tool to selectively undo the effects of the most recent operation. Unlike Edit⇨Undo, which undoes the entire operation, the Local Undo tool restores only the portion of the image you drag over. This tool is especially useful for erasing small portions of a line you just finished drawing. I rate this tool very useful.

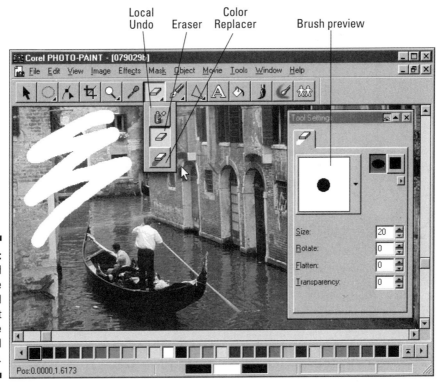

Local Undo   Eraser   Color Replacer   Brush preview

Figure 16-4:
Click and hold on the Eraser tool icon to get to the more useful erasers.

✔ The standard Eraser tool paints a hard-edged line in the background color. You can't even soften the eraser to make the lines less jagged. I rate this tool a complete and total waste of time.

If you want to paint in white (the default background color), change the foreground color to white and use the Paint tool, which is infinitely more versatile.

✔ As you drag with the Color Replacer tool, Photo-Paint replaces all occurrences of the foreground color (and colors similar to it) with the background color. For example, if you want to change a red line to green, change the foreground color to red, change the background color to green, and trace over the line with the Color Replacer tool. This tool can be moderately useful, but it still produces jagged results. Photo-Paint is incapable of softening any eraser effect.

✔ For the most part, the options in the Tool Settings roll-up let you change the size and shape of the eraser. Click on the big brush preview (labeled in Figure 16-4) to display a pop-up menu of preset eraser shapes. You can also edit the Size, Rotate, and Flatten values to create a custom brush, but Photo-Paint provides you with so many presets that you probably won't need to bother.

✔ When using the Eraser tool, you get a <u>T</u>ransparency option box in the Tool Settings roll-up. Raise the <u>T</u>ransparency value to mix the background color with the existing colors in the image. Higher values — up to 99 — make the background color more translucent. This option makes the Eraser tool slightly more useful, but not much.

✔ When using the Color Replacer tool, you can control how many colors in the image get changed to the background color. The value in the Tolerance option box, in the lower-left corner of the Tool Settings roll-up, determines how close a color has to be to the foreground color to be replaced. Higher values cause more colors to be replaced; lower values replace fewer colors.

✔ Double-click on any of the eraser icons to apply that tool's effect to the selected portion of the image. (I explain how to select stuff in the next chapter.) If nothing is selected, Photo-Paint applies the effect to the entire image.

For example, if you double-click on the Color Replacer icon, Photo-Paint replaces all occurrences of the foreground color throughout the image to the background color. Double-clicking on the Eraser tool icon fills the entire image with the background color; double-clicking on the Local Undo icon is just like choosing <u>E</u>dit⇨<u>U</u>ndo.

In order to double-click on a tool icon, it has to be visible in the toolbox. You can't double-click on a flyout icon.

Strangely enough, the best eraser tool isn't an eraser tool at all. It's a special function of the Clone tool called the Eraser brush. Read the "Painting One Portion of an Image onto Another" section at the end of this chapter to find out all about it.

Reviewing the history of your image

As long as we're on the subject of undoing things, I should mention that the Undo command works a little differently in Photo-Paint than in CorelDraw. In CorelDraw, you can choose <u>E</u>dit⇨<u>U</u>ndo several times in a row to undo one operation after another. In Photo-Paint, choosing <u>E</u>dit⇨<u>U</u>ndo once undoes the operation; choosing the command twice undoes the undo.

To undo more than one operation, you have to resort to the Undo List. Choose <u>E</u>dit⇨Undo <u>L</u>ist to display the Undo List dialog box shown in Figure 16-5. In the dialog box, Photo-Paint lists every single operation that you've performed while working on a photograph.

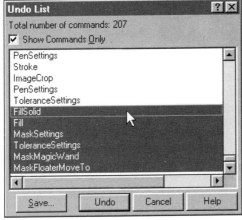

Figure 16-5:
Click on an
operation in
the list to
undo that
operation
and all
those that
followed it.

This list can be rather complicated — it may include things that you didn't even know you did, along with a bunch of meaningless numerical data. To get rid of the numbers — they aren't the least bit helpful — select the Show Commands Only check box, as I have in the figure. Things suddenly become easier to decipher.

Next, scroll through the list until you find the specific operation — however long ago — that you want to undo. Then click on it. Photo-Paint selects that operation and every one that follows it. It's important to remember that like CorelDraw, Photo-Paint undoes sequential operations only; you can't undo a single operation and leave the ones after it intact.

After you select the commands that you want to undo, click on the Undo button or press Enter. Photo-Paint sets about undoing the selected operations. Actually, that's not quite right. It really reperforms all the operations that you *didn't* undo. Depending on how long you've been working on the image, the process can take a few minutes, so be patient.

Make very sure that you want to undo the selected operations in the list, because you can't reverse the Undo List command by using Edit⇨Undo.

Drawing Pointless, Jagged Outlines

From that headline, you may get an inkling that I don't care for the tools I'm about to discuss. In fact, I think that they are wholly without merit. If you value your time, skip this section. However, if you want to learn about every Photo-Paint tool regardless of what I think of it — or you think that a few paragraphs of tactless prose might be worth a couple of chuckles — continue reading.

The tools I'm leading up to are the three outline tools. The first, the Line tool, appears in the toolbox by default. (It looks like a pencil drawing a line.) If you click and hold on the tool, you get a flyout menu that contains two alternates, the Curve and Pen tools.

✔ Drag with the Line tool to draw a straight line between two points. Click with the tool and then keep clicking at different locations to draw a free-form outline with straight sides. Each time you click, you set a corner in the shape. Double-click to end the line.

When the Line tool is selected, you can select the Anti-Aliasing check box in the Tool Settings roll-up to create soft lines. Unfortunately, this is not an option for the Curve and Pen tools, which is one of the reasons why they're so unspeakably awful.

✔ The second tool in the flyout is the Curve tool. This tool existed in previous versions of Photo-Paint, but it has changed in Version 6. Drag with the Curve tool to draw a free-form line. After you release, Photo-Paint displays the line as a path complete with nodes. Drag a node to move it. Select the node to get to its control points (which let you bend the segments between points, as explained in Chapter 5). You can even drag a segment to bend it. When you're satisfied with the curvature of the line, click anywhere in the image window to convert it to pixels. Ta da! Photo-Paint gives birth to a jagged, ugly line.

✔ Drag with the Pen tool to create a free-form line. You can't edit the line as you can lines drawn with the Curve tool. Photo-Paint lays down the pixels right away. The thought that some poor soul may actually use this tool in a naive attempt to enhance an image makes me shudder. Don't *you* do it, I beg of you.

Even though the Pen tool is Photo-Paint's least useful tool, it's also one of the easiest to access. Just press F5. Too bad Photo-Paint doesn't offer shortcuts for tools that you might actually use, like the Hand and Eyedropper tools.

Hard-edged lines have no business populating your photographs. After all, they interrupt the seamless blend between pixels that is the hallmark of computer images. Certainly, I commend the Line tool for its soft edges. And I would even recommend using it if you could assign arrowheads to the lines. But you can't, so I don't. Phooey to all the outline tools and a pox upon their houses.

Drawing Semi-Pointless Geometric Shapes

The simple shape tools — the next tools in line in the toolbox — are mostly worthless. Photo-Paint offers three simple shape tools, which you access by clicking and holding on the Rectangle tool icon. I labeled these tools in Figure 16-6.

✔ The Rectangle tool lets you draw rectangles. Ctrl+drag to draw squares; Shift+drag to draw the shape outward from the center. You can select the Rectangle tool by pressing F6.

✔ The Oval tool draws ovals. Ctrl+drag to draw circles; Shift+drag to draw from the center out. Press F7 to select the Oval tool. (Yet another waste of a keyboard shortcut.)

✔ The Polygon tool draws orange hamsters dressed in festive German drinking costumes.

No, sorry, my mistake. After reviewing my notes, I find that the Polygon tool actually draws free-form shapes with straight sides. This means that it's less like the Polygon tool in CorelDraw and more like the Line tool in Photo-Paint. You click to add corners and double-click when you're finished.

By default, Photo-Paint fills the shapes with the fill color. But you can also request no fill or some special fill by using the options in the Tool Settings roll-up (again, labeled in Figure 16-6). Click on the Fountain Fill icon, for example, to fill the shape with a gradation. Click on the X icon to make the fill transparent. Each one of these icons directly corresponds to a special fill function in CorelDraw, as described in the last section of Chapter 7.

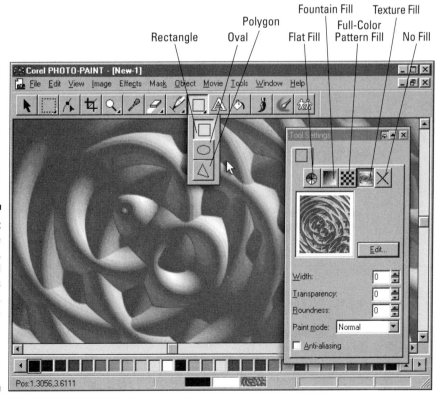

Figure 16-6: The simple shape tools, the Tool Settings options, and an interesting background created with a texture fill.

Although the special fill options are certainly attractive, they can't gloss over the simple fact that geometric shapes lend themselves to image editing about as well as vampire bats lend themselves to deep-sea diving. Their harsh corners and high-contrast curves interrupt the naturalistic appearance of just about any image.

So if you don't want people to be able to see from several miles off that you've been mucking about in an image, don't use the simple shape tools. The only exception is the Rectangle tool, which has two beneficial applications:

✔ First, you can use it to draw an outline around your image. Select the X icon in the Tool Settings roll-up, enter a Width value to set the outline to the desired thickness, and then draw a rectangle around the entire image.

✔ Second, you can create custom backgrounds. In Figure 16-6, for example, I've entered a Width value of 0 to eliminate the rectangle outline. Then I selected the Texture Fill icon, clicked on the Edit button to select the texture I wanted to use, and dragged across the screen with the Rectangle tool to fill the image with the texture.

Isn't it inspiring when the simplest tool produces the most useable results? I told you that less is more.

Plunking Down the Paint

The next tool on our hit parade is the Fill tool, which looks like a tipped bucket with paint dribbling out of it. You click with the Fill tool to replace an area of continuous color with the fill color.

In Figure 16-7 — which comes from image 079033b in the Europe folder — I set the fill color to white and clicked with the Fill tool inside the archway. Photo-Paint replaced the previously black pixels with white, making the archway look like it goes right through the page. If you use your imagination, that is.

To control the range of colors affected by the Fill tool, enter a value into the Tolerance option box, found in the bottom-left corner of the Tool Settings roll-up. You can also select an Anti-Aliasing check box to soften the edges of the filled area. (In Figure 16-7, the Tolerance value was 10, and Anti-Aliasing was turned on.)

You can also change the fill color from a flat fill to a gradation or texture by selecting the icons along the top of the Tool Settings roll-up. These are the same icons labeled back in Figure 16-6.

Fill tool cursor

Figure 16-7:
An area of black before (left) and after (right) clicking on it with the Fill tool.

The No Fill icon is absent; after all, replacing an area with a transparent fill doesn't make any sense. I mean, what is there to see behind the image? The Windows 95 desktop? The motherboard and other yucky computer innards? The center of the Earth? Without the No Fill icon, we'll never know.

Painting with a Tackle Box Full of Brushes

Using the Paint tool is simplicity itself. You merely drag around inside the image to lay down strokes of foreground color.

However, adjusting the properties of the Paint tool in the Tool Settings roll-up can be a nightmare. Quite simply, the roll-up offers far more options than you will ever exploit — assuming, of course, that you have a life.

So rather than explain each and every option that's available, I'll limit my discussions to the handful of options that matter most:

✔ As shown in Figure 16-8, three tab icons appear along the Tool Settings roll-up. You can click on one of these tabs to switch between the three panels of Paint tool options. But don't. The second and third panels are filled with goofy options you'll never use in a billion years.

✔ Beneath the tab icons is a row of four slightly larger icons. These icons represent the predefined brushes. Though you can see only four brushes at a time, Photo-Paint 6 offers a total of 15 brushes. To scroll from one row of brushes to the next, click on the arrowheads to the right of the icons.

Instead of explaining how each of the 15 brushes work, I show lines painted with the brushes in Figure 16-8. Each brush is pictured and labeled next to its line. The Paint tool always paints in the foreground color, except when you use the Water Smudge brush (second from the bottom). This brush smears existing colors in the image as if the colors were wet.

✔ Below the brush icons is a Type pop-up menu. If you're looking for a slightly different effect than what is offered by the 15 brushes, you can select a different effect from this menu.

✔ To mix the foreground color with the existing colors in an image in wacky and unusual ways, select an option from the Paint pop-up menu. To explain how all these options work would take five more books. But I do want to call your attention to three fun options: Add, Subtract, and Color.

Select the Add option to lighten the colors in an image as you paint over them. This option works especially well with the Hi-Liter brush and a dark foreground color. Select Subtract to darken colors — great for use with the Felt Marker and a light foreground color. And select Color — much farther down the menu — to colorize an image with any brush. (By colorize, I mean to add color to a black-and-white image or replace the color without affecting the detail in a color image.)

✔ To change the size and shape of the brush, click on the brush preview (labeled in Figure 16-8) to display a pop-up menu of alternatives. You can also adjust the values in the five option boxes below and to the right of the preview, but you can generally rest assured the pop-up menu offers every brush size and shape you'd ever want.

✔ Folks who are serious about painting generally prefer to work with a cursor that represents the brush size and shape. To swap the silly paint-brush cursor for a size and shape cursor, press Ctrl+J (or choose Tools⇨Options), select the Use Shape Cursor check box, and press Enter. This option affects the cursors used by the Paint and Effect tools, as well as all the erasers and line tools.

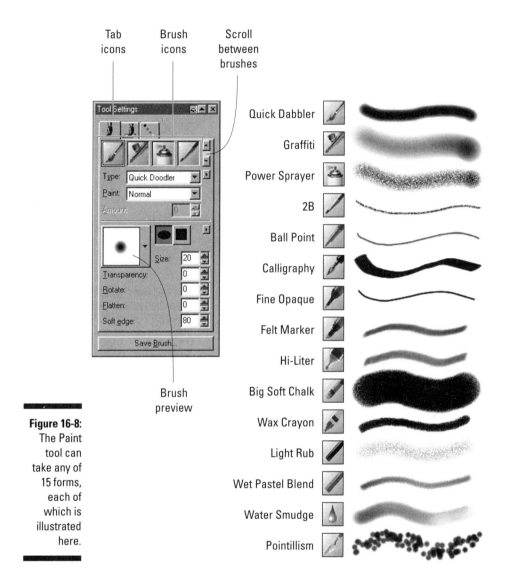

Tab icons   Brush icons   Scroll between brushes

Quick Dabbler

Graffiti

Power Sprayer

2B

Ball Point

Calligraphy

Fine Opaque

Felt Marker

Hi-Liter

Big Soft Chalk

Wax Crayon

Light Rub

Wet Pastel Blend

Water Smudge

Pointillism

Brush preview

Figure 16-8:
The Paint tool can take any of 15 forms, each of which is illustrated here.

Smudging, Lightening, Colorizing, and Blurring

The second-to-last tool is the Effect tool. As you do with the Paint tool, you use the tool by dragging across your image. And as you can with the Paint tool, you can adjust the way the Effect tool works by selecting different brushes from the Tool Settings roll-up.

Altogether, the Effect tool supplies ten brushes, displayed and labeled in Figure 16-9. Because many of the brushes work only in color, I can't show you how they work as I did for the Paint tool brushes back in Figure 16-8. So you'll have to experiment and rely on the following descriptions:

✔ The first thing I should mention is that you can change how each brush behaves by selecting an option from the Type pop-up menu. I can't tell you how every single option works — we'd be here till next Saturday (whenever that is) — but I can tell you how the brushes function in general, regardless of which Type option is active.

✔ The Smear brush smears colors in the image. Sometimes, it smears colors as if they were wet; other times, it takes the pixels at the beginning of your drag and repeats them over and over throughout the drag.

✔ The Smudge brush mixes pixels from one area into another. It does this rather randomly, creating a rough, gritty effect. Try dragging two or three times in the same direction for the best results.

✔ Use the Brightness brush to brighten the area you drag over. Change the Amount value under the Paint pop-up menu to increase or decrease the lightening effect. You can also darken pixels by selecting Darken from the Type pop-up menu or entering a negative value into the Amount option box.

✔ Select the Contrast brush to increase the contrast between light and dark pixels. Again, change the Amount value to increase or decrease the effect. In fact, that goes for all the other Effect tool brushes.

✔ The Hue brush is really dumb. It changes every color you drag over to a different color. Red changes to green, green to blue, blue to red, and everything else to other colors in between. Now, that'll come in handy.

✔ The Hue Replacer brush replaces every color in the image with the foreground color. This brush may sound even dumber than the Hue brush, but it's actually pretty useful. It's just the thing for colorizing a color image. For example, you could change a blue dress to orange without otherwise changing the way the dress looks.

✔ If the colors in your image are too vivid or too faded and drab, you can downplay or bolster them by dragging over them with the Sponge brush. If the Amount value is negative, the sponge sucks color out of an image; if the value is positive, the sponge puts color in.

✔ The Tint brush is the perfect tool for colorizing a grayscale photograph. After converting the image to color — by choosing Image⇨Convert To⇨RGB Color (24-bit) — you can select a foreground color and paint with the Tint brush. But be sure to decrease the Amount value to 50 or lower to allow the highlights and shadows to show through.

✔ Paint with the Blend brush to blur the pixels in an image, giving the photograph a softer quality. It's just the thing for getting that Vaseline-on-the-lens effect that was so popular in the Sixties.

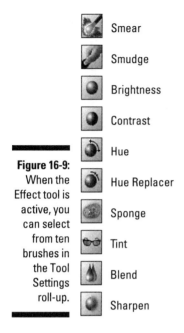

Smear

Smudge

Brightness

Contrast

Hue

Hue Replacer

Sponge

Tint

Blend

Sharpen

Figure 16-9:
When the Effect tool is active, you can select from ten brushes in the Tool Settings roll-up.

✔ You could use the Sharpen brush to sharpen the focus of an image. But it doesn't work worth a hill of beans. The much better way to enhance the focus of a photograph is to choose Effects⇨Sharpen⇨Adaptive Unsharp, as described in the "Bringing an image into sharper focus" section of Chapter 17. (I know that it sounds hard, but it's not.)

Painting One Portion of an Image onto Another

The tool whose icon looks like a couple of paper dolls is the Clone tool, which lets you copy one portion of an image onto another just by dragging. You can use the tool to duplicate portions of the image — take one cow and turn it into a herd, for example. Or you can cover up scratches and bits of dust that sometimes get scanned along with an image.

To use the tool, Shift+click to specify the portion of the image that you want to clone. A blinking cross appears in this spot. Then move your cursor to a different spot and drag to clone the image. The cross moves with your cursor to show what is being cloned. You can change the clone spot any time by again Shift+clicking.

When the Clone tool is selected, the Tool Settings roll-up offers four brushes, displayed and labeled in Figure 16-10. They work as follows:

> ✔ The Normal Clone brush clones the image normally. This is the brush you'll want to use most often.

Figure 16-10:
Though the four Clone tool brushes feature ghostly silhouettes that may frighten those with faint hearts, they are in fact quite harmless.

 Normal Clone

 Impressionism Clone

 Pointillism Clone

 Eraser

> ✔ The Impressionism Clone brush paints multiple lines at a time in different colors. The lines weave back and forth, so I guess you're supposed to think that Van Gogh might have used this brush. But come on, just because the guy cut off his ear doesn't mean that he was *totally* insane. This brush is too goofy.

> ✔ If the Impressionism Clone brush captures the spirit of Van Gogh, the Pointillism Clone brush embodies Georges Seurat. The brush lays down a bunch of differently colored dots. If you're painting a Hawaiian lei or a DNA molecule, it'll come in quite handy. Otherwise, not.

> ✔ In fact, the only Clone tool brush you're likely to use other than the Normal brush is new to Photo-Paint 6. I speak of the Eraser brush, which erases pixels back to the way they looked when you last saved the image to disk. Between you and me, this is an exceedingly useful brush. It stands on its own as one of the most useful tools Photo-Paint has to offer.

So why didn't Corel include the Eraser brush with the other erasers instead of with the Clone tool? Perhaps it was because the brush clones pixels from the saved image onto the version shown on-screen. But that reasoning also applies to the Local Undo tool, which is classified as an eraser. So my theory is that Corel buried the feature so that you'd have to read my book to find out about it. Wow, those guys. You gotta love 'em.

Chapter 17

Twisting Reality around Your Little Finger

- -

In This Chapter

▶ Using Photo-Paint's mask tools

▶ Softening the edges of a selection

▶ Changing the sensitivity of the Lasso Mask and Magic Wand Mask tools

▶ Adjusting the outline of a selection

▶ Moving and cloning selections

▶ Cropping an image

▶ Sharpening focus

▶ Making the colors bright and perky

▶ Converting selections to objects

▶ Transforming an object

▶ Creating and editing text in Photo-Paint

- -

*T*he Photo-Paint stuff I've explained so far qualifies as mildly interesting. Though rather easy to use, the functions covered in Chapters 15 and 16 aren't terribly powerful. Where Photo-Paint really shows off its muscles is in the features covered in this chapter. In these mild-mannered pages, you learn how to isolate portions of the image that you want to edit, change the focus, balance the colors, and even slap colors onto different backgrounds. The tools and commands are a little bit harder to use than those discussed in earlier chapters, but they can deliver some amazing results. It makes me giddy just thinking about it.

Specifying Which Part of the Image You Want to Edit

The first three tools in the toolbox let you select and manipulate portions of your image. If you click and hold on the second tool down, you get a flyout menu of six alternative tools. Altogether, these nine tools — all labeled in Figure 17-1 — represent the most important collection of tools Photo-Paint has to offer.

These tools fall into three categories:

- ✔ The Arrow tool — which Corel calls the Pick tool — lets you manipulate selections that you've converted into objects. Very likely, you have no idea what I'm talking about, which is why I examine this tool in the "Setting Your Selections Free" section toward the end of this chapter.

  To switch from the selected tool to the Arrow tool, press the spacebar. To switch back to the selected tool, press the spacebar again.

- ✔ The seven mask tools — all available from the flyout menu shown in Figure 17-1 — let you select portions of the image. (A *mask* is Corel's fancy word for a selection outline.) I discuss these indispensable tools in the very next section.

- ✔ The Path Node Edit tool is twice as complicated as its name makes it sound. You draw a CorelDraw-like path one node at a time. Then you fuss around with the nodes and control points using a collection of buttons straight out of Draw's Node Edit roll-up. And finally, you convert the path to a selection outline that you could have more easily drawn with one of the mask tools. If you don't mind a little advice, I suggest that you run fast, run far, and avoid this tool like the plague.

Carving out a little bit of imagery with the wondrous mask tools

As in CorelDraw, you have to select a portion of an image in Photo-Paint if you want to manipulate it. But instead of selecting discrete objects — you know, such as rectangles, polygons, and letters of text — you select free-form areas of the image, much as if you were cutting patterns out of a bolt of fabric.

Photo-Paint provides you with six different types of scissors to cut with; they come in the form of the first six mask tools labeled in Figure 17-1. (The seventh mask tool — Mask Transform — lets you modify selection outlines. I cover it separately in the next section.) Here's how these six slick scissors stack up:

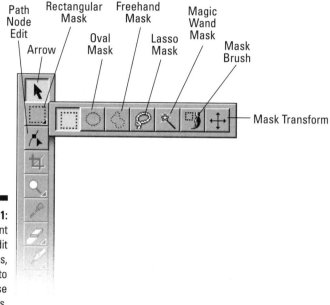

Figure 17-1:
If you want to edit photographs, learn how to use these tools.

✔ Drag with the Rectangular Mask tool to select a rectangular portion of the image. (Corel calls this the Rectan*gle* Mask tool, but Rectan*gular* Mask is more accurate. Small point, but I just didn't want you to get confused by my nit-picking.) Ctrl+drag with the tool to create a square selection. Shift+drag to draw the selection outward from the center.

✔ Drag with the Oval Mask tool to select an oval area of the image. (Corel calls this tool the Circle Mask tool, but it only draws circles if you press the Ctrl key.) Ctrl+drag to draw a perfectly circular selection; Shift+drag to draw the selection from the center out.

✔ Use the Freehand Mask tool to create a free-form selection outline with straight or curved sides. To draw straight sides, click to set the first point and then continue clicking to add corners to the polygon. To draw curved sides, just drag with the tool. When you finish drawing your outline, double-click to convert it to a selection.

Before you double-click to convert the outline to a selection, you can delete the last corner or node in the outline by pressing Delete. You can even press Delete several times in a row to delete the last few corners or nodes. This is a good way to fix portions of the selection outline that you don't like. Try it out with curved or straight-sided outlines.

✔ The Lasso Mask tool works similarly to the Freehand Mask tool: You click to add corners or drag to create a curved outline and then you double-click to convert the outline to a selection. The difference is that when you double-click, the Lasso Mask tool tightens the selection around a specified background color. In other words, it adjusts your selection to home in on a specific portion of the image.

Perhaps an example will help to clarify: Suppose that you want to rope a calf set against an alfalfa-green background. (Ya see how I'm gittin' into the lassoin' spirit, here? Yeehaw!) If you begin dragging on the alfalfa, Photo-Paint sets green as the background color and tightens around the calf. If you begin dragging on the calf, Photo-Paint sets calf brown as the background and tightens on the alfalfa.

✔ Click with the Magic Wand Mask tool to select an area of continuous color. In the first example in Figure 17-2, I opened a photograph that's cleverly named 085044 and found in the People folder on the third CD-ROM. I then clicked in the center of the kid's forehead, at the location shown by the cursor in the second example in the figure. Photo-Paint selected a range of colors in the kid's face, extending all the way from the top of his cranium down to the base of his chin. Just to make the selected area more obvious, I pressed Delete to fill it with white.

The Magic Wand Mask tool can take a few moments to work because it involves complex mathematical operations that tax Photo-Paint's tiny brain. Try to be patient.

✔ To create a selection outline with the Mask Brush tool, you just drag as if you were painting with the Paint tool. In the first example in Figure 17-3, I dragged around the perimeter of the kid's head. Photo-Paint traces the selection around the brushstroke. To more clearly demonstrate the selection, I pressed Delete to get the second example in the figure.

Regardless of which tool you use to select your image, Photo-Paint displays an animated conga line of dots around the selected area. These hyperactive dots are known far and wide as *marching ants*. Honest, that's what they're called. Everyone thinks that computer jargon has to be obscure and intimidating, but sometimes it's just plain silly.

If the marching ants begin to annoy you or prevent you from seeing some portion of the image that you want to scrutinize, choose Mask➪Marquee Visible to turn the command off and hide the ants. The selection is still there — you just can't see it any more. To bring the ants back so that you know where the selection is, just choose the Marquee Visible command again.

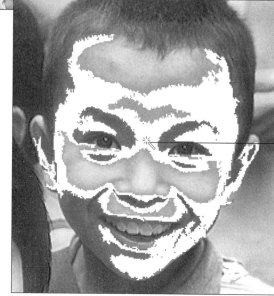

Magic Wand
Mask cursor

Figure 17-2:
After
opening
image
085044 in
the People
folder (top), I
selected an
area of
continuous
color with
the Magic
Wand Mask
tool and
pressed
Delete
(bottom).

—Marching ants

—Mask Brush cursor

Figure 17-3:
Here I drew
a selection
outline using
the Mask
Brush tool
(top) and
then
pressed
Delete to
fill the
selection
with white
(bottom).

Fine-tuning your selection outline

If the methods just described were your only means of creating selection
outlines, Photo-Paint would be a pretty poor excuse for an image-editing
program. After all, it's not as if you can expect to draw a selection outline and
get it just right on the first try. Suppose that you wanted to select that kid's
head in Figure 17-3 and then plop it onto a baby fur seal, as I did in Figure 17-4.
(By the way, that seal is image 041078b in the Animals folder.) Creating a
selection this perfect requires a little effort. You have to spend a lot of time
refining the selection until you get every hair, ear, and whisker just the way you
want it.

Original
baby seal

Figure 17-4:
Before I
could
plaster the
kid's face
onto this
innocent
arctic
critter, I had
to spend
lots of time
perfecting
the
selection
outline.

After
expert
cosmetic
surgery

That's where Photo-Paint's Tool Settings roll-up, Mask Transform tool, and Mask menu come in. These items enable you to modify selection outlines in ways too numerous to mention. I wanted to take a stab at mentioning a few of them anyway, which is why I came up with the following list:

✔ When you use the Oval Mask, Freehand Mask, Lasso, or Magic Wand tool, the Tool Settings roll-up includes a check box named Anti-Aliasing. This strange word is one of the most cherished terms in all of computer-dweebdom because it sounds really technical and it means something very simple — soft edges. Unless you want jagged edges around your selection, turn the check box on for each and every tool. (According to Corel's typically inverted logic, each and every check box is turned off by default.)

By the way, the Anti-Aliasing check box is dimmed when you work on black-and-white, 16-color, or 256-color images. Photo-Paint can only soften selections in grayscale or full-color images.

✔ If you draw a selection with the <u>A</u>nti-Aliasing check box turned off, don't think that you can go back and soften it by choosing Mas<u>k</u>⇨<u>S</u>hape⇨<u>A</u>nti-Alias. Tragically, this command is absolutely worthless. (It's not Corel's fault; it's just that the command is trying to do something that's fundamentally impossible.)

✔ You can, however, blur the selection outline after creating it. (Figure 17-5 demonstrates the difference between softening and blurring.) Choose Mask⇨<u>F</u>eather to display the Feather dialog box. Then enter a value between 1 and 200 into the <u>W</u>idth option box. Larger values produce blurrier selections. To get the right-hand effect in Figure 17-5, I entered a value of 12.

The <u>D</u>irection pop-up menu determines whether Photo-Paint blurs outward away from the selection outline or inward toward the center. When in doubt, select the Middle option. And always select Soft from the <u>E</u>dge pop-up menu. The Hard option creates harsh edges inside the blur, a singularly unattractive effect.

✔ When you select the Lasso Mask or Magic Wand Mask tool, the Tool Settings roll-up also includes the Tolerance slider bar. Move the slider handle to the right to raise the Tolerance value. A high Tolerance value for the Lasso Mask tool causes the selection outline to shrink farther and avoid more background colors. In the case of the Magic Wand Mask tool, a higher Tolerance value causes Photo-Paint to select a wider range of related colors. Try raising and lowering the value while using each tool to get a sense of how this option works.

✔ When you're using the Mask Brush tool, the Tool Settings roll-up lets you change the size and shape of the brush. Fatter brushes result in fatter selection outlines. Though the roll-up offers quite a few options for creating a customized brush, I recommend that you just click on the big brush preview on the left side of the roll-up and select an alternative brush from the pop-up menu. Unless you get seriously interested in this tool — which is unlikely — the predefined brushes should prove more than adequate.

✔ After you create a selection outline, you can move, scale, rotate, or skew it independently of the image using the Mask Transform tool. Drag the selection with the tool to move it. Drag one of the handles around the selection to scale it.

Click on the selection with the Mask Transform tool to switch to the rotate and skew mode. Then you can drag a corner handle to rotate the selection outline or drag a top, bottom, or side handle to slant it.

You can also use the options in the Tool Settings roll-up to move, scale, rotate, and skew the outline numerically. These options work just like their counterparts in CorelDraw, which I explain in the early pages of Chapter 9.

Figure 17-5:
A softened
and blurred
selection
placed
against a
white
background.

Softened (Anti-Aliasing)   Blurred (Mask⇨Feather)

✔ To select all colors throughout the image that are similar to the selected colors, choose Mask⇨Similar. This is a great way to expand the colors selected with the Magic Wand Mask tool. Suppose that you're working on a map in which all the water is blue and the land is green. If you click with the Magic Wand Mask tool inside a lake, you select just the lake. But if you then choose the Similar command, you select all the water on the map, whether it's surrounded by land or not.

✔ You can increase the size of a selection by choosing Mask⇨Shape⇨Expand and entering a value in the ensuing dialog box. Larger values increase the selection by larger amounts. To similarly decrease the size of the selection, choose Mask⇨Shape⇨Reduce.

✔ To select everything that's not selected and deselect everything that is — in other words, to *invert* the selection — choose Mask⇨Invert.

✔ To deselect everything, choose Mask⇨None or just click outside the selection with any of the mask tools.

✔ To select every last pixel in the image, choose Mask⇨All. Or double-click on the mask tool icon in the toolbox.

Making manual adjustments

All the selection modifications I've mentioned so far are automatic. You tell Photo-Paint what to do, and it does it. But what if you want to make more precise adjustments manually? Suppose that you select a kid's head but you miss his ears. Sadly, Photo-Paint does not offer Mask⇨Add Ears. So how do you add the ears to the selection?

The answer lies in the Mask⇨Mode submenu. Choosing one of these four commands turns the others off. Also, each command remains in effect until you choose a different one.

✔ By default, Mask⇨Mode⇨Normal is active. In this mode, every time you create a new selection outline, you deselect the rest of the image.

✔ If you want to increase the size of the selection, choose Mask⇨Mode⇨Add To Mask. To select the kid's ears without deselecting the head, for example, you'd choose this command, drag around one ear, and then drag around the other.

✔ To decrease the size of the selection, choose Mask⇨Mode⇨Subtract From Mask. Now you can carve areas out of the selection outline using a mask tool.

✔ The last command — XOR Mask — is kind of weird. It lets you find the intersection of two selection outlines. For example, if you draw a rectangular selection, choose XOR Mask, and then draw an oval selection around the rectangular selection, you get a rectangular outline with the corners shaved off.

You can also access these commands by pressing shortcuts on the keypad (the right-hand portion of the keyboard with the numbers on it in). Press Ctrl+plus (+) to choose the Add To Mask command. Press Ctrl+minus (–) for Subtract From Mask or Ctrl+asterisk (*) for XOR Mask. And press Ctrl+slash (/) to return to the Normal mode.

Things to Do with a Selected Image

It's been about 15 billion pages since I started this chapter, and all I've managed to explain is how you select part of an image. In Chapter 4, I was able to sum up how you select an object in CorelDraw in a single sentence: "Select the Arrow tool and then click on a shape to select it." In Photo-Paint, obviously, the process is a little more involved.

The good news is that after you select a handful of pixels, you can manipulate them with absolute impunity. Not only can you do things to Photo-Paint pixels that would make Draw objects stare with wonder, you can perform these edits with relatively little effort.

For starters, the following list describes a few of the minor modifications you can make to images (the kind of stuff you can do almost without thinking):

TIP

TIP

✓ Drag the selection with any mask tool other than the Mask Brush or Mask Transform tool to move it to a new location. Photo-Paint leaves a background-colored hole in the wake of the moved selection, as demonstrated in Figure 17-6. (In the figure, white is the background color, as by default. The image is file 046093b in the People folder on the third CorelDraw CD.)

✓ You can also nudge a selected area when one of the mask tools is selected by pressing an arrow key. Remember, a mask tool must be selected if you want to nudge.

✓ To clone the selected area and leave the image unchanged in the background, Alt+drag the selection using a mask tool. The bottom image in Figure 17-6 illustrates what I mean.

White hole   Moved selection   Cloned selection

Figure 17-6:
Drag with a mask tool to move a selection (top); Alt+drag to clone the selection (bottom).

- ✔ You can also paint inside a selection with one of the painting or effects tools described in Chapter 16. The selection acts as a stencil, preventing you from painting outside the lines. (Artists also call such stencils *masks,* which is why Corel calls the selection tools *mask tools.*) Try painting inside a selection, and you'll quickly see how it works.

- ✔ To get rid of all the stuff outside the selection outline, choose Image⇨Crop⇨To Mask. This technique allows you to focus in on a detail in the image. All the images in this chapter, for example, have been cropped to some extent.

You can also crop an image using the Crop tool — located between the Path Node Edit and Zoom tools. Drag with the tool to surround the portion of the photograph you want to retain. You can adjust the size of the cropping boundary after drawing it by dragging the square handles around the boundary. You can drag inside the boundary to move it. When you're finished, double-click inside the boundary to crop away excess pixels.

Correcting Focus and Contrast

You can also correct an image and apply special effects to it by choosing one of the many commands from the Effects menu. All told, this menu contains more than 70 commands. Most commands are the kinds of effects that you can have a lot of fun playing around with but serve little practical purpose. For examples of a few of the more interesting effects, read Chapter 19.

Despite the profusion of commands in the Effects menu, only a couple of them are useful on a regular basis: the Adaptive Unsharp and Equalize commands. Though they have weird names, these effects enable you to correct an image and make it look better rather than weirder. I'd be surprised if you didn't find yourself using these commands at least once every single time you use Photo-Paint, which is why I discuss each of them a little later in this section.

Reapplying an effect

Before I explain the Adaptive Unsharp and Equalize commands, I feel obliged to share one tidbit about the Effects menu. After you apply any one of the more than 70 effects, Photo-Paint displays that effect as the first command in the Effects menu. This way, you can easily reapply the effect by choosing the first command or simply pressing Ctrl+F.

Just about every Effects command brings up a dialog box so that you can mess around with a few settings. If you simply choose the command at the top of the Effects menu or press Ctrl+F, Photo-Paint reapplies the effect using the last settings that were in force. If you want to change the settings, press the Alt key when choosing the first command in the menu or press Ctrl+Alt+F.

Bringing an image into sharper focus

The first practical Effects command — Effects⇨Sharpen⇨Adaptive Unsharp — sharpens the focus of an image. That's right, you can actually sharpen the focus after the photo comes back from the developer. You can't bring out details where none exist — if the camera was way out of focus when you shot the picture, there's not much you can do — but you can sharpen photos that are slightly soft. In fact, you'll probably want to sharpen every single photograph you open in Photo-Paint.

Though Photo-Paint provides many sharpening commands, Adaptive Unsharp does the best job of combining ease of use and good results. So choose Effects⇨Sharpen⇨Adaptive Unsharp to display the Adaptive Unsharp dialog box shown in Figure 17-7. Here you find two previews — before and after — plus Hand and Zoom tools for navigating inside the previews and a Percentage slider bar. These options work like so:

✔ Drag the Percentage slider handle to decide how much you want to sharpen the image. Or enter a value between 1 and 100 into the option box to the right of the slider bar. The higher the value, the sharper your image gets.

For reference, Figure 17-8 features image 016042b from the People folder on the third CorelDraw CD. The top picture shows the photo as it appears when first opened. The image is surprisingly soft. The left examples show the results of applying Percentage values of 50 percent and 100 percent.

Because 100 percent is the highest value permitted, you may have to apply the command more than once. The right examples in the figure show the results of applying the command two and three times in a row. If you start seeing jagged pixels, as in the last example, you know that you've gone too far.

✔ To preview the effect, click on the Preview button. The right preview shows the sharpened image; the left preview shows the soft one.

✔ If you want Photo-Paint to automatically update the preview every time you change the Percentage value, click on that little lock icon to the right of the Preview button. This locks the preview function on so that you never need click on the Preview button again.

322 **Part IV: Corel's Other Amazing Programs**

Before   After

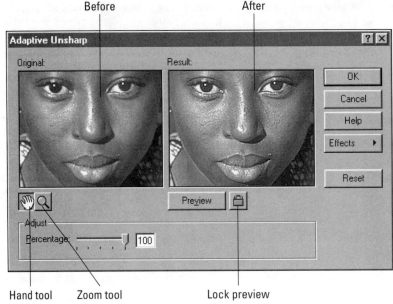

Figure 17-7:
Adaptive
Unsharp is
Photo-
Paint's most
straight-
forward and
capable
sharpening
command.

Hand tool   Zoom tool   Lock preview

➤ Only so much of the image fits into the preview windows. To preview a
different portion of the photograph, select the Hand tool and drag inside
the left preview window.

➤ To see more of the image at a time, select the Zoom tool and right-click
in the left preview to zoom out. To magnify the preview, just click with
the tool.

➤ Though you use the Hand and Zoom tools in the left preview, Photo-Paint
automatically updates the right preview as well.

➤ To close the dialog box and apply the sharpening effect, press Enter or
click on OK.

Making an image less dark and murky

Most photographs look bright and perky on-screen. But when you print
them, they typically darken up and fill in, which can lead to muddy colors and
murky detail. That's where Photo-Paint's second practical Effects command,
Effects⊏>Color Adjust⊏>Equalize, comes in handy.

Original

50% once

100% twice

Figure 17-8:
Like all of
Corel's
stock
photographs,
this one
benefits
from
sharpening.
But be
careful that
you don't
oversharpen,
as in the
bottom-right
image.

100% once

100% three times

Again, Photo-Paint offers plenty of different commands under the Effects⮕Color
Adjust submenu, but they are either monumentally complicated or grossly
inept. Equalize is the exception. It's also worth noting that the commands under
the Effects⮕Color Transform submenu are strictly designed for creating special
effects.

Choose Effects⇨Color Adjust⇨Equalize to display the Histogram Equalization dialog box shown in Figure 17-9. Now, naturally, when you see a term like *histogram* right there at the top of a dialog box, your first inclination is to sweat, wring your hands, and wail pitifully. But it's not as bad as it sounds. As labeled in Figure 17-9, the histogram is that mountain of spiky lines in the lower-right corner of the dialog box. It's a graph of the colors in the image, with the darkest blacks on the left side of the graph and the lightest whites on the right.

Because this dialog box is rather dense, I'm going to step you through the process of using it:

1. **Turn off the Flat Equalization check box.**

   If you haven't already figured this out, I don't always approve of Corel's default settings, and this check box is a primo example. The option should be called Make Your Image Exceedingly Ugly because that's exactly what it does. Corel turned it on just to provide you with a challenge.

Histogram

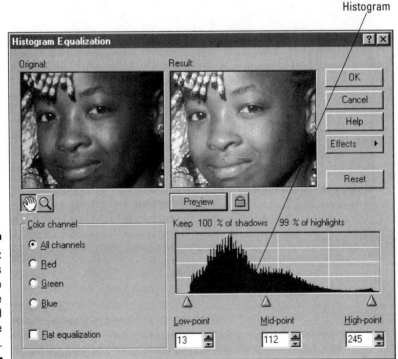

Figure 17-9: Use this dialog box to increase the contrast and lighten the image.

After that little bit of sarcasm, you may be wondering what the check box does (besides offend yours truly, that is). When it's turned on, Photo-Paint tries to even out all the colors in the image from light to dark, which results in some pretty drastic color modifications and unrealistic effects. When it's turned off, Photo-Paint just goes ahead and does what you tell it to do without making any bad guesses of its own.

2. **Drag the Low-Point slider triangle to the right until it meets with the beginning of the histogram.**

   See those three triangles under the histogram? They let you darken the blacks, adjust the grays, and lighten the lights, in that order. To make the darkest colors in the image black — not some wishy-washy gray — drag the first triangle slightly to the right so that it lines up with the left edge of the big histogram mountain.

3. **Drag the High-Point triangle to the left until it meets with the right end of the histogram.**

   This step makes the lightest colors in the image white. It's just the thing for whitening eyes and teeth to make it appear as though the folks in the photograph brush regularly.

4. **Drag the Mid-Point triangle to the left to lighten the image or drag it to the right to darken the image.**

   This middle triangle controls the lightness or darkness of the medium color that is absolutely smack dab between black and white. In all likelihood, you'll want to lighten the image a little, so drag the triangle to the left.

   Keep in mind that the image looks brighter on-screen than it will print. Monitors project light, but the printed page reflects it. So it's best to make the image look a little too light on-screen. Make a few test prints to be sure.

5. **Use the Preview button, lock icon, and Hand and Zoom tools as explained in the preceding section.**

   These options just help you get an idea of how your correction will look before you apply the command.

6. **Press Enter or click on OK.**

   Photo-Paint adjusts the contrast and lightness of the image according to your settings.

The top example in Figure 17-10 shows the 016042b image as it appeared when I first opened it and converted it to a grayscale image by choosing Image⇨Convert To⇨Grayscale (8-Bit). It's dark, it has bad contrast, and it's soft. The second image shows the results of applying Effects⇨Color Adjust⇨Equalize and Effects⇨Sharpen⇨Adaptive Unsharp. Needless to say, I wouldn't dream of printing an image without these helpful commands.

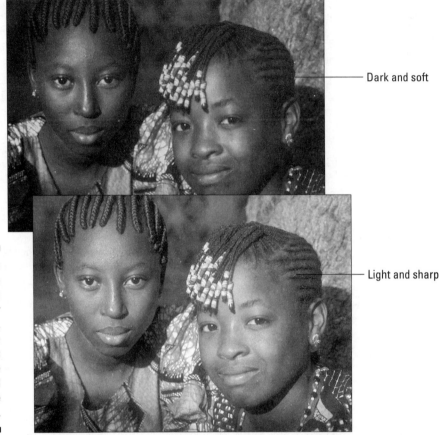

Dark and soft

Light and sharp

Figure 17-10:
If you do nothing else to your photograph, make sure that you correct the colors and sharpen the focus.

Setting Your Selections Free

There comes a time in every selection's life when it yearns for independence. You can grant this independence by turning the selection into a free-floating object. You can then select and manipulate the Photo-Paint object by simply clicking on it with the Arrow tool, just as you can with an object in CorelDraw.

For example, after putting all that time into selecting the kid's head back in Figure 17-4, I don't want to have to go through all that effort again if I decide to plop the head on the body of some other unwitting creature. By converting the head to an object, I make sure that I don't have to. As an object, the head remains intact and independent forever. (Ooh, sounds like a great idea for a horror story. "The Floating Photo-Paint Head." Could be quite gruesome.)

Making an object

To convert a selected area into an object, do any one of the following:

✔ Choose Object➪Create From Mask. Photo-Paint surrounds the selection with eight handles, just like an object in CorelDraw. It even automatically selects the Arrow tool, which is the primary tool for editing objects.

✔ But converting a selection to an object leaves a background-colored hole underneath, just as when you drag a selection. If you'd rather clone the object as you convert it, choose Image➪Preserve Image to turn the command on. Now choose Object➪Create From Mask to clone the selection and convert it to an object.

(Image➪Preserve Image stays on after you choose it, so you don't have to choose it every time you convert a selection to an object. If you decide you don't want to clone a selection when converting it, choose the Preserve Image command again to turn the command off.)

✔ If all that stuff is too complicated, just copy the selection by pressing Ctrl+C and then paste it by pressing Ctrl+V. (If you prefer commands over shortcuts, choose Edit➪Copy and then choose Edit➪Paste➪As New Object). Photo-Paint pastes the new object right in place and automatically selects the Arrow tool so that you can play with the object.

Manipulating an object

After you make your object, you can scale, rotate, and skew it just like an object in CorelDraw. Note that these transformations are different than those that you perform with the Mask Transform tool (as described in the earlier section, "Fine-tuning your selection outline"). Instead of affecting the selection outline without changing the image inside the selection — as is the case with the Mask Transform tool — these transformations affect the object itself.

In fact, before you can scale or rotate part of an image in Photo-Paint, you must first convert it to an object.

Of course, before you transform an object, you have to select it. If you just created the object, it's already selected. If you have multiple objects floating around inside your image and you want to select a different object, just click on the object with the Arrow tool.

As in CorelDraw, you can select multiple objects by clicking on one and Shift+clicking on the others. Or you can drag around the objects with the Arrow tool to surround them with a marquee.

After you select the objects you want to modify, you can change them like so:

- Move the selected object by dragging it with the Arrow tool. (Remember, you can get to the Arrow tool by pressing the spacebar.) Because the object floats above the background image, the background remains unaffected.

- When the Arrow tool is selected, press the arrow keys to nudge the selected object in one-pixel increments.

- Alt+drag the object to clone it.

- Drag a corner handle to scale the object proportionally. Drag a side handle to scale horizontally; drag the top or bottom handle to scale vertically.

- Click again on the selected object to display the rotate and skew handles. Drag a corner handle to rotate the object; drag a top, bottom, or side handle to slant the object.

Keep in mind that pixels are always square and upright. So when you rotate or skew an object, you don't actually rotate or skew the individual pixels. Rather, you force Photo-Paint to recolor the pixels to best represent the rotated or skewed image.

The practical upshot of this is that each and every rotation or skew causes a tiny bit of damage to the image. The recolored pixels don't look quite as good as the original ones did. If you rotate or skew the object many times in a row, it starts to look blurry and jagged. Figure 17-11 compares an image rotated three times to an image rotated the same amount once.

- Click a third time on the image to get a third set of handles you don't see in CorelDraw, the *distortion handles.* Drag one of these four corner handles to stretch the image any which way. As demonstrated in Figure 17-12, you can create perspective effects much as you can with the Add Perspective command in CorelDraw.

- When the Arrow tool is selected, the Tool Settings roll-up includes five panels of options that let you move, scale, rotate, and slant the object numerically. (Sorry, no numerical distortions.) These options work just like their counterparts in CorelDraw, as explained in Chapters 6 (in "The big move") and 9 (in "The provocative S&M roll-up" and "The not so provocative R&S roll-ups").

- As if all this weren't enough, you can flip an object horizontally or verti-cally by choosing one of the commands from the Object⇨Flip submenu. And you can rotate an object in 90-degree increments by choosing a command from the Object⇨Rotate submenu. (Object⇨Rotate⇨Free just displays the rotate and skew handles, as if you had clicked a second time on the image.)

- To delete a selected object, just press Delete.

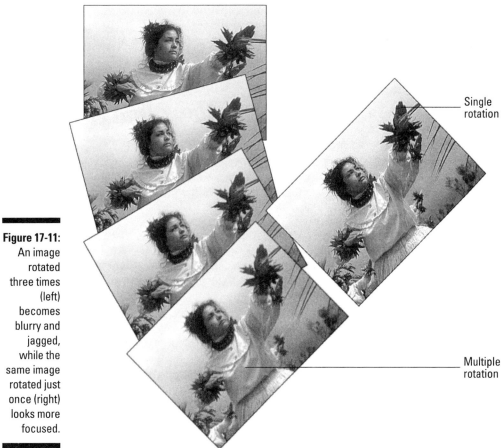

Single
rotation

Multiple
rotation

Figure 17-11:
An image
rotated
three times
(left)
becomes
blurry and
jagged,
while the
same image
rotated just
once (right)
looks more
focused.

Figure 17-12:
Drag the
distortion
handles to
create
perspective
effects.

To hide those distracting marching ants around the boundaries of your objects, choose Object⇨Marquee Visible to turn the command off. (If marching ants remain on-screen, they surround areas selected with the Mask tools.) To bring the marching ants back, choose the command again.

Stamping Some Text into Your Image

The Text tool — the one that looks like an *A* in the toolbox — lets you add text to your image. Because type in Photo-Paint is made up of pixels, you should only use it to create large letters that you want to embellish in ways that CorelDraw doesn't permit. (In Photo-Paint, small text comes out jagged and illegible because there aren't enough pixels to adequately represent the letters.) For example, after creating text in Photo-Paint, you can paint inside the letters to add stripes. You can also apply special effects from the Effects menu.

If you want to label an image, create a caption, or add other commonplace text, do it in CorelDraw. For best results, drag and drop the image as an object into CorelDraw, as described in Chapter 14.

Adding and modifying text

If you decide, after thoughtful consideration, to go ahead and create your text in Photo-Paint, you can select the Text tool by pressing F8 (the same shortcut used in CorelDraw to select the Artistic Text tool). Then click with the tool in the image and enter text from the keyboard. Photo-Paint colors the text in the current foreground color.

As shown in Figure 17-13, the Tool Settings roll-up contains formatting options when the Text tool is selected, so you can change the typeface, size, and justification of type after you enter it from the keyboard. Be sure to select the Anti-Aliasing check box to soften the edges of the letters.

At this point, you may be wondering why I'm discussing text in a chapter about selections and objects. Well, it's because text in Photo-Paint is an object. When you select the Arrow tool, Photo-Paint automatically surrounds each letter of text with marching ants (assuming that Object⇨Marquee Visible is turned on). Click on the text with the Arrow tool to select it and display the standard object handles. You can then move the text, scale it, rotate it, and so on.

If you ever want to edit the characters or change the formatting or color of the text, click on the text object with the Text tool. (You know that you've properly activated the text when the marching ants disappear and a big rectangle surrounds the letters.) You can't drag across letters to highlight them as you

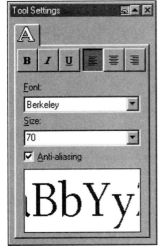

Figure 17-13:
Use these options to change the font, size, and justification of active text.

can in CorelDraw, but you can move the insertion marker around using the left- and right-arrow keys as well as add and delete characters from the keyboard. Click on a swatch in the color palette to change the color of the text. And adjust the formatting options in the Tool Settings roll-up to change the font and size.

Painting inside text

The following is a little exercise that demonstrates something you can do with text in Photo-Paint that you can't do in CorelDraw. The steps explain how to paint inside and behind type.

1. **Create a few characters of text.**

   Format and color it as desired. Be sure to make the text *really* big by entering a Size value of 200 or more. That may sound excessive, but 200 is the size of the type in Figure 17-14. You may also want to click on the B icon to make the text bold. And for a nice effect, select red from the color palette.

2. **Select the Arrow tool.**

   Photo-Paint makes the text into an object.

3. **Convert the text to a bunch of selection outlines.**

   Just as you can convert a selection to an object, you can convert an object to a selection by choosing Mask⇨Create From Object(s).

4. **Change the foreground color.**

   Click on a swatch in the color palette. Make sure that the new foreground color contrasts well with the text color. Might I suggest yellow?

Figure 17-14:
To get these
effects, I
created
some red
text (top),
painted
inside the
letters with
yellow
(middle),
and painted
behind the
letters with
black
(bottom).

5. **Select the Paint tool.**

6. **Paint inside the text.**

   The yellow stays entirely inside the selection boundaries; no paint escapes outside the letters. If you followed my color recommendations, you now have red text with yellow stripes, similar to the second example in Figure 17-14.

7. **Choose Mask⇨Invert.**

   This command selects the area outside the letters.

8. **Change the foreground color to black.**

   This color will serve as the shadow color.

9. **Select the Airbrush icon in the Tool Settings roll-up.**

   That's the second bluish icon from the left.

10. **Trace around the letters to add a shadow behind the letters.**

    I demonstrate this step in the last example of Figure 17-14.

Now *there's* something you can't do in CorelDraw.

Chapter 18

Do Dogs Dream in Three Dimensions?

CorelDream 3D is CorelDraw 6's most impressive acquisition. Although Draw and Photo-Paint have seen their fair share of modifications, Dream 3D is altogether new to CorelDraw 6.

As I mentioned a few hundred pages ago in Chapter 1, Dream 3D is a three-dimensional drawing program that enables you to create astoundingly realistic graphics. You draw and arrange shapes in 3-D space, assign textures to the shapes, and capture the final scene as an image file that you can then turn around and edit in Photo-Paint.

Sound exciting? You bet. Sound complicated? And how. It takes much longer to get to first base with Dream 3D than either Draw or Photo-Paint, and it takes weeks or even months to master the program. Three-dimensional drawing programs are among the hardest pieces of software to use in the universe. Occasionally, they have the distressing habit of baffling long-time computer artists like me.

In this chapter, I concentrate on getting you midway to first base by walking you through the process of assembling a 3-D scene. Don't get discouraged if you have to experiment to figure out how a feature works. And don't expect to learn it all overnight. By the time you finish this brief introduction, you should have a pretty sound idea of how the program works and whether or not you want to integrate it into your artistic regimen.

The Dream That Starts Like a Nightmare

Now that I've nearly frightened you into swearing off Dream 3D forever, I'd like to scare you a little further by having you start the program. Just choose Start➪Programs➪Corel Applications➪CorelDream 3D from the menu in the bottom-left corner of the screen. After a few moments, the Dream 3D interface takes over your screen, as shown in Figure 18-1.

Some portions of the screen are familiar. Dream 3D offers a bunch of menus, a ribbon bar, a toolbox, and a status bar, just like Corel's other programs. But the four windows in the middle of the screen herald a decidedly different artistic approach. Sure, they're weird, but you have to get used to them:

Work area   Working box   Hierarchy window

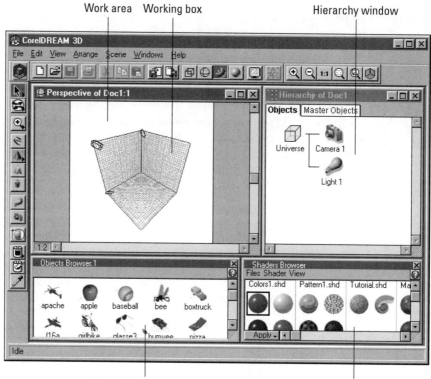

Figure 18-1: In Dream 3D, you create and edit shapes in the work area.

Objects Browser window   Shaders Browser window

✔ The *work area* is where you create your drawing. It's like the drawing area in CorelDraw, except this one shows your objects in perspective.

✔ To demonstrate the perspective scene, Dream 3D throws in something that it calls a *working box,* which looks like a chicken-wire cage that's missing a top and two sides. The remaining three sides represent the three *planes* of 3-D space. The edges where the planes meet are known as *axes.*

✔ The window to the right of the work area shows the hierarchy of the objects in the work area. (Now let's try that sentence again, but in English.) See, it's easy to lose items in a complex 3-D drawing. The Hierarchy window lists the names of objects and other items so that you can easily locate and select them without having to waste time searching for them in the work area.

✔ The Objects Browser window, below the work area, contains a handful of predrawn 3-D objects. Called *models,* these objects include an apple, a bike, and a chair. To use one of these objects, just drag the object out of the window and drop it into the work area.

✔ The Shaders Browser window includes colors, patterns, and textures. Click on a shader and then click on the Apply button in the bottom-left corner of the Shaders Browser window to apply the shader to the selected shape in the work area. Or you can drag the shader and drop it right onto the object.

In all likelihood, you have no immediate need for the Hierarchy window. So you can cut down on the screen clutter by clicking on the Maximize button in the top-right corner of the work area window. The work area expands to fill the entire screen. The Hierarchy window is covered up, but the Objects Browser and Shaders Browser windows remain visible. If you ever need to get to the Hierarchy window later on, just choose the Hierarchy command from the Windows menu.

You may also want to resize both Browser windows and move them into the upper-right corner of the screen to get them out of the way of the scroll bar. (Check out the upcoming Figure 18-2 if you want to see how I did it.)

A Beginner's Guide to 3-D Objects

Dream 3D provides two ways to add objects to a drawing. You can either draw the objects from scratch or select from the hundreds of predrawn objects that Corel includes on CD-ROM.

Three panes of pure drawing pleasure

Dream 3D's working box is really an average, everyday dimensional grid. You know how a bar graph has a horizontal X axis and a vertical Y axis? Well, the only difference between that bar graph and the working box — besides a complete absence of bars — is the addition of a third axis, called the Z axis. The X axis points to the right, the Y axis goes straight up and down, and the Z axis shoots off to the left.

Each of the planes is connected to two of the axes. The right-hand plane borders the X and Y axes, for example. As a result, it's called the

X,Y plane. (Uninspired, but accurate.) Similarly, the left-hand plane is called the Y,Z plane, and the bottom one is called the X,Z plane.

In CorelDraw, you have two dimensions: width (X) and height (Y). Therefore, you have just one plane, the X,Y plane. By adding a third dimension — depth (Z) — you add two additional planes — X,Z and Y,Z — to your drawing area. This is why Dream 3D presents you with the 3-D working box instead of the flat drawing area you see in CorelDraw.

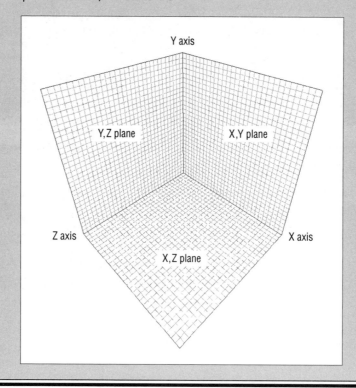

To import an object, you can drag it from the Objects Browser and drop it into the work area. But the Objects Browser contains only 12 models. More models are included on the third CD-ROM in your CorelDraw 6 box. To see some of these models, choose File⇨Browse 3D Clipart or press Alt+F1. A tiny Directory Selection dialog box comes up. Open up the 3dmodels folder on the CD-ROM. Then double-click on a folder name that looks interesting — such as Aircraft or Fashion — and press Enter or click on the Select button. Dream 3D displays a new Objects Browser window that contains lots more objects. It may take forever, so have patience.

Importing and magnifying an object

For an example of how to use Dream 3D, drag the Vicchair item from the default Objects Browser window and drop it into the work area. A 3-D chair appears in the work area, surrounded by a box shape with handles in each corner. The box and handles show that the chair is selected.

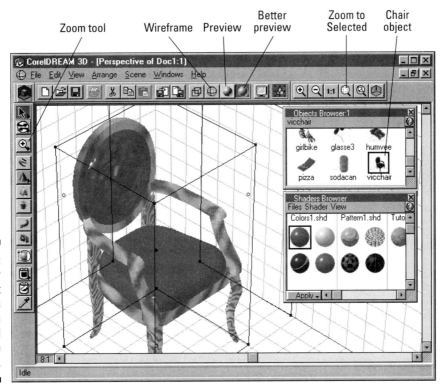

Figure 18-2: The Vicchair object as it appears when imported into the work area.

To get a closer look, press Shift+F2 to magnify the selected portion of the drawing. This keyboard shortcut is the same one used in CorelDraw. In fact, all the CorelDraw shortcuts explained in the "Lightning-fast zooms" section of Chapter 3 work in Dream 3D.

If you don't like shortcuts, you can click on the zoom icons on the far right side of the ribbon bar. The Zoom to Selected icon, which lets you zoom in on the chair, is labeled in Figure 18-2. You can also use the Zoom tool, which is the third tool down in the toolbox. To zoom out, Alt+click with the Zoom tool.

Changing how the object looks on-screen

You can also change the way Dream 3D displays the model on-screen:

✔ The default view mode is the *preview mode,* which shows the object in color but does not accurately show textures and other realistic stuff. You can return to this mode at any time by clicking on the Preview icon in the ribbon bar (labeled in Figure 18-2). You can also choose View⇨Default Quality⇨Preview or press Ctrl+Alt+Shift+Y.

✔ If things seem to be happening too slowly, you can speed them up by switching to the *wireframe mode.* This mode displays coarse, chicken-wire versions of the objects without any color. Although it's not terribly accurate, this mode is much faster. To make the switch, you can click on the Wireframe icon in the ribbon bar, choose View⇨Default Quality⇨Wireframe, or press Ctrl+ Shift+Y.

✔ If you own a powerful computer, such as a Pentium, or you simply want to see more detailed versions of your objects, click on the Better Preview icon in the ribbon bar. When you work in this so-called *better preview mode,* you can see surface textures and shadows, as demonstrated in Figure 18-2. If the ribbon bar isn't quite your style, choose View⇨Default Quality⇨Better Preview or press Ctrl+Alt+Y.

Moving an object in 3-D space

To move an object, you drag it with the Arrow tool — the one at the top of the toolbox — just as in CorelDraw or Photo-Paint. The only trick is figuring out where the heck you're dragging it. I mean, how do you move an object side to side, forward and backward, and up and down when the only directions you can move your mouse are side to side and forward and backward? Sadly, you can't lift your mouse and expect the object to levitate in 3-D space.

Based on the way other programs work, you may think that up and down motions would be a breeze; but if you do, you're not thinking in 3-D. Granted, when you move your mouse forward and backward on the mouse pad, your cursor moves up and down on-screen. So over time, you've come to associate forward and backward mouse movement with up and down object movement.

Not so in Dream 3D. In this program, you have to imagine that the mouse pad is sitting on the bottom plane (X,Z). When you drag the object, it doesn't move up and down, it moves back and forth. The object never moves off the ground when you drag it.

In Figure 18-3, for example, I dragged the object down. But the object moved toward me, just as my mouse moved toward me. How can I tell? By watching the *tracking boxes* on the two other planes (as labeled in the figure). The tracking boxes move along with the object to show how it aligns with the planes, much as the tracking lines in CorelDraw's rulers move with an object. Because the tracking boxes remain firmly fastened to the X and Z axes, I know that the chair does not move upward.

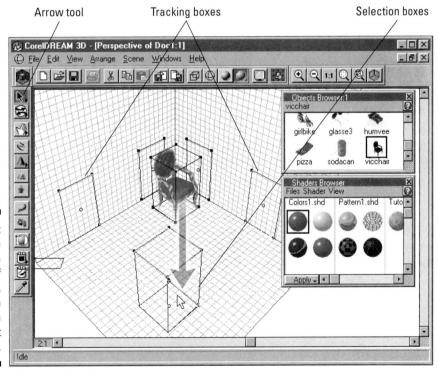

Figure 18-3: In the strange world of Dream 3D, dragging an object down moves it forward.

So how do you move an object up and down? Well, it turns out that you can drag a tracking box directly. When you drag a tracking box, the corresponding object follows along with your move — on the same plane as the tracking box. In Figure 18-4, for example, when I dragged the right tracking box up, the chair moved upward into 3-D space. Because a tracking box always adheres to its plane, you can move it in only two directions: up and down or left and right.

Moving an object by dragging a tracking box is frequently easier than dragging the object directly, because you don't have to translate your 2-D mouse movements into 3-D space. So when in doubt, drag a tracking box.

Scaling and spinning the object

You can also scale and rotate objects inside Dream 3D. To scale an object, drag the corner handles around the selection box. You can also drag the corner handles of one of the tracking boxes.

Tracking box

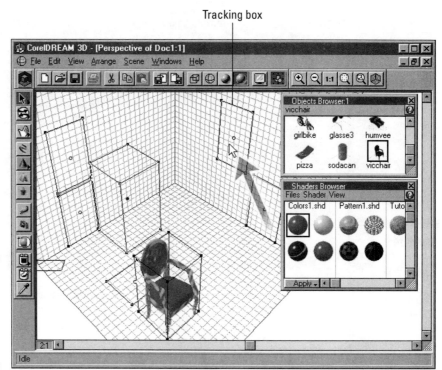

Figure 18-4:
Drag the tracking box upward to levitate the object.

To rotate an object, use the Virtual Trackball tool, the one below the Arrow tool. Though the tool has a name that's nothing short of ridiculous, it can be very useful. Drag the selected object to spin it around in 3-D space, as shown in Figure 18-5. With the Virtual Trackball tool, you can't drag the tracking boxes as you can with the Arrow tool — you can drag only the object itself. This is one tool you'll definitely want to try out for yourself.

Every Object Needs a Look

As I mentioned earlier, you assign colors and textures to objects using the options in the Shaders Browser window. Dream 3D calls these items *shaders* because they not only affect the color and texture of an object, but also the translucency, reflectivity, and all kinds of other properties. (Okay, so *shader* doesn't necessarily conjure up colors, textures, and all that other stuff in your mind, but it did to some daffy program manager at Corel. Unfortunately, the industry-standard term, *texture maps,* doesn't make all that much more sense.) Using shaders, you can make an object appear as if it were made out of glass, wrapped in burlap, or covered with mud.

Virtual trackball

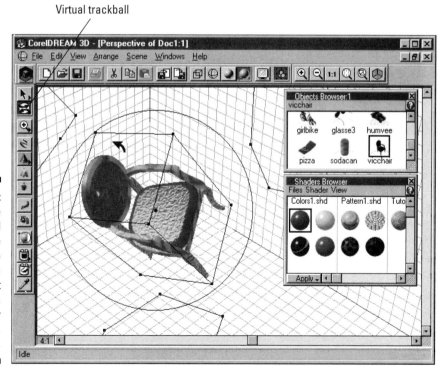

Figure 18-5:
Use the
second tool
in the
toolbox to
twirl an
object
around in
any
direction
you please.

Corel's predrawn objects comprise many separate objects, each of which you can color separately. The chair, for example, has plush blue fabric applied to the cushions and wood grain applied to the legs and trim.

In Figure 18-6, I changed the bottom cushion to stone by dragging the first shader from the Tutorial column in the Shaders Browser and dropping it onto the cushion. This step colored only the bottom cushion; I had to drag the stone shader and drop it onto the back cushion separately. To change the wood grain trim and legs to the striped pattern, I had to drag and drop the same shader onto ten different sections of the chair.

The End of the 3-D Highway

When you finish a drawing in CorelDraw, you print it. When you finish editing a photograph in Photo-Paint, you print it. But as you may have already noticed, the Print command in Dream 3D is dimmed.

A 3-D drawing is so vast and complex that it would take far too long to print it out. So you have to perform an intermediate step called *rendering,* in which Dream 3D converts the drawing to pixels and saves it as separate image file.

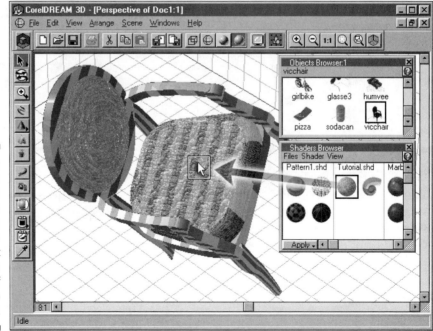

Figure 18-6: Drag a shader and drop it onto a shape in the model to change that shape from one type of material to another.

Before rendering, it's a good idea to save your drawing to disk. Though Dream 3D saves the rendered image to a separate file, you don't want to lose your work if something goes wrong.

Here's how to render a 3-D drawing:

1. **Choose Scene⇨Render Setup⇨Final.**

   Up comes the Artwork Settings dialog box, which enables you to specify the resolution of the final image.

2. **If you have a specific resolution in mind, enter it into the Resolution option box.**

   Otherwise, just select the Medium Resolution radio button.

3. **Click on the Estimate Time button at the bottom of the dialog box.**

   Dream 3D estimates the amount of time it will take to create the image. In all likelihood, you're looking at several minutes. Complex scenes with lots of objects can take more than an hour. Images with higher resolutions take longer as well.

   If the estimate is more than 20 minutes, you may want to start the rendering process at the end of the day. Heck, you could even let Dream 3D work while you sleep. That's what the professionals do. It's no coincidence that 3-D software is sometimes called *sleeperware.*

4. **Press Enter.**

   Or click on OK to close the dialog box.

5. **Press Ctrl+R.**

   Or choose Scene⇨Render⇨Preview. Dream 3D renders a tiny version of the drawing to show you what it will look like. This process should take only a minute or so.

   If you don't like how things look, close the image by clicking on the Close button or choose File⇨Close and make the necessary changes. If you do like the image, close it and proceed to the next step. Either way, there's no sense in saving the preview, so click on the No button when the save message comes up.

6. **Choose the Perspective option from the bottom of the Windows menu.**

   Dream 3D has the irritating habit of returning you to the wrong window after rendering. Choose Perspective (followed by the name of your drawing) to get back to the work area.

7. **Choose Scene⇨Render⇨Final.**

   This command tells Dream 3D to begin rendering. It takes a long time, so be patient. If you decide to skip it for now, press Esc to cancel the rendering.

By the way, you don't have to sit on your hands while you wait for Dream 3D to complete the image. Thanks to Windows 95, you can keep working in the program or switch to a different program and work in it. Unfortunately, Dream 3D renders more slowly if you make your computer do other stuff, and it may even cause the other program to pause intermittently and, in the worst cases, crash. Despite Windows 95's swell new multitasking capabilities, it's better to let Dream 3D do its stuff unhampered.

As Dream 3D works away, it shows you the portions of the image it has finished.

8. When the image is complete, save it to disk.

Choose File⇨Save or press Ctrl+S. The Save dialog box appears. Enter a name for the image and select a format from the Save as Type pop-up menu. I heartily recommend that you select the last option, Tiff (Cor) (*.tif), but you can select any format you like. Then press Enter or click on the Save button.

Figure 18-7 shows the final chair image as it appeared after I opened it in Photo-Paint, cropped it to get rid of the extraneous background stuff, and enhanced the brightness and contrast as explained in Chapter 17. And on my speedy Pentium, the image took only three minutes to render.

Figure 18-7: Rotating through 3-D space, my stripey chair with stone cushions is truly a sight to behold but probably not too comfy to sit in.

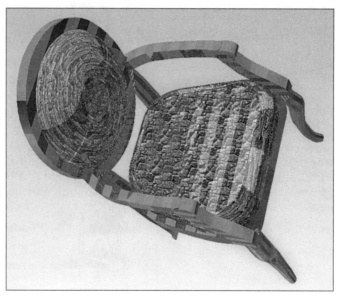

Part V
The Part of Tens

The 5th Wave   By Rich Tennant

THE GREAT THING ABOUT THIS DRAWING PROGRAM IS, IT'S MADE CREATING SALES FLIERS AS EASY AS PUTTING ONE FOOT IN FRONT OF THE OTHER.

In this part . . .

Sure, sure, we're all addicted to statistics and sound bites — so much so that no one knows the full story about anything. But I figure what's good enough for Moses is good enough for me. I mean, the guy kept it simple — two tablets, ten factoids — and everybody ate it up. "Thou shalt not kill" kind of sticks in your mind. It has a certain undeniable directness that's downright impossible to argue with. You can toss it out at a party or share it with a friend in a time of need.

Jill:	I swear, Jack's driving me nuts. I'm about ready to strangle the chump in his sleep.
Humpty Dumpty (a friend from a neighboring story line):	Now now, Jill. (Wagging finger.) "Thou shalt not kill."
Jill:	Oh, right, I forgot about that one. (Considers.) But I can wallop him with my pail, right? It doesn't say anything about walloping folks with a pail, does it?
Humpty Dumpty:	No, I believe that's acceptable.

Of course, the following lists don't quite measure up to the Ten Commandments (or Mother Goose, for that matter). In fact, they're more the *Guinness Book of World Records* variety of list. But they're still lots of fun and, wow, talk about memorable! You can even toss them out at a party, assuming that you want to look like a total geek.

Chapter 19
Ten Way-Cool Special Effects

∙ ∙

In This Chapter

▶ Draw a planet with a ring around it

▶ Morph between two shapes

▶ Create a shadow for your text

▶ Make type bulge like a balloon

▶ Wrap paragraph text around a graphic

▶ Put your message in the sky

▶ Wallpaper your drawing with a patterned backdrop

▶ Shuffle the colors in a photograph

▶ Make the pixels beg for mercy

▶ Design your own repeating pattern

∙ ∙

Some folks characterize CorelDraw as a functional and powerful tool for creating business graphics. They say that CorelDraw lets you assemble drawings and edit images in an efficient and timely manner. They add that CorelDraw enables you to store and catalog your graphics quickly and conveniently.

Well, I say bugger. Sure, I guess all that stuff is true, but who gives a rat's fanny? Especially when you consider the real potential of CorelDraw: It enables you to take cheesy little shapes, text, and stock photos and turn them into bizarre artistic monstrosities that overflow with an excess of special effects.

Enticed? That's where this chapter comes in. I hereby invite you to abandon all pretense of good taste and go on a computer graphics binge. Some of the techniques presented in the next few pages are based on ideas I covered in previous chapters, but don't expect any warmed over repeats. This is your chance to indulge in some purely frivolous and largely irrelevant special effects.

Draw a Planet with a Ring around It

I'd like to start things off with a razzle-dazzle project. But instead, the following steps tell you how to create something that looks vaguely like the planet Saturn, as in Figure 19-1. Isn't it a beauty? Can't you imagine spying that baby through the viewport of your rocket ship? Or perhaps losing communications with an unmanned probe in the vicinity of this gorgeous orb?

1. **Inside CorelDraw, draw a circle.**

   You do this by Ctrl+dragging with the Oval tool. Saturn is very big, so make your circle nice and big.

2. **Press F11 or select the Fountain Fill icon from the Fill tool flyout menu.**

   The Fountain Fill dialog box appears.

Figure 19-1: Scientists aren't sure whether this is Saturn or just a sphere playing with a hula-hoop.

3. **Select Radial from the <u>T</u>ype pop-up menu.**

   This setting creates a radial gradation that progresses outward in concentric circles, as in Figure 19-1.

   The way things stand now, the white spot is dead in the center of the gradation, as the preview in the upper-right corner of the dialog box shows. That doesn't look right. It needs to be up and to the left a little, maybe. You can move the white spot using the <u>H</u>orizontal and <u>V</u>ertical options in the Center Offset area.

4. **Enter a value of –20 in the <u>H</u>orizontal option box and 20 in the <u>V</u>ertical option box.**

   Or just drag inside the preview in the upper-right corner of the dialog box to move the white spot up and to the left.

5. **Press Enter.**

   CorelDraw exits the dialog box and returns you to the sphere, which should look like the one in Figure 19-1, but without the ring.

6. **Draw a short, wide oval centered on the sphere.**

   Using the Oval tool, Shift+drag outward from the center of the sphere. This new oval represents the planet's rings. Or at least one ring, anyway.

7. **Select the second-to-fattest line width from the Pen tool flyout menu.**

   It's the one that's 16 points thick.

8. **Select the Shape tool.**

   You can do this by pressing F10.

9. **Drag the node at the top of the oval down and to the right.**

   This step creates a rift in the outline of the oval. Make sure to keep the cursor outside the oval so that you get an arc instead of a pie. Drag until the outline of the ring no longer overlaps the top portion of the sphere.

   By the way, my instruction to drag the node down and to the right assumes that you drew the oval from left to right. If you drew it from right to left, drag down and to the left with the Shape tool.

10. **Drag the other node down and to the left.**

    Again, keep the cursor outside the oval and drag until the ring no longer overlaps the sphere. You should now have an arc that looks more or less like it circles around the front of the sphere.

11. **Press F12 or select the Pen icon from the Pen tool flyout menu.**

    The Outline Pen dialog box appears.

12. **Select the second Line Caps radio button.**

    This option is the round cap.

13. **Press Enter to exit the dialog box.**

14. **Press Ctrl+C and then press Ctrl+V.**

    This step copies the arc and then pastes it right in front of the original.

15. **Right-click on the white swatch in the color palette.**

    This step makes the pasted arc white.

16. **Select the middle line width from the Pen tool flyout menu.**

    I'm talking about the 8-point line width.

You could, of course, create a true 3-D sphere in Dream 3D, draw a bunch of really sophisticated rings around it, and make it look just like the real Saturn. But that would take a lot longer. And besides, you'd ruin that special Ed Wood feel of your current planet.

Morph between Two Shapes

CorelDraw enables you to create your own custom gradations using the Blend roll-up. In essence, you can blend a shape that's filled with one color into a different shape that's filled with a different color. Here's how it works:

1. **Draw two shapes.**

   For this example, draw a large rectangle with the Rectangle tool. Then use the Oval tool to draw a smaller oval that fits inside the rectangle.

2. **Select white from the color palette.**

   Because you just finished drawing the oval, it should be selected. So clicking on the white swatch fills the oval with white.

3. **Right-click on the X icon on the left side of the color palette.**

   This step deletes the outline from the oval, which is a very important step when creating custom gradations. If you don't delete the outline, borders will appear between the colors in the gradation.

4. **Select the rectangle with the Arrow tool, select black from the color palette, and right-click on the X icon.**

   The rectangle is now black with no outline.

5. **Use the Arrow tool to select both the rectangle and the oval.**

   Assuming that the rectangle is still selected, you just have to Shift+click on the oval.

6. **Press Ctrl+B.**

   Or choose Effects⇨Blend to display the Blend roll-up.

7. **Click on the Apply button in the Blend roll-up.**

   CorelDraw automatically creates a gradation between the two shapes, as illustrated in Figure 19-2.

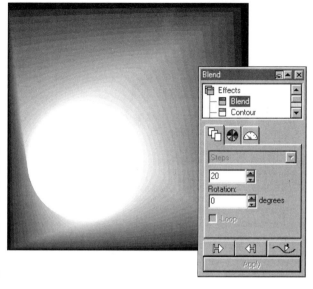

Figure 19-2:
Use the
Blend roll-
up to create
gradations
between
two shapes.

CorelDraw makes this gradation by generating 20 transitional shapes between the rectangle and oval, each shaped and filled slightly differently. If you want to increase the number of shapes to create a smoother gradation, increase the value in the Steps option box in the middle of the roll-up and then click on the Apply button again.

Create a Shadow for Your Text

Folks invariably ooh and ah when they see the effect shown in Figure 19-3, but it's really easy to create. Here's how:

1. Press the Caps Lock key.

This effect works best when you use capital letters only. Lowercase letters sometimes descend below the baseline, ruining the shadow effect.

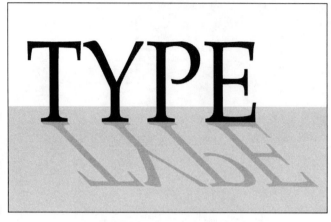

Figure 19-3:
No program
does type at
dusk like
CorelDraw.

2. Create some text with the Artistic Text tool.

Press F8 to get the tool. Then click in the drawing area and type in one short line of text.

3. Use the Text palette to enlarge the type size to 100 points or so.

You display the Text palette by right-clicking on the edge of the toolbox and selecting the Text option from the pop-up menu. Then enter 100 in the type size option box and press Enter.

4. Select the Arrow tool.

Pressing Ctrl+spacebar is the fastest way to select the tool. The text becomes selected.

5. Press Alt+F9 or choose Arrange⇔Transform⇔Scale and Mirror.

This command displays the Scale & Mirror roll-up.

6. Click on the vertical mirror icon.

This is the icon to the right of the V option box.

7. Click on the Apply To Duplicate button.

This step creates a duplicate of the text block as it flips the block.

8. Press the down-arrow key until the baselines of the two text blocks align.

In other words, the bottom of the letters in the different text blocks should touch.

9. Click on a light gray color in the color palette.

The flipped text changes to gray.

10. Click on the flipped text block.

The rotate and skew handles appear.

11. Drag the bottom handle to skew the text.

This step makes the shadow appear at an angle. To complete the effect shown in Figure 19-3, I added a rectangle, filled it with light gray, and pressed Shift+PgDn to send it to the back of the drawing.

Make Type Bulge Like a Balloon

CorelDraw is one of the few programs that lets you create type that bulges off the page, as shown in Figure 19-4. This interesting text effect is remarkably easy to create using the Envelope feature.

1. Repeat the first four steps from the preceding section.

Press the Caps lock key, click with the Artistic Text tool, enter a word or short line of text, increase the type size to 100 points or so, and select the Arrow tool.

Figure 19-4:
This text
looks like it's
about ready
to pop.

2. **Drag up on the top handle of the text block until it's roughly as tall as it is wide.**

   The text stretches vertically.

3. **Press Ctrl+F7 to display the Envelope roll-up.**

   Or choose Effects⇨Envelope.

4. **Click on the Add New button.**

   This step displays a dotted outline and special handles around the text.

5. **Click on the single-arc icon.**

   It's the second icon below the Create From button.

6. **Drag the top handle upward; drag the bottom handle downward; drag the left handle farther to the left; and drag the right handle to the right.**

   Don't drag any of the corner handles. Ultimately, you're trying to turn the square confines of the text block into a circle.

7. **Click on the Apply button in the Envelope roll-up.**

   The text now puffs out like you're viewing it through a fish-eye lens.

Wrap Paragraph Text around a Graphic

You've seen it in national magazines, newspapers, and slick fliers. Now you can join in on the fun. CorelDraw 6 lets you wrap paragraph text around a graphic, which is just the thing for designing nifty documents that'll make your friends and coworkers drool with envy.

1. **Create a few lines of paragraph text.**

   Press Shift+F8 to select the Paragraph Text tool. Then drag in the drawing area and enter some text from the keyboard. Any old text will do.

2. **Draw the graphic you want to wrap the text around.**

   Or import a piece of clip art. If you want to wrap the text around several objects, be sure to group them first by choosing Arrange⇨Group or pressing Ctrl+G.

3. **Right-click on the graphic.**

   CorelDraw displays a pop-up menu of options.

4. **Select the Properties option.**

   It's the one at the bottom of the pop-up menu. The Object Properties dialog box leaps onto the screen.

5. **Click on the General tab and then select the <u>W</u>rap Paragraph Text check box.**

   Look for the check box in the bottom-left corner of the panel.

6. **Press Enter.**

   Or click on OK. CorelDraw closes the dialog box and wraps the text around the graphic.

From now on, you can move the graphic anywhere on the page, and all paragraph text — including other text blocks on the page — will automatically wrap out of the graphic's way. It's as if the graphic has some kind of force field around it. Too bad you can't apply this feature to yourself and have people wrap out of your way on the subway.

Put Your Message in the Sky

You can use CorelDraw's Add Perspective command and Extrude roll-up to create text that appears to zoom across the screen. Figure 19-5 shows an example in which a consumer-oriented message demands the reader's immediate compliance.

Figure 19-5:
An important 3-D message solicits the attention of an eager audience.

1. **Use the Artistic Text tool to create some text.**

   This time around, you can use lowercase letters if you want to. Furthermore, the type size doesn't really matter because you'll end up stretching the type all over the place anyway.

2. **Choose Effects⇨Add Perspective.**

   Four handles appear in the corners of the text block.

3. **Drag the handles until you get the desired effect.**

   Experiment to your heart's content.

4. **Click on red or some other garish hue in the color palette.**

   This step colors the text so that no one will accidentally overlook it.

5. **Press Ctrl+E or choose Effects⇨Extrude.**

   CorelDraw displays the Extrude roll-up so that you can add depth to the text.

6. **Drag the vanishing point to get the desired depth.**

   The vanishing point is that X you see in the drawing area.

7. **Click on the light bulb icon at the top of the Extrude roll-up.**

   You now see the lighting options.

8. **Click on the first light bulb icon on the left side of the roll-up.**

   It's the one with a 1 in it. This step turns on the first light. Drag the little 1 in a black circle down to the lower-right corner of the box on the right side of the roll-up.

9. **Click on the Apply button.**

   Your text now appears in 3-D.

If you accidentally click off the text and the vanishing point goes away, just click on the Edit button in the Extrude roll-up to continue changing the depth of the letters.

Wallpaper Your Drawing with a Patterned Backdrop

Full-color patterns are new to CorelDraw 6. Though you probably won't want to fill too many complex shapes with the patterns — especially if you want the drawing to print without a hitch — you can set a pattern behind other shapes so that it can serve as an interesting background. These exciting colors and festive prints are sure to brighten up the drabbest of documents, and all without synthetic fibers.

1. **Draw an enormous rectangle.**

   Make it as big as the page. You want it to cover the entire background.

2. **Press Shift+PgDn.**

   This step sends the rectangle to the very back of the drawing.

3. **Select the Full-Color Pattern icon from the Fill tool flyout menu.**

   It's the third-to-last icon in the flyout, right below the big X. Clicking on this icon brings up the Full-Color Bitmap Pattern dialog box.

4. **Select the desired pattern.**

   Click on the big pattern preview and then select from the ten patterns in the pop-up menu.

   If you don't like any of the patterns, you can import patterns from disk. Click on the Import button. Then open the Tiles folder inside the Corel60 folder. Inside, you'll find several more folders, each of which contains more patterns.

5. **Press Enter.**

   CorelDraw applies the pattern to the selected rectangle, resulting in a breathtaking wallpapered background.

Wouldn't that look lovely in the den?

Shuffle the Colors in a Photograph

In Photo-Paint, you can apply some serious special effects to images by choosing commands from the Effects menu. Figure 19-6 shows just a few examples from the Color Transform submenu, which automatically shuffles the colors in an image. The labels indicate the commands used, which work as follows:

- ✔ The Invert command changes all the light colors to dark and all the dark colors to light, as in a photographic negative.

- ✔ Posterize decreases the number of colors in a selected area to any value between 2 and 32. It's great for creating high-contrast effects.

- ✔ The Psychedelic command thoroughly jumbles the colors, thus fooling the viewer into seeking medical attention. You can apply this command to color images only.

Original

Posterize

Invert

Psychedelic

Figure 19-6:
The original
image
058053b,
followed by
three differ-
ent effects
chosen from
the
Effects⇨Color
Transform
submenu.

Make the Pixels Beg for Mercy

Photo-Paint stores its most amazing special effects in the 2D Effects and 3D
Effects submenus in the Effects menu. Figure 19-7 demonstrates four effects
from the 2D Effects submenu; Figure 19-8 demonstrates a few from the 3D
Effects submenu. Though most of the effects in these submenus are incredibly
difficult to apply — sometimes involving specialized selection outlines or
other prerequisites — the eight commands demonstrated in the figures are
straightforward and produce intriguing, unusual, and occasionally even
attractive results.

✔ The Edge Detect command traces around high-contrast areas in your image, which is ideal for changing photographs into line art. You can trace with white, black, or the foreground color.

For a really cool effect, set the foreground color to some bright color, such as orange or blue. Then choose Effects⇨2D Effects⇨Edge Detect and select the Paint Color radio button in the Edge Detect dialog box.

✔ Choosing Effects⇨2D Effects⇨Swirl curls the image toward its center, as if the image is twisting down a drain. You specify the amount of curl. Negative values curl the image counterclockwise; positive values curl it clockwise.

Edge Detect

Swirl

Figure 19-7:
A few fascinating effects from the Effects⇨2D Effects submenu.

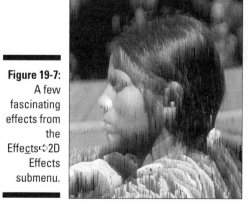

Wet Paint

Wind

✔ The Wet Paint command melts your image as surely as water melts Wicked Witches of the West. Raise the <u>P</u>ercent value to make the drips stand out more. A positive <u>W</u>etness value makes the light colors run; a negative value makes the dark colors bleed.

✔ Choose the Wind command to blast the image with a hurricane-force gale. A high <u>S</u>trength value smudges the pixels farther. Adjust the <u>O</u>pacity value to mix the blasted pixels in with the original colors in the image.

✔ Choose Effe<u>c</u>ts⇨3D Effects⇨Emboss to make a photograph appear carved out of stone. You can adjust the color of the Emboss effect or select the <u>O</u>riginal Color radio button to retain the original colors in the image. You can also adjust how deeply the image is carved by changing the <u>D</u>epth value and specify the direction of the light that shines on the image using the Dire<u>c</u>tion arrows.

Emboss

Page curl

Figure 19-8:
Four examples of what happens when you choose a command from the Effe<u>c</u>ts⇨3D Effects submenu.

Pinch/Punch

Whirlpool

✔ Effects⇨3D Effects⇨Page Curl turns up the corner of your photograph as if it were a curled page.

For the best results, isolate the corner you want to curl by selecting a small area with the Rectangular Mask tool before applying the command. In Figure 19-8, for example, I selected the bottom-right area, starting at the point where the curl starts. If you don't make a selection, the curled corner can take over your image.

✔ Pinch/Punch distorts your image inward or outward. A positive Punch/Pinch value (in the Pinch/Punch dialog box) sucks the pixels toward the center. A negative value bows the image outward, as if it were projected on a balloon.

✔ Choosing Effects⇨3D Effects⇨Whirlpool brings up one of Photo-Paint's most complicated dialog boxes. Still, you can have fun messing around with the options, and nothing you do can cause any harmful effects until you click on the OK button. Even then, you can press Ctrl+Z to undo the damage. So relax and experiment.

Design Your Own Repeating Pattern

My favorite special effects command in Photo-Paint wasn't created by Corel. It comes from a company called Xaos (pronounced *chaos*) Tools. The command, Effects⇨Artistic Effects⇨Terrazzo, enables you to design totally wild patterns by repeating small portions of your image. Here's how to put this wonderful effect to work:

1. **Choose Effects⇨Artistic Effects⇨Terrazzo.**

   Photo-Paint displays the busy dialog box pictured in Figure 19-9.

2. **Click on the Symmetry button in the middle of the dialog box.**

   Another dialog box appears, offering several different ways to repeat your image as a pattern. Select the option that looks interesting — you can always come back and select a different Symmetry option if you change your mind — and press Enter. In Figure 19-9, I selected the Whirlpool option.

Tile   Sizing   Symmetry   Pattern
boundary   handle   button   preview

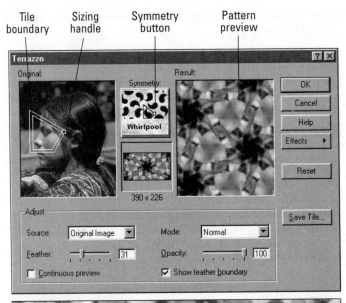

Figure 19-9:
By fooling
around with
the options
in the
Terrazzo
dialog box
(top), I was
able to
create a
kaleidoscope-
like effect
(bottom).

3. **Edit the pattern tile boundary in the left-hand preview to select the area
   you want to repeat.**

   Drag the tile boundary to move it. Drag the sizing handle (labeled in
   Figure 19-9) to stretch or shrink the tile.

4. Adjust the Feather value to soften the transition between tiles.

A low Feather value creates abrupt transitions between one repeating tile and the next; a high value results in soft transitions. Keep an eye on the right-hand preview to see how your changes affect the pattern.

5. Lower the Opacity value if you want to blend the pattern in with the original image.

I just wanted to see the pattern, so I left the value set to 100 percent.

6. Press Enter to apply the pattern.

My completed pattern appears at the bottom of Figure 19-9. Who needs a kaleidoscope when you have CorelPhoto-Paint?

If you're working on a speedy computer such as a Pentium, you can get immediate feedback in the right-hand pattern preview by selecting the Continuous Preview check box in the Terrazzo dialog box. On a less powerful computer, the option slows things down considerably, so you will probably want to turn it off.

Chapter 20

Ten Time-Saving Shortcuts

*A*nd now, from the ridiculous to the sublime. In between having fun with CorelDraw and creating every wacky special effect you can think of, you may as well work in a little productivity so that you don't go completely broke and have to put the kids up for adoption or rent them out for scientific research. To that end, this chapter presents ten time-saving mouse and keyboard equivalents (and then some). Absolutely every CorelDraw user should memorize these shortcuts — and get in the habit of using them on a regular basis.

File Menu Stuff

Ctrl+O, Ctrl+N

To open a document in any Corel program, press Ctrl+O. Press Ctrl+N to create a new document.

Ctrl+S

To save a document in any program, press Ctrl+S. Do this early and often.

Ctrl+P

You can print a document from just about any Corel program by pressing Ctrl+P. (Dream 3D is the only program that generally refuses to print, requiring you to render your drawing instead.)

Ctrl+F4

To close a document in Draw, Photo-Paint, and Dream 3D, press Ctrl+F4 or click on the Close button in the upper-right corner of the document window. If you haven't saved your most recent changes, press Y or Enter to do so.

Alt+F4

To quit a program and return to the Windows 95 desktop, press Alt+F4. Again, press Y or Enter to save your most recent changes.

Ctrl+Esc, Alt+Esc, Alt+Tab

Ctrl+Esc displays the Start menu so that you can start another program if you like or shut down your machine.

Alt+Esc cycles through the buttons in the taskbar at the bottom of the screen. It's a handy way to switch from one program that's running under Windows 95 to another.

But my favorite program-switching shortcut is Alt+Tab, which lets you switch to a specific program or directory window. Hold down the Alt key and then press Tab. A small window appears listing the program or window you can switch to. If you don't want to go to that program, press Tab to go to the next one. When Windows 95 lists the desired program, release the Alt key.

All of these shortcuts are applicable not only to CorelDraw programs, but to any program that runs under Windows 95.

Navigating Inside Dialog Boxes

You can move around a dialog box without ever using the mouse. To activate the next option in a dialog box, press Tab. To return to the previous option, press Shift+Tab.

To display the pop-up menu for an active option, press Alt+down arrow. Then use the up- and down-arrow keys to highlight the desired option and press Enter to select it. You can also use the up- and down-arrow keys in scrolling lists.

To select a specific option, press the Alt key in combination with the underlined letter in the option name.

Displaying Menus

To display any menu, press Alt. Then type the underlined letter in the menu name. After the menu is displayed, press the underlined letter in a command name — no Alt key required — to select the command.

The Control menu is a special case. Press Alt+spacebar to display this menu.

In some cases, you may be more comfortable navigating through the menus with the arrow keys. Press and release the Alt key to highlight the first menu in the menu bar. Then press the left- and right-arrow keys to highlight different menu names. Press the up- or down-arrow keys to display a menu and highlight different commands. If a highlighted command brings up a submenu, press the right-arrow key to display it. Press the left-arrow key to hide the submenu.

Press Esc or press Alt again to hide the menus and deactivate the menu bar.

Zooming from the Keyboard

F2, Shift+F2, F3

In CorelDraw, press F2 and click to magnify the drawing area to twice its previous size. In Photo-Paint and Dream 3D, just press F2; you don't have to click.

To zoom in on a selected object in either CorelDraw or Dream 3D, press Shift+F2.

To reduce the view size to half the current level of magnification, press F3. No clicking is required.

Ctrl+1

To see one pixel in a Photo-Paint image for every screen pixel, press Ctrl+1.

F4, Shift+F4

In CorelDraw, press F4 to zoom to the maximum view size at which you can see all objects in the drawing area. In Photo-Paint, press F4 to fit the image on-screen.

To zoom out so that you can see the entire page in CorelDraw or the entire work area in Dream 3D, press Shift+F4. In Photo-Paint, Shift+F4 resizes the window to fill the screen but does not zoom the image.

Selecting Tools

Spacebar, Ctrl+spacebar

To switch between the selected tool and the Arrow tool in any Corel program, press the spacebar. The first press of the spacebar selects the Arrow tool, and the second press returns you to the previously selected tool.

If text is active in CorelDraw, you can press Ctrl+spacebar instead.

F10

In CorelDraw, press F10 to select the Shape tool and edit a path.

F5, F6, F7, F8, Shift+F8

You can also select a few tools common to CorelDraw and Photo-Paint by using the following function keys.

- ✔ Press F5 to select the Pencil tool in Draw or the Pen tool in Photo-Paint.
- ✔ Press F6 to select the Rectangle tool. Press F7 to select the Oval tool.
- ✔ Press F8 to select the Artistic Text tool in Draw and Photo-Paint. Shift+F8 selects the Paragraph Text tool in CorelDraw only.

Undoing a Mistake

Ctrl+Z, Alt+Backspace

To undo a mistake in any Corel program, press Ctrl+Z or Alt+Backspace.

If the Undo command changes to Redo after you choose it, as in Photo-Paint or Dream 3D, you can restore an operation that you undid by pressing Ctrl+Z or Alt+Backspace again.

Ctrl+Shift+Z

In CorelDraw, you can redo an undone operation by pressing Ctrl+Shift+Z.

Ctrl+R

For extra credit, you can repeat an operation in CorelDraw by pressing Ctrl+R.

Manipulating Objects with the Arrow and Shape Tools

Shift+click, Shift+drag

To select an object in CorelDraw, Photo-Paint, or Dream 3D, click on it with the Arrow tool. To select multiple objects, click on the first object you want to select and Shift+click on the others.

You can also begin dragging on an empty portion of the document and drag around multiple objects to surround them in a marquee. Press Shift while marqueeing to add objects to the selection. In order to select an object, you must completely surround it with the marquee.

To deselect specific objects that are currently selected, Shift+click on them.

Alt+drag

In CorelDraw 6, you can Alt+drag to select all objects that even partially fall inside the marquee. This technique is a great way to select objects when you're zoomed in very close to them and can't marquee all the way around them.

Ctrl+drag, arrow keys

Drag an object to move it. Drag and then press and hold Ctrl to move the object strictly horizontally or vertically. To nudge a selection a few fractions of an inch (as specified in the Options dialog box), press one of the arrow keys.

Ctrl+click

In CorelDraw, you can select an object inside a group by Ctrl+clicking on it. This technique is also a useful way to select text on a curve independently of its path.

All of these techniques also work when you're editing nodes with the Shape tool in CorelDraw. Furthermore, you can double-click on a node to display the Node Edit roll-up.

Making Copies of Objects

Ctrl+C, Ctrl+X, Ctrl+V

In all Corel programs, you can copy one or more selected objects to the Clipboard by pressing Ctrl+C. To cut an object from the document and transfer it to the Clipboard, press Ctrl+X. To paste the contents of the Clipboard into the document, press Ctrl+V.

Ctrl+Insert, Shift+Delete, Shift+Insert

Or you can stick with the old keyboard shortcuts that folks used in Windows 3.0. Copy by pressing Ctrl+Insert, cut by pressing Shift+Delete, or paste by pressing Shift+Insert.

Ctrl+D, Alt+drag

In CorelDraw and Dream 3D, you can bypass the Clipboard and make an immediate duplicate of a selected object by pressing Ctrl+D. In Photo-Paint, Alt+drag the object to a new location to duplicate it.

Changing the Stacking Order of Objects

Shift+PgUp, Shift+PgDn

To bring a selected object to the front of the stacking order in CorelDraw or Photo-Paint, press Shift+PgUp. To send it to the back of the document, press Shift+PgDn.

Ctrl+PgUp, Ctrl+PgDn

You can also scoot a selected object one object forward or backward by pressing Ctrl+PgUp or Ctrl+PgDn, respectively.

Neither of these shortcuts works in Dream 3D because front and back are true spatial concepts that you adjust by dragging objects around. It's a whole different ball game.

Activating Buttons

Enter

Remember, pressing the Enter key always activates the button that's surrounded by a heavy outline. This button is usually the OK button, but there are times — especially when you're working in a complex dialog box — when pressing Enter activates a button other than OK.

Esc

To activate the Cancel button or cancel just about any activity, press Esc. In fact, rely on Esc to get you out of just about any weird situation when you don't know what to do. If you don't recognize a dialog box, press Esc to get out of it. If all the menus and other interface elements disappear, press Esc to bring them back. If you start rendering a drawing in Dream 3D and decide that you don't want to waste the time, press Esc. This key almost always returns you to familiar territory.

Chapter 21

Ten Little-Known, Less-Used Features

. . . .

In This Chapter

▶ Understanding layers

▶ Fathoming the Blend feature

▶ Making small sense of combining objects

▶ Gaping in wonderment at CorelMemo

▶ Catching on to object databases

▶ Grasping at color trapping

▶ Assimilating the mysteries of color channels

▶ Getting the drift of scanning

▶ Wrapping your brain around lights and cameras

▶ Giving up on OCR

. . . .

*I*n case you haven't figured it out yet, CorelDraw 6 is a veritable grab-bag of graphics functions. For $500 or whatever you paid, you get more programs and features than you get with any other software package I can think of. But let's face it. Like any grab-bag, CorelDraw is split evenly between essential capabilities and extravagant, super-complicated excess.

This chapter is about the latter. I introduce ten features that you'll probably never use. But, by gum, you paid for them, so you may as well know about them. I'll start with the borderline excess and move my way up to functions that you never, ever in a billion years expected to find in a drawing package.

Turning CorelDraw into a Parking Garage

You find layers in just about every drawing program with high-end pretensions, but only a handful of experienced artists use layers on a regular basis. Granted, those experienced artists swear by layers. They'll tell you how layers saved their artwork from certain, overwhelming confusion. But for my part, I can take or leave layers. Except for using them to create master layers (as explained in Chapter 12), I would never recommend them to anyone who isn't drawing vast blowouts of manifold exhaust systems, or tubercular cancer cell networks, or something equally complicated and mind numbing.

Still, I'm a simple guy with simple tastes. You may enjoy complexity. So here's how layers work: Imagine that all the objects in a CorelDraw document are cars. Sure, the cars come in various shapes, sizes, and colors, and they're heaped all over each other, but they're still cars. Flat cars without engines. And no drive train warranties. Anyway, one day, you realize that you have way too many cars, and you think to yourself — because you're some kind of city official or something — "How can I sort out these cars to make things more efficient and less of a screwball mess?" The answer is to build a multilevel parking garage.

Well, that's layers. By choosing Layout⇨Layers Manager (Ctrl+F3) in CorelDraw, you display the Layers roll-up, which lets you divide your document into a transparent, multilevel parking garage viewed from a helicopter. Each layer contains a bunch of objects — as many as you want — that are fully segregated from objects on other layers.

Unless you specify otherwise, objects on different layers don't look different, and they don't print differently. They're merely organized into separate banks to help eliminate confusion and provide greater control and flexibility. For example, you can hide different layers to get them out of your face; you can print only certain layers to isolate others; you can lock the objects on a layer to prevent accidental alterations; and you can make objects on layers appear in different colors. The icons in the Layers roll-up assist you in determining what's locked, visible, printable, and so on.

Blending between Objects

I sort of spoiled the surprise with this one when I mentioned blending as a way to create custom gradations in Chapter 19. Luckily, there's more to blending than just creating gradations. In fact, blending is one of CorelDraw's most complicated functions. You can do all kinds of things with this feature that you never wanted to do and you never will do — so it fits right in with the tone of this chapter.

As described in Chapter 19, you display the Blend roll-up by choosing Effects⇨Blend or by pressing Ctrl+B. Then you select two objects, click on the Apply button, and watch CorelDraw create a bunch of intermediate objects (called *steps*) between the two. The steps gradually change in form and color as they progress from the first object to the last. You can specify how may steps Draw creates, you can rotate the steps, you can make the steps follow a path, and you can even control the amount of space between steps.

Blending is sort of like morphing — the effect you see when all those faces change into each other at the end of that Michael Jackson video. But instead of each step occurring in a different frame of videotape — creating the effect of a gradual transition — all the steps in CorelDraw appear in the drawing area at the same time. As a result, no one uses blending for any other purpose than creating custom gradations.

Taking the Old Blowtorch to Your Objects

In Chapter 17, I explain that you can manually adjust selection outlines in Photo-Paint. You can add one selection outline to another, delete a chunk from a selected area, or find the intersection of two selection outlines. (Read "Making manual adjustments" in Chapter 17 for how-to's.) Well, you can do the same thing in CorelDraw, except with objects.

Let's say that you want to create a snowman, for example. You can take one circle and weld it to another. How? Why, by choosing Arrange⇨Weld, of course. If you want to subtract a small circle from a large circle to create a doughnut, you choose Arrange⇨Trim. And to make a circle with a flat bottom — you know, like a Magic 8-Ball — you can take a circle and a rectangle and choose Arrange⇨Intersection.

Though these are inherently useful commands, CorelDraw handles them in a really weird way. First you select just one of the objects that you want to add, subtract, or intersect. Then you choose the command to bring up a roll-up. You click on a button in the roll-up — Weld To, Trim, or Intersect With — and then click on the other object. It would be much easier if you just selected two objects and chose a command to merge them, but simplicity is rarely Corel's style.

Slapping a Few Post-its onto Your Drawing

Ever wish you could explain how something in your drawing is put together so that the next person to work on it would know what's going on? No? Didn't think so, but that's exactly what you can do with the new, mostly useless CorelMemo function.

Inside CorelDraw, choose Edit⇨Insert Memo. This command starts the CorelMemo program, which shows a Post-it-like note on-screen. Enter a title at the top of the note and enter some information-rich text in the lower portion. You can change the color of the text, the font, and the color of the note. When you're done, choose File⇨Exit & Return to leave the Memo program and place the Post-it into CorelDraw.

The problems with this ridiculous function are numerous. First, Draw places the memo right in the middle of your page, which is not necessarily what you're looking at on-screen. I've seen folks place three or four memos in a row, thinking that the feature isn't working properly. Unlike Photo-Paint, which is smart enough to edit embedded images right inside Draw (as I describe in Chapter 14), CorelMemo starts up as a separate program and wastes plenty of your time while it's at it. And finally, the actual memo takes up a ton of room in your drawing. If you reduce it, you can't read it anymore except by magnifying it, in which case it takes up a ton of room on-screen again. The point is, you can rarely read the memo and view the portion of the drawing that the memo concerns at the same time.

I'm reminded of an old Eddie Murphy sketch in which he's advertising protective Plexiglas domes that you can put over your home. Midway through the sales pitch, he interrupts himself with, "Are you crazy? You don't need no dome over your house! How's anyone going to get inside?" Well, if you don't need a dome over your house, you certainly don't need a lot of Post-it notes cluttering up your drawing. How's someone supposed to get to the objects with all those Post-its in the way?

Backing Your Objects with Data

Here's an obscure one. CorelDraw lets you link data to any object in the drawing area. Select an object and choose Tools⇨Object Data. After the Object Data dialog box appears, click on the little data icon just below the title bar. The Object Data Manager dialog box appears, sporting a miniature spreadsheet window that's right out of Microsoft Excel.

Here you can enter any data you want about the selected object. For example, you can assign it a name, type in its phone number, or enter the name of the closest relative to contact in case of emergency. You can associate any data you want with the object.

Why on earth would you want to do this? Well, Corel's example is catalogs. If you had a drawing of a rotary combine engine, for example, you might want to write down the name and price of the product along with a few comments. Later you could print this information or export it for use in a different program.

Yeah, I'm always wishing I could do that.

Trapping Colors

Sounds like we're going on a little hunt, huh? Well, not really. You may remember the "Printing full-color artwork" section of Chapter 13, in which I discuss how to print color separations. Cyan, magenta, yellow, and black primaries are printed on separate pages and reproduced in separate passes. First all the cyan pages are printed, then the magenta ink is added, then yellow, and finally black.

It turns out that this is the same process used to print the Sunday comics in your local newspaper. Actually, nearly all color newspaper and magazine art is created this way, but the comics are the best example because they invariably have *registration* problems. Maybe the red in Hagar's beard is printed on Helga's face, or perhaps Robotman's outfit is leaking yellow onto a neighboring panel. These errors are caused by the fact that the cyan, magenta, yellow, and black inks aren't aligned properly.

CorelDraw enables you to compensate for bad registration by overlapping the colors a little. For example, imagine a circle with a cyan fill and a black outline. If the colors don't register exactly right, a gap occurs between the fill and outline colors. CorelDraw can fill in this gap by spreading the colors. The black outline becomes slightly thicker, and the cyan fill becomes slightly larger. This process is known as *color trapping*.

To activate CorelDraw's trapping function, do the following:

1. **Press Ctrl+P or choose File⇨Print.**
2. **Click on the Options button in the Print dialog box.**
3. **Click on the Separations tab to switch panels.**
4. **Select the Print Separations check box.**
5. **Select both the Always Overprint Black and Auto-Spreading check boxes in the Auto Trapping area.**
6. **Press Enter twice to start printing.**

Phew, what a lot of work. Might as well get out your crayons and draw the artwork from scratch. It'd be equally as convenient.

Separating Color Channels in Photo-Paint

CorelDraw offers some rarefied features, but it's not until you leave Draw and explore the other Corel programs that the features become truly obscure. In Photo-Paint, you can take a color image and view it as several separate images called *channels*, each of which represents a primary color. For example, a CMYK image has four channels — one each for cyan, magenta, yellow, and black — just as you have four plates when printing color separations. You can view any of three channels in an RGB image — one each for red, green, and blue, the primary colors of light.

To view the different color channels in an image, press Ctrl+F9 or choose View⇨Roll-Ups⇨Channels. Then click on one of the options in the Image Channels list in the Channels roll-up. Photo-Paint displays the channel as an ordinary grayscale image.

What's the point of all this channel segregation? Well, you can apply a special effect to a single color channel to get a doubly weird effect. In addition, if a color image looks a little fuzzy, it may turn out that only one of the color channels needs sharpening. You might also want to create a psychedelic effect by selecting part of one channel and rotating it independently of the other channels.

In other words, you'll never use this function.

Scanning Directly into Photo-Paint

All right, here's something you might actually do one day. If you sunk a few hundred bucks into a scanner, you can scan images directly into Photo-Paint. See, scanners convert photographs — *real* photographs, the kind you shoot with a camera — into on-screen images.

To take a bit of real life and make it appear magically on your computer screen, choose File⇨Acquire Image⇨Acquire. Then click on the Scan button inside the Corel TWAIN dialog box. When the scanner is done working, your photograph appears on-screen.

If you don't have a scanner, however, nothing happens. You can try smushing the photograph against the screen, but I don't think that Corel has figured out how to make Photo-Paint read images that way. Maybe if you tried smushing the photo and shouting at the same time. It's worth a try.

Assembling Your Own 3-D Movie Stage

Dream 3D lets you clutter your drawing not only with three-dimensional objects, but also with two additional kinds of items — lights and cameras. Lights shine on the objects so that you can see what's going on. Without lights, you couldn't see anything. (That's why Dream 3D throws in an automatic light in the upper-left corner of every drawing.) The camera controls what Dream 3D renders. Just as the audience at a movie sees what the camera films, your audience sees what Dream 3D's camera shoots.

Dream 3D offers two tools for adding your own lights and cameras. These are the Create Light and Create Camera tools, found roughly in the middle of the toolbox. Both lights and cameras show up as 3-D rectangles. It's virtually impossible to tell what direction they're pointing unless you're working in the better preview mode (which is accurate but very slow on most machines). Moving the lights and cameras around and turning them toward objects is just as difficult as moving and rotating any other objects (as I describe in Chapter 18).

If, despite these hazards, you want to edit a light, double-click on it. You can then select from different kinds of lights, control the range and brightness, add gels, and generally perform half a dozen modifications that are every bit as bewildering as they sound, if not more so. To switch to a different camera, press Ctrl+E (or choose Scene⇨Camera Settings) and select the desired camera from the Name pop-up menu. You can even change the lens on the camera from Normal to Telephoto.

Then again, you can accept Dream 3D's default lighting and camera settings and consider yourself lucky that you can draw some halfway decent-looking objects (if you indeed can).

Attempting Optical Character Recognition with CorelTrace

After scanning a typewritten page, CorelTrace can recognize the characters in the scanned image and generate a text document that you can open in a word processor such as WordPerfect or Microsoft Word. This is absolutely the last function that I expected to see worked into what is ostensibly a drawing package. Face facts, it'll be a cold day in Port-au-Prince before you decide to use this function.

Chapter 22

Ten File Formats and Their Functions

● ●

In This Chapter

▶ Native CorelDraw: CDR and CMX

▶ Encapsulated PostScript: EPS and AI

▶ Metafile formats: CGM and WMF

▶ AutoCAD: DXF

▶ CorelPhoto-Paint: PCX

▶ Tag Image File Format: TIFF

▶ Windows Bitmap: BMP

▶ CompuServe Bitmap: GIF

▶ Joint Photographic Experts Group: JPEG

▶ Kodak's Photo CD: PCD

● ●

CorelDraw supports more file formats than any other graphics program for the PC. This fact means that you can create a graphic in just about any program on an IBM-compatible or Macintosh computer and open it or import it into CorelDraw. Likewise, you can export an image from CorelDraw so that it can be opened in just about any program. If CorelDraw were a person, it would be able to speak every language but . . . well, any language I mention would be politically incorrect, so I'd better keep my mouth shut.

Native CorelDraw: CDR and CMX

CDR is the *native file format,* which means that if you just choose File⇨Save As, enter a name, and press Enter, CorelDraw uses the CDR format. This format retains every little shred of information about your drawing, including nodes, segments, fills, outlines, layers, and anything else you can imagine. Unless you plan on sharing your drawing with another user or opening it in another program, stick with this format.

A variation on CDR is CMX, the Corel Presentation Exchange format. Like CDR, CMX saves all information about a drawing. However, the format results in smaller files than native CDR, which is why Corel has stored all the clip art on the fourth CD-ROM in CMX. Besides, it keeps users of non-Corel programs from opening the clip art. To open a CMX image in CorelDraw, you have to use File⇨Import.

Encapsulated PostScript: EPS and AI

PostScript is the printer language I mention in Chapter 13. *Encapsulated PostScript* (EPS) is a file format that contains a complete PostScript definition of the graphic right in the file. It's as if the artwork contains a little PostScript capsule. When you print an imported EPS file from CorelDraw or some other program, the program just sends the PostScript capsule to the printer and lets the printer figure it out.

However, the printer has to support PostScript in order to print EPS graphics. If you don't own a PostScript printer, don't use EPS.

The Adobe Illustrator (AI) format is an editable variation on the EPS format. You see, when you import an EPS graphic into a program, you can't edit it. You can display the graphic inside your document, but you can't manipulate the paths, or reformat the text, or do anything else. You can just place the graphic on the page and print it.

But when you import an AI file into CorelDraw, you can edit every little bit of it. This format is ideal if you want to share your artwork with someone who works on a Macintosh computer. It's also widely supported by other Windows programs.

Metafile Formats: CGM and WMF

CGM (*Computer Graphics Metafile*) is a dinosaur-like file format that's certified by the American National Standards Committee. Predating the EPS format, CGM is preferable to EPS when you're printing to non-PostScript printers. It's also very popular within large institutions where the wheels grind very slowly, such as the U.S. Government.

The *Windows Metafile Format* (WMF) is the rough equivalent of CGM in the Windows environment, though no institutions have come out to certify it. WMF is the format used by the Windows Clipboard. If you plan on transferring a drawing to another Windows program and you'll be printing to a non-PostScript printer, you may want to give WMF a try.

AutoCAD: DXF

AutoCAD may be the most venerable graphics program for the PC. Technically, AutoCAD is a computer-aided design (CAD) program created with engineers, architects, and other precision-oriented professionals in mind, but the program's been around so long that even amateurs and novices sometimes get into the act.

The AutoCAD format, known as DXF, is widely supported by CAD programs. It is also supported to a lesser extent by desktop publishing and drawing programs. Much to its credit, both CorelDraw and Dream 3D can import and edit DXF graphics. However, unless someone specifically tells you that they need a graphic in the DXF format, you shouldn't export your drawings in this format.

CorelPhoto-Paint: PCX

The formats covered from here on out — PCX, TIFF, BMP, GIF, JPEG, and PCD — are image file formats. They save artwork as pixels, not as objects. Though CorelDraw is perfectly capable of importing these formats, you should *not* export to them unless you want to convert your graphic to pixels. However, it is perfectly acceptable to both open and save in these formats in CorelPhoto-Paint because Photo-Paint works with pixels exclusively. You can also use the formats to save an image created and rendered in Dream 3D.

The PCX format was originally designed for PC Paintbrush and is now the most widely supported graphics format on the PC. When in doubt, save your image in the PCX format.

Tag Image File Format: TIFF

TIFF (*Tag Image File Format*) was developed to be *the* standard image file format, even more of a standard than PCX. Although it still plays second fiddle to PCX in terms of raw support on the PC, TIFF is more likely to be supported by programs running on other kinds of computers, namely the Mac. Furthermore, if you're exporting an image for use in a mainstream desktop publishing program such as PageMaker, QuarkXPress, or (gad!) CorelVentura, TIFF is the way to go. It's generally a more reliable format than PCX and it offers compression options to reduce the size of the image on disk.

Windows Bitmap: BMP

BMP is the native format of the squalid little Paint program that comes bundled with Windows. The only reason Corel supports BMP is for importing purposes. Besides, it's a Microsoft format, and when Microsoft does something, all the other software vendors follow along like mindless little sheep. I don't recommend exporting to the BMP format unless . . . gee, I can't think of a reason.

CompuServe Bitmap: GIF

The GIF format was created especially for trading images over CompuServe, which is a mammoth on-line service that you can access via modem. Anyway, GIF offers compression capabilities, but it only supports 256 colors. Like BMP, it's generally for importing purposes only.

These days, lots of folks use GIF for artwork they want to post on the Internet. But the format discussed next, JPEG, is better because it lets you save 16 million colors and yet it creates smaller files on disk. Frankly, GIF is an antiquated geezer of a format. (No offense to antiquated geezers, of course.)

Joint Photographic Experts Group: JPEG

The new format among ultra-high-end users is JPEG (or JPG), which stands for the *Joint Photographic Experts Group,* which is the group of folks who came up with the format. JPEG is designed to compress huge images so that they take up much less space on disk. Compression-wise, JPEG wipes the floor with TIFF and GIF. However, you actually lose data when you save to the JPEG format. Usually, the loss is nominal — most users can't even see the difference — but it's something to keep in the back of your mind.

Generally speaking, you don't need to worry about the JPEG format unless you start creating very large images — say, larger than 400K — with Photo-Paint or Dream 3D.

Kodak's Photo CD: PCD

CorelDraw and Photo-Paint can import Kodak Photo CD files. Neither program can save to the format because Kodak won't let them. Photo CD is what is known as a *proprietary format*.

In case you haven't heard of it, Photo CD is the latest thing from Kodak, and it's designed for storing photographs on compact discs. You take a roll of undeveloped film to a service bureau, give the technician $30 or so, and the technician scans your photos onto a CD. As long as you own a Photo CD-compatible CD-ROM drive — which includes just about every CD-ROM drive manufactured in the last two years — you can then open and edit the images in Photo-Paint. What will they think of next?

Appendix

Installing CorelDraw 6

• •

***O**ne thing you can say about Windows 95 is that it makes installing software a heck of a lot easier than it used to be. And when a behemoth program like CorelDraw becomes easy to install, you know that the computer gods are smiling.*

If You Build the Computer, CorelDraw Will Come

Let's start off by reviewing what you need in order to install CorelDraw 6:

- ✔ **CorelDraw 6:** You need the CorelDraw 6 package with all the CD-ROMs and other goodies inside. Osmosis simply won't work.

- ✔ **A 486 or Pentium computer:** It's not that CorelDraw 6 positively won't run on a 386, but it will creak along so slowly that slugs and inert pieces of cardboard will laugh at your misfortune.

- ✔ **Windows 95 or Windows NT:** None of this Windows 3.1 stuff for CorelDraw 6. Even if you curse and swear every time you hear those "Start Me Up" commercials, you'll have to join the Windows 95 bandwagon if you want to run CorelDraw 6.

- ✔ **A large hard drive:** You need a lot of space for CorelDraw 6. You can probably get by with an older 200MB hard drive, but a 1GB hard drive is best. (If you don't know what size drive you have, I tell you how to figure it out in a minute.)

- ✔ **Lots of memory:** You need at least 8MB of RAM to run CorelDraw 6. (Again, I explain how to confirm this shortly.)

- ✔ **A CD-ROM drive:** CorelDraw 6 is so enormous, it's available only on CD. If you don't have a CD-ROM drive, rest assured that it's a great purchase — one you'll come to love, and not just for CorelDraw 6.

You can see what kind of machine you have by looking at the front of it. If you see the words *486* or *Pentium*, you're in business. But checking the size of your hard drive and memory is a little more involved.

Checking your memory

At the Windows 95 desktop, choose Start⇨Settings⇨Control Panel. Inside the Control Panel window, double-click on the System icon. Inside the System Properties dialog box, click on the Performance tab. The first item in the Performance panel is Memory. If the value is 8.0MB or more, you're okay. If not, you need more RAM. Talk to your local computer wizard to find out how to get the precious memory into your machine.

In case you're not up on the latest terminology regarding digital storage space, here's how it works. A *byte* is a unit of space that's big enough to hold one letter of text. A *kilobyte*, or *K*, is about a thousand bytes. (It's actually 1,024 bytes, but who cares?) A *megabyte*, abbreviated *MB*, is equal to 1,000K or a million bytes. And a *gigabyte*, or *GB*, is 1,000MB, which is a billion bytes. That's mighty big.

Inspecting the hard drive

To move on from checking your RAM to checking your hard drive space, press Esc to close the System Properties dialog box. Then double-click on the My Computer icon in the upper-left corner of your screen. Click on the icon that represents drive C to select it. In the lower-right corner of the My Computer window, you should see two messages about your hard drive. One message includes a Free Space value, and the other lists a Capacity value.

The Capacity value should be 200MB or more. (If the value is 1GB, that's even better.) The Free Space value is even more important because it tells you how much room on the hard drive is available for use by CorelDraw. If the value is more than 100MB, skip to the next section. If it's more than 200MB, you're really in good shape. If the value is less than 100MB, however, you probably need to delete some files before you can install CorelDraw 6.

If you don't know what to delete or how to delete it, get that computer wizard on the phone and beg for some attention. Or just hunt and peck around your files to see what you can throw away. Unfortunately, there's no magic formula you can follow. It's like cleaning out your closet; some things just have to go.

Insert the CD and Watch the Sparks Fly

Assuming that your computer is now prepared to install CorelDraw 6, the following steps tell you what to do:

1. Put the first of the CorelDraw 6 CDs in your CD-ROM drive.

On some CD-ROM drives, you eject a tray and then place the CD in the tray, just as you do with the CD player on your stereo. Others require you to put the CD in a caddy and stick the caddy in the drive. Do whatever you need to do.

A few seconds after you stick the CD in the drive, a Welcome to CorelDraw 6 window appears. That's right, Windows 95 is smart enough to automatically run the installation program off the CD. (Did I just use the words *Windows* and *smart* together in the same sentence? What is the world coming to?)

If the Welcome to CorelDraw 6 window does not pop up automatically on your screen, double-click on the My Computer icon in the upper-left corner of your screen. Then double-click on the icon for your CD-ROM drive, which is most likely drive D. The window should then appear.

2. Click on the Setup button.

A Setup message wastes your time for a few moments. Then a larger window set against a blue background takes over your screen.

3. Click on the Next button or press Alt+N.

The window is filled with text you don't need to read, so perform this step to get rid of it. A new window appears asking who you are.

4. Enter your name, press Tab, enter your company name, press Tab, and enter your phone number.

I know that a lot of folks are starting to get paranoid about programs asking for personal data, but you have to do it to install the program. Besides, unless you register the program, your personal data doesn't leave the confines of your computer.

Check out that lady next to the question mark. Ooh, nice graphic. Corel always manages to pick its worst artwork for these things.

5. When you're done, click on the Next button or press Alt+N.

Corel asks you to confirm your information. Press Alt+N to tell it to take a hike.

6. Copy down the serial number.

In the next screen, the installation program automatically assigns you a serial number. You'll need this number if you ever have to call Corel's technical support line for assistance. After you scribble down the serial number — preferably on something inside the box — press Alt+N to continue to the Setup Options screen.

7. Select the desired kind of installation.

You can select from four radio buttons to decide which CorelDraw 6 files you want to install:

- • <u>F</u>ull: Select this option if you want to install everything and you have at least 200MB of free space on your hard drive. I doubt that you'll ever use most of the stuff, but you never know.

- • C<u>u</u>stom: If you don't feel like wasting vast amounts of hard disk space on a bunch of silly programs, you can select this option to specify exactly what you do and do not want to install. If, like me, you're not a big fan of letting automated installation programs put whatever they like on your hard drive, this is the best option.

- • <u>M</u>inimum: If you don't want to put a lot of time and effort into deciding what to install and what not to install, but you're low on hard drive space, you can select this radio button. It copies all programs but leaves off a lot of support files that you generally don't need. This option requires just under 70MB of free disk space.

- • C<u>D</u>-ROM: This option copies just enough files to your hard drive to run CorelDraw off the CDs. It only needs about 30MB of disk space, but it means that CorelDraw, Photo-Paint, Dream 3D, and other programs run very slowly — far too slowly to be acceptable. Do not select this option.

After you make your decision, press Alt+N to advance to the next screen.

8. Decide where to put CorelDraw 6.

The installer asks you to specify a directory for CorelDraw. But most likely, you'll be happy with the program's default suggestion, so just press Alt+N again.

9. Turn off the specific programs you don't want to install.

If you selected the C<u>u</u>stom radio button back in step 7 — good job! — a list of check boxes appears on-screen. If you selected one of the other radio buttons, skip to step 10.

Turn off check boxes depending on how much space you want to save on disk. You can also click on the <u>D</u>etails button or double-click on an item to control exactly which files do and do not get installed with each program. I recommend the following choices. (Keep in mind that you can always come back and install something later.)

- Start by double-clicking on the Utilities name — not the check box — to get to the Details screen. Turn off all check boxes in the Utilities Options screen except Dictionaries. Then click on the Continue button.

- If you won't be creating any presentations, turn off the CorelPresents check box. That move alone saves you over 40MB.

- If you won't be tracing any scanned images to convert them to drawings (very few people do), turn off the CorelOCR-Trace check box. This step saves another 8MB.

- Do you plan on cataloging all your graphics, images, and multimedia files? No? Then turn off the CorelMultimedia Mgr. option to free up another 10MB.

- Before you set your sights too high on the wonderful world of 3-D graphics, read Chapter 18, which explains Dream 3D. In the meantime, turn off CorelMotion 3D and CorelDepth. This step saves nearly 14MB.

- If you follow all the preceding recommendations, the remaining program files will consume 101MB of disk space. If you trust me to explain CorelDraw and Photo-Paint adequately in this book — and I think you should — you can get rid of Corel's on-line help files (which aren't always very accurate anyway). Double-click on the CorelDraw name and turn off Help Files, Samples, and Tutorial. Then click on Continue. Next, double-click on the CorelPhoto-Paint name, turn off Help Files and Samples, and click on Continue. For CorelDream 3D, you should probably leave the Help Files and Tutorial options on, but you can save a lot of space by turning off Samples.

- Finally, click on the Import/Export Filters name and then click on the Details button. These filters let you open and edit drawings and images, which is very important. But some of the options are unnecessary. Turn off the Presentation Filters, Animation Filters, Sound Filters, and Text Filters check boxes. The last three options turn gray instead of hollow when you click on them because a couple of filters stay on regardless of your choices.

These settings bring the requirements for installation down to 77MB. (Actually, it'll take up less room than that. The installer pads the total value a little just to make sure that it has more than enough wiggle room.) Press Alt+N to move onward.

10. **Select the Temp check box.**

CorelDraw likes to create temporary files on disk. Select the check box for your drive C and press Alt+N to continue.

11. **Name the Corel program folder.**

The installer wants to put all your program icons in a central place called Corel Applications. Press Alt+N to make it so.

12. Press Alt+N for the billionth time.

This step tells the installer to complete the installation. Assuming that you have enough space on disk and nothing is wrong with your CD, you can go to lunch. It takes a long time to install the software — anywhere from five minutes to an hour, depending on the number of files you're installing and the speed of your computer. But the good news is, you don't have to swap any disks as you did when installing previous versions of CorelDraw from floppy disk. All the program files for CorelDraw 6 are stored on the first CD-ROM. The second, third, and fourth CDs contain clip art and that kind of stuff.

13. Click on the Register or Finish button.

If you want to register your program with Corel and you have a modem hooked up to your computer, click on the Register button and follow the instructions. Otherwise, press Alt+F to quit.

That's it. You're done. You can now begin using CorelDraw, Photo-Paint, and Dream 3D as explained in the pages of this fair book. Oh, and have a great time.

If you ever want to install additional programs or files — such as Motion 3D or one of the on-line help files — just reperform the steps in this appendix, taking special care to select the Custom radio button in step 7 and installing the missing stuff in step 9.

Index

(continued)